LEEDS UNITED IN PURSUIT OF THE PREMIERSHIP

LEEDS UNITED IN PURSUIT OF THE PREMIERSHIP

One fan's game by game record and reflections on watching Leeds United in the 2010/2011 season.

David Watkins

First published 2011
This paperback edition published 2011

Copyright © 2011 by David Watkins

ISBN 9781849141284
10 1849141282

Self Published with
Completelynovel.Com

http://www.completelynovel.com/people/davidwatkins--2

ACKNOWLEDGEMENTS

Thanks to everyone I have met on my travels this season, many of you are mentioned within these pages, but many more are not. You have all helped to make this season memorable. Special thanks to Mark for proof reading the whole book and without whom the season would only have been half as enjoyable! Thanks to Suzi for keeping Mark on the straight and narrow. Thanks also to my wife Karen who has diligently worked her way through the book, proof reading, and to Adam, who, despite what he tries to make out, is just as big a fan as the rest of us. Most of all, my thanks to Leeds United and to all Leeds fans everywhere. We are Leeds!

Momentum

The start of our journey back to the big time began on that amazing afternoon last May at Elland Road. It was May 8th 2010, and my eldest son Mark, his girlfriend Suzi, and I, had just witnessed one of the most incredible football come backs of all time. Down and out at half time, not playing well, a man down after Max Gradel's stupid retaliation and subsequent antics, and results elsewhere in the country all going against us. That we won the game and with it promotion back to the Championship, is now history of course, but that game seemed to suggest that it was meant to be, and there was not only relief all around Elland Road that afternoon, there was something else. There was a sense that the tide had turned, we were on our way, and there was a momentum that we all felt would become hard to resist.

I have been a Leeds United supporter most of my life, going back to the late 60's, but until last season, I only got to see a handful of games each year, a few at home and a few away games if tickets were available from fans of the home side, or if as in the 70's you could pay cash at the turnstiles for the home enclosures at the ground. I have watched and supported Leeds from many of the great vantage points of British football, standing on the Kop in Liverpool, the Kippax at Maine Road, the Gwlady's Street Stand at Goodison, the Directors box at Villa Park and yes, even from the Stretford End. In the "old" days I was not a member or a season ticket holder, I don't even recall if there was a membership scheme in those days, and so watching from the home sections was the only way I could see Leeds away. I also managed to scrounge quite a few games with hospitality offers from work contacts.
When I was a student in Manchester in the late 70's, I saw plenty of home games; I would get that old slow train across the Pennines from Victoria station to Leeds Central every

other weekend. I would walk with the other Leeds fans, usually with a mounted Police escort, all the way to the ground, or sometimes get a ride on one of the match-day buses. I would take my favoured position in front of the stand and at the very top of the terracing on the Lowfields Road side of the ground, where the East Stand is now. Believe it or believe it not, I had not taken my place on the Kop at Elland Road until last season, and that will remain one of the biggest regrets of my football following life, as I would now not sit (or stand if the stewards aren't pestering us) anywhere else.

My first Leeds game seen live in the flesh was at The Hawthorns in 1969, just a few games before we were crowned Champions for the first time. I was 12 years old and had been following Leeds for a few seasons already, but I lived with my Mum and Dad in Worcestershire, and hence it was always likely to be a game in the Midlands that took my Leeds virginity. I can still remember my Dad coming home one night from work, and telling me that a mate of his was going up to the game the following week, it was a Wednesday night league game, and did I want to go? *Did I want to go?* I couldn't wait. I was Leeds mad. I kept a scrapbook with cuttings of every game and a little black book with all the results, scorers, and attendances. I had my white Leeds shirt, the one with the round neck and the old owl badge, and I had even glued the club crest onto my green grammar school tracksuit top. That caused me a bit of a problem at school since I was told in no uncertain manner that unless I was actually a member of the team whose badge it was, I couldn't have the badge on my school kit! I had to try to remove the badge, but it had been glued on so well that I was left with a patch of backing material and dried glue for the next two years until I grew out of the tracksuit! I also had my Leeds United tie, bought through the post from Jack Charlton's shop, they sent me a printed autograph sheet with the tie, which I still have to this day.

We travelled up the M5 from Worcester to West Bromwich in a battered old bottle green, hand painted, ex Post Office Morris Minor van, me on the bench seat on one side in the back, hanging on for grim life and swinging like a deranged monkey, as we went round corners. Dad's mate was a Baggies fan of course, so we watched the game from behind the goal at the Birmingham Road end with the rest of the Baggies fans, even though I had bought a big Leeds poster outside the ground, and then carried it under my arm for the rest of the night. Any old fans will surely remember the one; it had postcard sized head and shoulders photos of the first team squad of the time, in glossy black and white. Only problem with it was that it included Jimmy Greenhoff, who had left us at the start of the season. I sorted that out during the next close season when I bought a picture of new signing Allan Clarke, and stuck that over Greenhoff's picture! The game with the Albion ended in a 1-1 draw with Eddie Gray grabbing our goal.

The most games I had seen in a season before this year, was during the spell I had in Manchester, as a student at UMIST, and particularly the 1976/77 season when I got enough programme vouchers (remember those?) to get tickets for the FA Cup quarter final tie with Wolves down at the Molineux. It was the day Eddie Gray got the only goal of the game at the end packed with the Leeds fans, and the match at which Wolves fans were throwing darts into the Leeds section. I also made it to the very disappointing Semi Final defeat to the Old Trafford mob, at Hillsborough that year. The Semi was during the Easter break from University, so I was at home revising, and had to get the train up to Sheffield from Worcester. That game was one of the most disappointing I have ever seen. We were 2 goals down inside 15 minutes and seemingly without hope, until Allan Clarke gave us just a glimmer of optimism late on with a penalty. The train ride home that day was one of the longest and most miserable journeys of my life.

My eldest son Mark began his student life at Leeds University (well, where else would he go?) studying History, in October 2009, and that was the opportunity for both he and I to watch many more games last season, as it was an opportunity not only to see the Whites, but also for me to pick up his fortnightly washing load, that his Mum would then sort at home ready to return at the following home game. Often his girlfriend Suzi (studying in Sheffield) would join us, or my other son, Adam, when he wasn't playing rugby for school, and when he could "be arsed", as he was very much the archetypal 17 year old at the time. We have had four memberships now for several years, but still the magic of away games had passed us by – we tried a few times to get tickets for away games during our spell in League 1, but we were seldom successful. Mark did manage to cadge a ticket for the January 3rd (remember the date, we beat the team that we f*****g hate….) FA cup tie at Old Trafford, from a Reds season ticket holder we know, but of course that was in amongst the home fans. The minimal ticket allocations we generally got in League 1, meant it was almost impossible to get tickets without being season ticket holders, but we continued to go to most of the home games including of course that magic afternoon on the 8th of May.

But this season was going to be different. We decided that we would apply for as many away games as possible, and try to do all of the home games. Mark was now living in a student house in Leeds, so it was still relatively easy for him to get to Elland Road, while I would drive up from our home in the Potteries, and meet him in the new Pavilion before each game. It quickly became apparent that the much bigger grounds and ticket allocations in the Championship would see us successful in getting away tickets for most of the games.

When the fixtures came out in the summer, we began planning our campaign to follow the Whites wherever and whenever we could for the season. We had no idea what the season would bring in terms of results, and back in the summer I guess we would have been happy with just consolidating our new status in the Championship, with a view to mounting a serious promotion push in the coming years. That was pretty much the clubs official line as well. The first competitive game of the season was at home to Derby County; it was to be shown live on BBC as part of their Championship coverage in their new 5:15pm slot on a Saturday evening. The season was underway.

Feeling our way

The Derby game on August 7th was still well before the universities and schools went back so we had bought 4 tickets for this one. This time they went to Mark, younger son Adam, who decided he "could be arsed" for this one, Mark's now long time girlfriend Suzi, and me. It is strange how the fixture computer throws up interesting games. This being our first match back in the Championship, we could all remember that it was against Derby that we played our last match in the Championship, 3 years ago, and of course Derby were now managed by one Nigel Clough, son of Brian of the 44 days infamy. We made the trip by car, and made our way to Billy's Bar for a few pints before the game. The previous season this had become our preferred pre match ritual, and with the new Centenary Pavilion still a few weeks away from completion, we saw no reason to change the routine. We took our seats in the Kop on row EE near the front, and with the goal to our left. We would try to keep our seats in that area all season, although we did eventually move back a couple of rows, as we got soaked at one game when the wind just happened to be blowing the rain towards the Kop. The match itself was a first taste of the excitement we were to see throughout the season. Derby were clearly more experienced contenders at this level, and Leeds had 5 new faces in the line up from the team that won promotion. Leeds also had to get used to playing without Jermaine Beckford of course, and we did look a little bit light in attack, with Becchio effectively playing on his own up front and with 5 in midfield. Mike Grella was the only other striker on the bench at the start of the season.
Incidentally, on Jermaine Beckford, the family is divided. Adam reckons that because he scored so many goals he was a big loss. Mark and I though felt that he missed 5 times as many as he scored, and that someone like Billy Paynter might be far more efficient in front of goal. Later in the season I would be speaking with an Everton fan and explaining this to

him, saying that he ought to watch out for the fact that Beckford would tend to miss about 5 good chances for every one he put away. In the very next match after we spoke, Everton got stuffed 4 – 1 at home to West Bromwich Albion and Mr. Beckford was in all the sports headlines for missing 3 gilt edged chances. As if to prove my point, in Everton's very next game at Stamford Bridge, Beckford only goes and scores a last minute equalizer! I can remember last season listening to fans at Leeds regularly saying things like "eh up Beckford's missed three or four now, must be about ready to score" ... and he usually did!

Leeds battled manfully throughout the game with Derby, and we were in contention right until the end, but they always looked capable of opening us up and were yards quicker in converting defence into attack. In the event it was Rob Hulse, well known to the Leeds fans of course, who scored the first Championship goal of the season at Elland Road, he picked up the ball on the right edge of the box, took a couple of strides and smashed the ball past Schmeichel right in front of the Kop after just 13 minutes. The fact that he failed to celebrate his strike, suggested that maybe the rumours that Grayson was interested in re-signing the big striker could be true, but as we now know, that proved wide of the mark and he joined QPR later in the season. In fact, he would be back at Elland Road with the Hoops in a few weeks time.
It did only take us 3 minutes to respond though, when Howson beat his man and squared the ball across to the unmarked Luciano Becchio, who slotted the ball home for 1 - 1. Leeds looked nervy at the back though, and after 29 minutes Lloyd Sam made a poor tackle on Cywka in the box and the referee awarded the Rams a penalty. Kris Commons wrong-footed Schmeichel to restore the visitors' one goal lead. It was "100 miles per hour stuff", as the Leeds website wrote after the game, and there were plenty of chances for both sides. Naylor and Collins of all people, both hit the woodwork for Leeds, and Schmeichel justified his inclusion in

the side ahead of Higgs, with a string of excellent saves. The second half picked up where the first had ended, with plenty of chances, and Leeds having the better part of the possession. When it mattered most though, in front of goal, we came up just short, and with no addition to the goals tally in the second half, the game ended in a 2 -1 defeat for the Championship new boys.

The feeling was that this was not a bad start, particularly since we were missing so many players through injury and suspension, notably Max Gradel who had had an excellent pre season. But Max was now paying the penalty for that indiscretion against Bristol Rovers, and Billy Paynter, who having been given the number 9 shirt was clearly expected to play a big part, was still several weeks away from recovery from his long term injury. Robert Snodgrass had injured a knee in Norway in pre season, and he was also going to be a big miss for a few weeks, and of course Patrick Kisnorbo was still missing with the injury that he suffered early last season. Driving home after the game, we felt that it was in defence that we had been weak, with an obvious inability to deal with long balls in the air, neither Collins nor captain Richard Naylor gave any confidence in that area. It was also apparent that Derby had been very quick in moving the ball forward when we lost it on the edge of their box, something that we didn't seem able to replicate. None-the-less, as Simon Grayson told BBC radio Leeds afterwards, there were lots of positives to take from the game, and it was a good learning experience. 26,761 were packed into Elland Road for the game, and the atmosphere had been excellent. The results elsewhere in the Championship gave little indication of things to come, though the results of QPR, 4 -0 winners over Barnsley, and Millwall's impressive 3 – 0 win at Bristol city, for whom David "Dodgy" James was making his debut, caught the eye.

The games come thick and fast once the season has opened, and the next Tuesday night saw a Carling Cup 1st round match against Lincoln City at Elland Road.

To make a 7:45pm kick off is always going to be difficult for me, unless I leave work early, living as we do in the Midlands. I took the afternoon off for this game, and Mark and I set off from home around 4pm, aiming to reach the ground at about 5:30pm, if the traffic on the M6 and M62 permitted. It wasn't too bad on this occasion, and we arrived in good time to take up our position in Billy's Bar, having first called in at McDonald's for a couple of burgers, another ritual that we had carried on for many years. When the boys were little they enjoyed the opportunity of a burger and chips now and again, and they both loved sitting in the Elland Road Macky Dee's on those high stools that were shaped like players legs. I always enjoyed looking at the huge pictures in there of the Revie team of the 70's, and it is something I do miss now that we have forsaken McDonald's for the Pavilion and its pie and peas option! I went back into McDonald's recently though and the décor has completely changed.

As we walked round from Billy's Bar, down Elland Road and then into the ground past the West Stand Ticket Office, that word momentum came to mind again. There was the most monumental queue for tickets, 2 or 3 wide, and stretching down the whole of the West side of the ground. No one was expecting a huge crowd for this fixture, but it was clear that a lot of people had decided at the last minute to come down for the match, and it seemed to me at least that they were getting wrapped up in the momentum that was starting to push Leeds United back to where they should be, amongst the elite of British football. We later found out, that of the 12,602 fans that saw the Lincoln match, an astonishing 4,500 bought their tickets on the night, and were in that queue. As we were going through our turnstile, the queue was still snaking past us, round the corner at the Kop end of the ground. There was no way they were all going to get in for kick off, as it was already 7:30pm.

Perhaps surprisingly Simon Grayson made only one change to the team that played on Saturday evening, bringing in Alex Bruce (son of Sunderland manager, Steve) for the rested Richard Naylor. Mark and I thought he might rest a few more, but equally we could see that it was another chance to get this selection to have a bit more competitive playing time together. I think it certainly helped in that respect and Leeds lost no time at all in getting going. We had a 2 goal lead inside 7 minutes, with first Howson, and then Becchio, getting on the score sheet with headers from close range. Those Leeds fans still queuing for tickets were going to be well upset. Lloyd Sam added a third after half an hour, again with a header. Leeds took their foot off the gas a bit in the second half and added just one more when Neil Kilkenny scored from the spot at the Kop end, after the very busy Sanchez Watt was brought down. Watt looked in a different class that night, and as the season progressed we both felt it was strange that he got so few opportunities to start. The one aspect that still didn't look right was that central defence pairing, this time of Collins with Bruce. They did well enough, but every now and again a long ball pumped down the middle seemed to cause confusion, and we often didn't deal with it well. This was a feature that would haunt us throughout the season. It didn't seem to matter which two Grayson chose to fill the roles out of Naylor, Collins, Bruce, or even O'Brien later in the year. Travelling home after the game we thought "So far, so good", the Lincoln game was a potential banana skin upon which we could have slipped, and Lincoln were talking a good game ahead of kick off, with manager Chris Sutton suggesting an upset was possible. 6 weeks later and Sutton walked out on Lincoln City, only 12 months after having gone there. Fickle old game.

Next up was Nottingham Forest at the City Ground, and once again we were live on TV. This time it was our old friends at Sky who were showing the game, in their Sunday lunchtime slot, kicking off at 1:15pm. We missed out on tickets for the Forest match; probably we applied too late, because we were not sure we were able to go until well after the tickets were offered to members. Since it was on TV anyway, it was no big disappointment, and so we settled down in front of the box to watch it.

Simon Grayson reverted to the team he had opened the season with against Derby, which meant slotting Richard Naylor back into the defence, instead of Bruce who had come in against Lincoln in midweek. We thought that was unlucky for Bruce, because he had a good game against Lincoln, albeit we had to acknowledge that it was not a big test. Nevertheless, we felt that Naylor struggled in the Derby game, and it was generally felt that Forest would come at Leeds like a train. And that is exactly what they did. I think most people thought Forest would be among the front runners this season, and that they only narrowly lost at Burnley in their opening fixture, seemed to support the view that they were a decent side. They are also known for having a great record at the City Ground. They only lost three there all last season, conceding just 13 goals.

For the first 20 minutes it did not look very promising for Leeds, as Forest dominated the possession and positively bombarded our goal. In Ken Bates programme notes for the following home game against Millwall, he described us as "playing like a pub team". It was inevitable that they would score during this spell, and on 9 minutes they did. Following a throw in on the right, Chris Gunter curled the ball into the box, and Dexter Blackstock glanced the ball across Schmeichel. There was no let up from Forest, and it was uncomfortable viewing from the sofa and for the 4,240 travelling Leeds fans, although they were making plenty of noise as they always do. Rob Earnshaw should have doubled

their lead when his shot beat Schmeichel but came back off the post. It didn't look too good at this stage.
I certainly didn't spot it at the time, but after the game Simon Grayson admitted to changing his tactics after that first 20 minutes, and he said we went 4 - 4 - 2. This was to be another constant debate in our household throughout the season. Often when we were forced to swap from 4 - 5 - 1, as a result of going a goal (or sometimes 2) down, we started to do much better operating in a 4 - 4 - 2 formation. It was proof that the "attack is the best form of defence" motto has some truth in it!
Gradually the pace of the game seemed to die down, and as it did Leeds started to get a better proportion of the possession. Becchio had a chance that he lifted wide, but then Bradley Johnson got hold of the ball on the left and somehow managed to clip a great cross into their box with his left foot. Lloyd Sam came on to it from a long way out with a late run, and his header was perfection. It was all square. Needless to say the mood in our front room was instantly improved, despite Mark jumping up and cracking his head on a light fitting in the centre of the room. The rest of the game was much more even, and indeed looking back at the match stats now, over the whole game we matched them on most counts, possession, attempts, corners, and of course goals. As the final whistle went we thought it had been a solid display, apart from that first 20 minutes, at a place where it was likely most teams would struggle to get anything. So, a week of the new season was over. Three games and we had managed a defeat, a win, and now a draw. It was starting to look as though we would be able to hold our own in the Championship despite the fact that it was our first season back. It was only six days now until the Millwall game, and the tickets were safely tucked away ready for the trip back to Leeds. I inspected my low hanging light fitting and declared there to be no damage. Mark was less sure about the state of his cranium!

Optimism

Millwall is a game we always look forward to. Let's face it we have had some battles over the years, both on and off the pitch. They include that disappointing Play Off semi final in May 2009, when the whole family was there to see Beckford miss that penalty. Then Becchio scored the priceless goal that evened up the two-match tie, only for Abdou to break all our hearts, and commit us to yet another season in League One. Mark and I had an even more vivid memory of a Millwall game though, and that was the home league game in the 2007-2008 season. It was a Saturday afternoon, 27th October, 2007, and we were making our way over to the ground after the usual Big Mac. We spotted the specially laid on buses that were bringing the 600 Millwall fans in from the station just arriving at the ground, and we could also see hundreds of Leeds fans, massed outside the superstore entrance and all around Billy's statue. The Leeds fans were chanting "Let's go f****** mental" and "Leeds, Leeds, Leeds" and were doing all they could to wind up the Millwall fans on the buses. All of a sudden, there was a shower of glass from one of the double-deckers, as the Millwall fans literally kicked the windows out from inside their own bus! Mark was 16 years old at the time and unlike me, he hadn't witnessed this sort of thing before, he was fascinated and I couldn't drag him away! For me though, it brought back memories of those very dark days of the '70's, when going to football was often a risky affair, as with those flying darts at that Wolves quarter final. For anyone interested, have a look at some of the YouTube videos from that 2007 game. There is one in particular that explains how the Leeds police tried to minimise the problems that day, by meeting the Millwall fans off the train, keeping them together in a pub next to the station, and then organising the buses for them to get to the ground. All the time the key was to try to keep the so-called "Leeds Risk" (known Leeds football hooligans) from getting to the Lions' fans.

I felt that this season the pre match entertainment might be a tad quieter, and thankfully it was. Millwall had, like ourselves, come up from League One to return to the Championship this year, albeit they had to do it via the Play Offs. They had started well this season, with two wins out of two, beating Bristol City by putting three goals past Dodgy James, on his debut at Ashton Gate, and then thrashing much fancied and recently of the Premier League, Hull City, 4 – 0 back at the New Den. Following up the East Midlands pair of Derby and Forest, every game looked tough in this division.

We arrived early at the ground for this game, and decided to wander round to the back of the West Stand to see if the Millwall Coach had arrived. There was still a big crowd waiting by the cordoned off area around the players entrance, so we waited with everyone else. It was interesting to see the players getting off the coach, and we joked that one or two of them looked half asleep. Kenny Jacket looked his usual dapper self in suit and club tie.

Leeds were unchanged from the Forest game, meaning that Collins and Naylor continued to fill those central defence roles, and Grayson was continuing with that 4 - 5 - 1 formation with Kilkenny, Howson, Johnson, Watt, and Sam, making up the 5 in the middle.

Our recent record against the Lions had not been good, and after 15 minutes, despite having had most of the early possession, it looked like that poor run would continue. Steve Morison looped a "donkey drop" cross over from the right wing and Richard Naylor rose as one with Kevin Lisbie, to beat the Millwall striker to the ball. His header though, flew straight past the rooted Schmeichel, in front of the Kop, and to the joy of the 566 Lions fans housed in the Cheese Slice corner, at the other end of the ground. What a bummer that was! Disbelief was voiced all around us, and there was not a little criticism of Naylor. Simon Grayson was diplomatic after the game, describing it as a freak goal. It was going to be an uphill battle now.

It had however been against the run of play, and if anything, the crowd got behind the team even more and the momentum was slowly rebuilt. Leeds played some excellent football, with Sam causing all sorts of mayhem down the left side, and Watt using his, at times, magical skills on the right. Becchio and Sam went close, and Howson struck a post, before the breakthrough came on 32 minutes, when Lloyd Sam completed another excellent passing move with a sweet right foot drive from the edge of the box. No one thought about it at the time I doubt, but that was the first league goal the Lions had conceded in the new campaign.

Leeds continued to press up to half time, with Neil Collins often finding himself in the opposition penalty area for corners and free kicks. He put one header inches wide from a free kick, and then another glanced off the cross bar from a corner. There was no disputing that Leeds were playing as well as we'd seen them for many a long month, probably back as far as that Old Trafford win on January 3rd (Remember the date etc. etc.)

Half time came at the wrong moment for Leeds, as it completely halted the momentum that we had built up in the first 45 minutes. The game was starting to become a bit of a stalemate, albeit with Leeds still playing all the football, when on 75 minutes Simon Grayson decided to go for gold, literally. He ditched the 4 - 5 – 1, in favour of 4 - 4 – 2, by substituting left back Federico Bessone with Davide Somma, complete with his golden yellow boots. Simon would try to stick with his original line up until the 75th minute in most games throughout this season.

Somma was something of an unknown to most of us, he had spent time last season under the tutorship of Chris Sutton when on loan with Lincoln City, and reportedly had been taken under Sutton's wing somewhat. That could only be good for Davide because Sutton was a very useful striker himself, part of the famous SAS (Sutton and Shearer) attack at Blackburn from 1994 to 1996. Somma scored plenty of goals during his spell with the Sincil Bank club, including some pretty spectacular efforts that helped him to third place in the Lincoln City Player of the Season vote! By his inclusion on the bench, he was obviously thought to be ready for his league debut for Leeds. He had been suspended for the first three games of the season.

Immediately, the new formation caused Millwall even more problems, and Leeds attacks rained down towards the Kop from all angles. On 79 minutes, and just 4 minutes into his league debut, Davide Somma smashed the ball in the net from about 12 yards with his yellow booted left foot, after it had been rolled across the face of the goal by Lloyd Sam out on the left wing. It was another one of those "meant to be moments", and the Kop went wild. Just to our left, one Leeds fan held up both his crutches, on which he was waving his White Leeds shirt emblazoned with the name "Stirk" and the number 14. Respect to that man! The sun was beating down, Leeds were playing as well as we could remember, and everything in the world was perfect! Could it get any better?
Leeds didn't let up and they continued to attack, much to the delight of the fans, and a Watt header rattled the post and came back off the besieged Millwall keeper David Forde, before Somma struck again in the 4th minute of injury time. This time a long diagonal ball (not dissimilar to the Howson ball that put Beckford in the clear at Old Trafford last January) found Somma raiding down the inside left channel. He was on the shoulder of a defender, but he jinked left, then right, and then unleashed an arrow of a shot from about 12 yards out that flew across the keeper into the opposite top corner. Superb strike! All the Leeds players celebrated right in front of us, in the northwest corner, and it was a remarkable atmosphere. We had gone up to 9th in the league with our 4 points from 3 games, and although we were already 5 points behind the early pace setters QPR, it was a steady start.

The inevitable question we were asking in the car going home was "Can we play like that every week?" We wouldn't have long to find out, as we were back on Tuesday night for the Carling Cup, second round game, with another one of our bogey teams, Leicester City.
Another of our bogey teams and another bogey Tuesday night game, although at the time we didn't know Tuesdays were going to be such a problem for us! We had beaten Lincoln City on a Tuesday night, but we were about to embark on a run of dire Tuesday night performances that would last until Tuesday March 8th 2011.

Grayson again rested Richard Naylor, as he had done for the first round game, and again it was Bruce junior who partnered the ever-present Neil Collins. Max Gradel was now available, having served his suspension for the Bristol Rovers sending off, and he went straight into the side with Lloyd Sam rested. Davide Somma kept his place in the starting line up after his super-sub performance on Saturday, replacing Sanchez Watt. Shane Higgs got a first start of the season, with Schmeichel on the bench. This had all the hallmarks of a proper 4 - 4 – 2, with Becchio and Somma up front.
It was an uneventful journey up to Leeds, with the only excitement being spotting (well, going past it really), the Shropshire Whites mini bus. It was to become a familiar sight as we began our tour of the country this season. Seemingly the same little bus is used every week. The Shropshire Whites is probably our closest members' branch, or it may be the Stoke Whites. We have often thought about joining one, as it would presumably make the sourcing of away tickets a bit easier. Anyway, we never have done, but it was always nice to spot the little white bus with its Shropshire Whites flag in the back window. We would also frequently see the huge Cheshire Whites metallic blue Mercedes bus, on our travels. Mark and I joked that the relative quality of the transport seemed to fit well with the relative prosperity of the two regions!

There was another long queue at the ticket office as we entered the ground, but we estimated not as big as that for the Lincoln tie. Clearly some fans had learned the lesson and had taken heed of Mr Bates' programme notes, in which he had pleaded for fans to buy their tickets in advance to avoid the queues.

Leeds failed to replicate Saturday's superb performance against the Lions, and the opening half an hour against the Foxes, with Leeds attacking the South Stand, was mostly frustrating. Gradel showed flashes of brilliance, and almost put Becchio in on one occasion, and at the Kop end, Shane Higgs showed his abilities with a fine save from the lively little Dany N'Guessan. Then, on 32 minutes, it was Higgs who lit the place up, not for his goalkeeping, but for a superb 50-yard pass! Kilkenny or Howson would have been proud of it. He tapped the ball forward out of the box, and then spotted Kilkenny out on the right wing, mid-way in the Leicester half. Kilkenny controlled the ball superbly from Higgs clearance, and then twisted past a Leicester defender, before poking the ball along the touchline a couple of yards to Gradel. Quick as a flash, Mad Max whipped the ball over into the centre with his first touch, Davide Somma rose to meet the ball, and he glanced a header past the keeper. A wonderful goal and Higgs rightly got the plaudits for the stunning pass.

1-0 at half time then, but Leeds were not playing that well, with passes going astray, and that familiar defensive frailty still looking likely to undo us at any minute. In the second half, Gradel continued his mazy runs down the right, often going past two or three defenders, but often then failing to find a teammate with his final ball. It was following one such run, that Becchio had a shot cleared off the line as the ref played advantage for various fouls on little Max. And then the inevitable happened and Leicester got an equaliser, and it was a real mess. Richie Wellens picked up the ball in his own half after a sloppy pass from Bessone, and moved it forward to N'Guessan. Howson and Johnson both had an opportunity to whack the ball away, but somehow they both failed, and eventually Wellens, who had continued his run, slotted the ball past Higgs. It was all down hill from there. Leeds continued to work hard, but without creating any real openings, and just as the game seemed to be heading for extra time... well, that defensive frailty came calling again. This time it was a real nothing ball into the box, aimed straight at Neil Collins. The ball did hop quite abruptly, straight up into the big defenders right arm in fact. Penalty! Steve Howard duly despatched the spot kick, hard to Higgs' right, with the Leeds keeper sadly diving full length to his left. 2 -1 and we were out of the Carling Cup. The game had been more like the Derby game than just the score; we just didn't seem to click tonight. We had the usual discussion on the journey home as to whether going out of the Carling Cup at this stage was a blessing or not, it is always the first thing we fans say, but we don't really mean it. We want to win every game.

We couldn't make it to the Watford game the next Saturday, even though we would only be a 17-mile car ride away ...at Wembley Stadium! As well as the whole family following Leeds United, we also have a bit of an affinity with Leeds Rhinos, the rugby league outfit. Once we knew that the Rhinos were going to Wembley, in the Challenge Cup final against Warrington on August 28^{th,} the boys decided that it would be a good birthday present for their Mum to take her to the game!

We do have previous for this sort of "birthday treat". The year before, for example, I had decided that the only way we would get the whole family together for the wife's birthday (which is actually 29th August by the way), was to find a football match that the boys were prepared to go to see! The missus fancied Barcelona for a weekend away, but when the La Liga fixtures came out that summer, it was Real Madrid who were at home, on what was to be the opening weekend of the 2009/2010 season. It was though, likely to be a very special game, as it was scheduled to be the Madrid debut game for the three big summer signings, Ronaldo, Kaka, and Xabi Alonso. They were playing Deportivo La Coruna at the Bernabeu. The boys were up for it. The missus was up for it. So I set about sorting out a long weekend in Madrid, and I managed to get tickets for the game on the Internet. It all worked out really well, and we not only got to spend an evening at the game in a packed Bernabeu Stadium, with 90,000 fanatical Spanish supporters, but we also got to see a real live bull fight, the following night, at La Plaza de Toros de Las Ventas del Espíritu Santo.

The score at the Bernabeu was a 3 – 2 win for Real. The score at Las Ventas was Bulls 0, Matadors 7, and that despite Mark and me giving everything we had in support of the bulls! Having never seen a bull killed in the ring before, even on TV, it was quite a shocking experience. There were many tourists at the bull fight, there presumably, like us, just to see what goes on. When the sword was thrust between the shoulders of the first bull, and he sank to the ground, dead, a significant number of the tourists got up and left, muttering and shaking their heads. We stopped until the end, all hoping that one of the bulls would turn the tables, but it was not to be. Would I ever go to a bull fight again? No thank you. If the odds were evened up a bit between bull and matador, then I might consider it, but this all looked a bit one sided to me.

What made it a truly excellent weekend though, was the news that Leeds had won 2 – 1 at Colchester!

On yet another birthday occasion, I took the missus and Adam away for a long weekend in Rome, and it just happened to coincide with an A S Roma home game, at the Stadio Olimpico! The singing of Roma, Roma, Roma, by the home fans, before the start of the game, is another of the great spectacles of world football that I will never forget.

So anyway, August 28th, a day before the wife's birthday, we are all heading down the Motorway to Wembley, while most travelling Leeds fans are making a very similar trip, but would veer off to Vicarage Road for the league game. We saw lots of them on the motorway, as there were 2,199 of them there. It might have been the fact that there were two such big games on in the vicinity that caused the traffic problems on the M1 that day. It was quite confusing trying to work out what fans were in what cars that morning, since the colours of United, The Rhino's, and Warrington Wolves, are all so similar. In fact at one point, we very nearly stopped to help; when we saw what we thought was that Shropshire Whites Mini bus, broken down in a queue of traffic on the M1. Just as we got to it though, it was clear that it was a mini bus full of Warrington Wolves fans …so we waved our scarves at them, and wished them good luck in getting to Wembley in time for kick off!

We thought we had left in good time, and we had pre booked a car park space at Wembley so we didn't have to mess about when we arrived, but it was so slow once we got close near the stadium, that we only arrived at the ground half an hour before kick off. There were 5 of us on this trip, including Mark's girlfriend Suzi, and we were all starved. We just had time to queue at one of the food points and get an assortment of burgers and fish and chips, before going to our seats. For anyone who hasn't been to the new Wembley yet, I can recommend the "gourmet" burgers! OK, they are expensive, but they are huge, and the portion of chips we got was massive as well. Well-done Wembley! Oh, another tip for new visitors, you can take your beer with you to your seat, at least you can at the rugby. We didn't know this, so Mark, thinking his would be confiscated, decided to knock back a quick pint in the few seconds we had before kick off. In his haste, he managed to pour much of it down his Rhino's shirt! When he got to his seat he saw that everyone else had their pints with them!

Sadly, the game didn't live up to the burgers, and was a total disaster for Leeds fans as the Rhinos never got started. They eventually lost, 30 points to 6, with Warrington's Chris Hicks scoring a hat trick of tries. At the start of the game there was a record (for rugby) 72,000 inside Wembley Stadium, but mid way through the second half, most of the Leeds fans had already left! So it was a very strange closing few minutes, as we were sat in a very sparsely occupied, and silent, Leeds end, while the other end remained packed with fanatical, singing, flag waving Wolves fans.

We were keeping up to speed of course with what was going on a few miles away, and it was only the fact that Richard Naylor had poked the ball in the Watford net, to give us 3 points, that made the trip home even partly bearable. We were able to fly our Leeds scarves from the car windows, and once we got far enough up the M1, passengers in passing cars must have assumed we had been to see United, and not the Rhinos!

For that game at Watford, Simon had once again reverted to the same team he had played in every league game, with Naylor and Collins in central defence; Connolly and Bessone at full back; Kilkenny, Sam, Howson, Johnson, and Watt across the middle; and Becchio up front. Schmeichel was back in goal. It was a combination that seemed to work, as we had now gathered 7 points from 4 games, and we were in 6th place in the table. This was great news, as we all knew that we still had Paynter and Snodgrass to come back from injury, Max Gradel was also available, and Somma was showing he was a valuable squad member too. It was starting to look like a strong package.

Next up was Swansea, at Elland Road, on 11th September, but again neither Mark nor I were there. Mark was away with Suzi on holiday in Bulgaria, while I had to host a retirement dinner and weekend away for a long-standing customer at work. I did get a first hand report on the game, from a mate at work who is also a life long Leeds fan, and who was at the game with his son in law who, strangely, lives in Swansea but is also a Leeds fan. I got them the tickets for the game. Their report was positive; we had won the game 2 – 1, in front of another big crowd of over 26,000. It didn't look like we were going to win it after 13 minutes though, when we were undone yet again by another long hopeful ball pumped down the inside left channel. It was there for Naylor to clear, but somehow the ball just skipped past him, and Stephen Dobbie ran on to collect it, and run with it into the box. He then had a simple task to side foot the ball across the keeper with his right foot, just inside the far post. When Mark and I eventually saw it on the TV, we just shook our heads in disbelief. How can experienced defenders allow that sort of innocuous ball to go past them? Anyway, on this occasion it was not disastrous, as in the second half, attacking the Kop, we managed to pull the game round. First a free kick from Gradel on the right was clipped in, and Naylor rose and headed firmly straight at the Swans keeper, only for him to pat it back to Johnson, who volleyed it into the net. That was on 56 minutes, and just 7 minutes later, Gradel was again the provider. This time he picked up the ball on the left wing ("He's here, he's there, he's every f*****g where"), jinked past a defender, pulled the ball back, and first Lloyd Sam had a shot that was blocked, then it went to Kilkenny who shanked his shot to the left. Howson had a swing at it, only for the keeper to push it into the path of Becchio, who finally, finally, found the net. Another three points and that momentum was still with us, though that defence still looked frail, and there was the fear that sooner or later it would cost us. We hoped it would not be at Barnsley, on Tuesday night...

Derby Days

Barnsley, our first Leeds away game where we would actually be with the Leeds fans, in their section. Mark and I had no idea what to expect, but we had been filled with anticipation since the tickets arrived, a few weeks earlier. In Ken Bates' regular sermon in the Swansea Programme, (my mate had bought me one) he had mentioned that over 6,000 Leeds fans would be travelling to the game "… the largest away contingent for a league game, since Wigan in 2005". Wow! What was that going to be like?

It was a lovely clear evening, as we set off in the car from our home in the Potteries, and we had the scarves flying from the car windows. We had no idea where we were going. We had the notes from the Swansea Programme, and we had the AA route map that I had printed off the Internet. Essentially, we were trying to get near junction 37 of the M1, and then follow the signs into Barnsley. Our route would take us up the M6, and via the M62, M60 and M67, eventually onto the A628; one of the most famous roads in Britain, going through some glorious scenery. It *was* glorious in the autumn evening sunlight that night. The A628 connects the M67 from Manchester, to the M1 in South Yorkshire. It is beautiful along the way, but it is also very frustrating for drivers, as it is a single carriageway road that twists and turns, following the contours of the landscape as it passes through such picturesque villages as Mottram, Hollingsworth, and Tintwhistle. It also passes through the Peak District National Park. It is said to be one of the most congested A-roads in the country, and that is pretty much our experience from that night. There was no way to overtake and it was very busy. Incidentally, this is the road mentioned in the Human League track titled "The Snake" – "The way to Hyde, the sixty-two or the six two eight, will do if you cannot be late". If you don't believe me, check it out by Googling "Human League, the Snake".

We got to the outskirts of Barnsley, and followed signs to the ground. We went through some local housing estates, and we were looking out for car park signs. Eventually, we spotted some Leeds fans parking, in what looked like a college car park, but as we couldn't see the ground yet, we carried on a bit further. Shortly after, we spotted the old Shropshire Whites mini bus, and we followed that for a while, joining a queue that was heading for "Barnsley FC" parking. We were still in plenty of time, but this queue was moving very slowly. We got to within 2 car lengths of the entrance, to what we later discovered was a piece of grassland that ran down to the ground. It was where all the Leeds official coaches would be parked after the game. For now though, the Police had decided they were not going to let any more private cars through! We wound down a window, and asked a friendly bobby what we should do. "No idea mate" he shrugs "you just need to find a spot wherever you can, everything is full up." "Bloody marvellous" we say to ourselves. Then we spot that the big black four by four in front of us is reversing, and it then turns left directly in front of us, down a bit of a track called Carey Avenue, by the side of a school playing field. It looks a bit dodgy but we didn't want to start roaming around Barnsley town centre at this time, so we did the same. We did a 7 or 8 point turn in the narrow dead end lane, so that at least we were facing the right way out after the match. I parked the car right up against the wall of a house that backed onto the lane, the other side to the school field. It looked OK. The Police didn't stop us so we assumed it was fine. We got coats and scarves out of the boot and made our way down to the ground. There was a great buzz amongst the fans walking to the ground; we seemed to have found the designated Leeds parking area by accident. Everywhere around us were Leeds fans, and all the way down to the ground there were mini buses from all over the country, including that Shropshire Whites bus with the big Leeds flag in the back window. None of the big coaches had arrived yet.

We bought a couple of burgers at a little mobile stand, just at the entrance to the car park, and we ate them as we carried on walking down to the ground. The man and wife running the stall had said it was getting cold, and Mark agreed, "Colder than bloody Bulgaria." He said. "Siberia, do you mean love" says Mrs Burger Seller trying to be helpful. "No, bloody Bulgaria, I was there last week" explained Mark. I think it was all pretty much lost on Mr and Mrs Burger Seller.

When we got to the bottom of the car park, we found ourselves at the corner of the ground, with the North Stand to our left, and the old West Stand, which ran along one side of the ground, to our right. From where we were standing, it didn't look all that impressive, but the main part we could see was the back of the West Stand, which is the oldest stand they have at Oakwell, dating from around 1900. We made our way in through a turnstile set in a wall surrounding that corner of the ground, and entered the "foyer" below the relatively new North stand. This was where the majority of the 6,700 Leeds fans were going to be housed. It was the normal sort of concrete concourse area, with a couple of fast food counters and a couple of televisions showing Sky TV. The area beneath the stand was very cramped, and when we discovered that there was an alcohol ban in that area, we fought our way back outside to the little bookies hut, that was situated at the entrance to the North Stand. I usually go for 4 – 0 Leeds (that is usually about 100/1 for a Leeds away game, and worth it if it comes up). Mark more often than not goes for a quid on the first scorer, and tonight he went for Jonny Howson at 16 /1.

Back in we went, but this time we made straight for our seats, that were about half way up and to the left of the stand, as we looked at the pitch. The view was very good, and it was obvious that the stand we were in was quite new. It was built in 1999/2000 apparently. It was already rocking up there, the lads round us had clearly been drinking at some local hostelry or other, as they were all well plastered, and some were having trouble even standing up, but it was all good natured stuff.

As the players came off after the warm up, they exited the pitch just underneath us, into the dressing rooms below, and as they did so the sprinklers started up to dowse the pitch for one final time. Leeds made just one change from Saturday, including Lloyd Sam from the start in place of Sanchez Watt. That meant that Shane Higgs was still in goal, with Schmeichel apparently still injured. I didn't mind that, as I always thought Higgs was a solid keeper with good hands.

The game started at a break neck pace, and there was a real frenzy about the place, with the Leeds fans making all the noise, and going through the complete repertoire of songs, over and over again, including "We filled your ground for you!" and "You're only here to watch the Leeds!" The Leeds end then went completely manic after just three minutes of the game, when Leeds took the lead. Kilkenny clipped a corner over from the right, and Jonny Howson rasped a shot into the net from an angle. Oh what delirium! "Let's go f****** mental" rang out loud and clear from the bouncing North Stand. It was a few minutes before we were aware that it was Howson that had scored, as this had all gone on at the far end of the ground. But when we did of course, Mark went mental too, as he realised he had turned a quid bet into seventeen! It felt like the best night ever for a few minutes, but gradually Barnsley got their composure back, and they carved out a few chances, enough to suggest that this game had a long way to run. We were a couple of minutes away from a breather at half time, when Bessone inexplicably passed the ball to a red shirt in the middle of the pitch. Red Shirt tore towards the massed Leeds fans in the North Stand and then, as he was challenged by Naylor, he nearly let the ball go dead over the goal line. Somehow, his hand scooped the ball back from the line. The Leeds fans went up as one with a shout of "Handball, f****** handball!!" but incredibly the game went on. The ball shot back to the debutant Barnsley striker, Garry O'Connor, recently arrived from

Birmingham City, and he fired the ball into the net. 1 – 1. It was heads in hands time.

We stayed in our seats at half time. Well, nobody had actually sat down at all in the first half, apart from the chant of "Sit down, if you hate Man U", so this was the first time we had really been in our seats, but we stayed up in the stand, rather than going down to the bogs or the food bar.

The second half of this game will go down as one of the worst performances I have ever seen, by any team, anywhere, although we were destined to see Leeds repeat the dose in exactly 2 weeks time, on another unforgettable (for the wrong reasons) Tuesday night.

As Leeds did in the first half, the Tykes did in the second, scoring after just three minutes. Adam Hammill had been a menace to us all night, and he broke away down the left again, and eventually, after almost overrunning the ball, he somehow found himself in front of Higgs. He poked the ball through Higgs, and there was Jim O'Brien to tap the ball into the now unguarded net.

Both sides toiled away for the next 20 minutes, but Leeds looked out of sorts and passes were going astray far too often. In the 65th minute the game was up. A corner seemed to pass straight through the gloves of the hapless Higgs, (that's the Higgs who I always thought had good hands!) and as he fell to the ground, the ball landed at the feet of Arismendi at the far post. He just lashed the ball straight back past Higgs, into the net. It was all happening at the South end of the ground of course, so it was difficult to see exactly what was going on, and even the big screen replays were not clear. Whatever it was though, it wasn't good! And it got even worse. Leeds looked to have all but given up at this stage. Davide Somma was brought on in place of Lloyd Sam, as Leeds tried to salvage something, but the damage was already done and Leeds confidence was shot to pieces. On 81 minutes Barnsley attacked again, this time a clipped cross from the left corner of the penalty area was deftly headed into his own goal at the near post by Neil Collins. "What the f*** is going on" was the chant now, a genuine question, from fans confused by the sudden disarray on the pitch. From where we were standing, it looked for all-the world that Collins had aimed his header to beat his own keeper, not dissimilar in fact to Naylor's effort for Millwall a couple of weeks before. No sooner had we lined up again than Hammill had stolen the ball inside his own half, and he then just ran though the Leeds team, straight down the inside left channel, took aim and fired the ball inside the left post, with Higgs just looking bemused. Somma did pull one back a few minutes later, and that did spark the Leeds fans to start singing "We're gonna win 6 – 5, 6 – 5 we're gonna win 6 – 5", but despite the brave words and faces, we were all pretty shocked by the capitulation in the second half. We applauded the team off, but even they looked embarrassed that we were all still there, and they trudged off as dejected as we all were. We made our way out and of course we stopped by the bookies shed, to collect Mark's seventeen quid. As the Leeds fans filed by, one or two saw us collecting, and asked incredulously if we had got the 5 – 2 score right. "You are joking mate, no, it was Howson for first goal" Mark told them. "Ah, Good call mate" they replied, and off they wandered.

It was a quiet journey back home that night, with neither of us having much to say. We headed down the M1, rather than going over the tops again. "We were shite tonight" Mark said after a long silence, "Yeah" I said, wondering whether the momentum had now been lost. We would soon find out because we were playing again on Friday night, live on Sky Sports ... and it was another Yorkshire derby, this time against Doncaster Rovers at their Keepmoat Stadium. We had failed to secure tickets for that one, and would not be among the 3,000 Leeds faithful to make that trip. We would be in front of the box again; at home with our fingers and toes crossed, that we would play better than tonight.

As reported on the Leeds website, Simon Grayson had demanded a response from the team, following the poor second half display on Tuesday night at Barnsley. He made several changes, resting Naylor and Becchio, and so Bruce and Collins were again the preferred central defence pairing, while Aidy White and Hughsey were paired at full back for the first time. Ross McCormack made his full debut, and Davide Somma was again up front. There must have been quite an atmosphere in the Leeds section again, as we took 3,297 to the game, although it didn't really come over on TV. The total attendance was only 13,293.

We watched nervously as the opening exchanges went to the home team, but gradually Leeds played themselves in, seeming to erase the memory of the Barnsley fiasco. Somma went closest early on, when Neil Sullivan (ex Leeds) was beaten, only for Somma's shot to strike the bar. Equally though, Shiels saw a delightful right foot curler hit the far post with Higgs beaten. Overall, we had the better of the possession and the attempts, and by the end it had to go down as a satisfying away point, at a ground where the home side was as yet undefeated, and they had beaten the likes of Norwich and Hull recently. Final score 0 – 0, move on. Next up it was the third Derby in a row, this time with Sheffield United visiting Elland Road, on Saturday 25th September.

The Sheffield game was one we looked forward to with even more relish than normal; this one was going to be special on a number of counts. Suzi joined Mark and I at this game, I think it being Sheffield swung it for Suzi, as she was studying at Sheffield Uni, and she was living just a stones throw from Bramall Lane. In fact, we joked that she should indeed throw some stones at it. It was also the first time that the new Centenary Pavilion was to be open for service. We didn't know what to expect from the Pavilion, and we thought it would be packed on the first day, so we kept to our usual ritual of doing McDonald's first, and then went into Billy's Bar for a pint. After that though, we strolled down to the Pavilion to see what all the fuss was about. Ken Bates said in his programme notes that we would be "gob smacked" by it, and indeed we were. We didn't immediately appreciate it, but having been in many times since then, we now understand what Ken meant. It has transformed the pre match experience for us, and I am sure it's the same for all the fans that use it.

Bates has talked many times about making a trip to a football match, a better all round experience; improving the standard of the toilets for example and the quality of the surroundings, and the choice of food. The Pavilion ticks all those boxes. I don't know whether all the fans appreciate the finer things about the Pavilion or not, but to me, treating us as human beings is important. Having good food available, proper cutlery, paper napkins, tables to eat and socialise at, a decent carpet on the floor, big screens with entertainment, and, probably most important, having one or two players or guests to speak from the stage, while we wait in there pre match. It all makes going to Elland Road that much more of an event, and as a good mate of mine often reminds me, that is what life is about, events. When you get older and you look back at your life, it's events that you will remember, and that's why they are important. Being able to see the players close up and for the kids to seek their autographs is also part of the entertainment experience. After all, it now costs an arm and a couple of legs to watch football at this level, so I think it is only right that clubs try to give us more than just 90 minutes of a game. Well-done Batesy – a great facility!

The only slight criticism we had of the Pavilion that day, was that it was just too popular! We rolled in there at about 2pm, and by then it was heaving! Sadly, we learned later that arriving so late, we missed appearances by Allan Clarke and Mick Jones, two of the Leeds legends that played under Don Revie, and possibly one of the best strike partnerships of all time. It was standing room only in the Pavilion and the queues for the bars were lengthy. We do have to remember though that there was a huge crowd expected for this game, they had opened up the top tier of the East Stand for this one, and it was thought that the crowd was likely to be 36,000 or more. In the event, it was only just over 33,000, but that was easily the biggest gate at Elland Road so far this season, and indeed was the biggest gate in the Championship so far.

I guess I should also mention that a lot of people were in there to see Lucas Radebe. The Chief had been launching his new biography in Leeds city centre, and in the club shop, and he put in an appearance on the Pavilion stage too. As Peter Lorimer was interviewing the popular ex Leeds defender, the audience broke into a spontaneous chant of "Chief, Chief Chief"!

However, we had a good look round, got our bearings, and decided that we would just have to get there a bit earlier in future to try to get a seat at one of the big round tables. I have to admit that since that day, we have always managed to get a seat, and we now have a new pre match ritual in which the trip to the Pavilion is central.

Another feature of being in the Pavilion is that you can place a bet in there, and they announce the team over the PA as soon as they have it. That means our pre match bet is made after rather more consideration than it was in the past, as previously we had to decide as we got to a betting point, often not knowing the team line up! It doesn't mean we get it correct any more often of course.

For this game we had a slightly more attacking look, with both Becchio and Somma starting, and with Sam and Gradel joining the ever present Howson and Johnson, in a midfield quartet. Incidentally, the only other ever present at this stage was Neil Kilkenny, but he was only on the bench today. George McCartney was making his full debut for Leeds today, on loan from Sunderland, so it was our first look at him.

We obviously lost the toss, as the two teams had to swap ends, with Leeds having to attack the Revie Stand in the first half rather than the second. As with all teams, Leeds prefer to kick towards the Kop in the second half. The sun was shining, the ground was nearly full, and it was all set for a great game. There was an added bit of spice, in that the two managers know each other really well. Apparently, they both signed their apprentice forms for Leeds on the same day, way back in 1984. The Blades manager was of course former Leeds midfielder Gary Speed, who was part of the team back in the late 80's and 90's that got us out of the old Second Division as it was then, with the likes of Gordon Strachan and Vinny Jones. I still remember those days, struggling to get promotion year after year, with a certain fondness. That was pre children of course, and in those days the wife and I would go to the games together. Gary Speed has always seemed one of the nice guys of football, of course he was destined not to stop with the Blades very long, as he was given the Wales job just a few weeks after his Sheffield team was at Elland Road.

It has to be said that it was not a great game. Both sides huffed and puffed, and there was plenty of aggression, as you would expect of a big Derby. Howson squared up with his opposite number at one point, 4 yellow cards were handed out, and 2 reds as well.
The referee didn't help; Mr Taylor was whistle-happy to say the least. We had already seen some appalling referees this season at Elland Road, and we were destined to see many more before the season was done.
The best move in the first half saw Max Gradel scamper down the left wing, check to get the ball on his right foot, and swing over an inch perfect cross, where Bradley Johnson met it with a fine header. We were sat right behind the goal for this game, and the ball was clearly heading for the top right corner from Bradley's view. Somehow Steve Simonsen (ex Stoke City keeper) managed to get one hand on it, to tip it round the post, whilst diving full length to his left. Other than that though, the first half was not memorable, and we

contemplated at half time why we couldn't replicate the form we showed against Millwall, just a few weeks ago.
Snodgrass, Kilkenny, and McCormack, all joined the fray during the last half hour, replacing Sam, Gradel, and Somma, respectively. Snodgrass immediately looked up for it, it was only his second game of the season following his long injury lay-off, so he was bound to want to make up for lost time. His first act though, was to plough through the back of Richard Creswell, another ex Leeds man, and that got him a yellow card. Leeds started to come under pressure, despite the substitutions, but it was from one spell of this Blades pressure that we got the break we needed. Ross McCormack tracked back to help out the defence, and when he intercepted the ball, he swivelled and whacked it clear from the edge of the Leeds box. There was no particular danger as Stephen Jordon shaped to swing a boot at the ball, which had reached the half way line. But Jordon inexplicably missed the ball completely, and suddenly Snodgrass was racing on to it and driving on into the Blades box. He twisted one way and then the other and got to the bye-line before pulling it back to the edge of the 6 yard box, right in the centre of goal. Bradley Johnson was there to bash it into the net through a couple of defenders on the line, with the keeper stranded on his near post.
Snodgrass then got his marching orders, when he blatantly blocked Kyle Bartley, just outside our area, and then shortly after that, Sheffield's Jamie Ward also saw red for a reckless challenge on Kilkenny. So it was a rather boisterous end to the game, but the huge crowd was, in the majority, well pleased with the result.
1 – 0, that will do nicely. It was not a great performance, but it kept us ticking over, and we ended the day in 5th place in the table on a respectable 14 points, just 2 points adrift of Cardiff in $2^{nd,}$ although already 8 points behind run away leaders QPR. Next game up was Preston North End, at Elland Road, next Tuesday. Preston were in 22nd spot, with just 6 points, and already there were calls for their manager Darren

Ferguson to resign. On paper it looked like a great opportunity to consolidate our top 6 position. As the man says though...we don't play on paper.

Knocked for Six

The Preston game was our 4th Tuesday night fixture, and the 3rd one at home, but we had lost the previous 2, to Leicester City in the Carling Cup, and then that disaster at Oakwell a fortnight ago. I had started to automatically get nervous about Tuesday night fixtures. It wasn't a superstitious thing, but you do just start to think that maybe Tuesday nights don't suit the team for some obscure reason. Maybe the players don't like the Tuesday menu at the players' canteen or something? Who knows, but it was starting to become a bit of a monkey on our backs. Reading Richard Sutcliffe's recent biography of Don Revie "Revered and Reviled", the various superstitions of the Don were discussed at length. It seems to me, that were he still at Elland Road today, he would be making sure all Leeds midweek games were held on days other than Tuesdays...just in case. Maybe we need to get that Gypsy back to lift the curse again.

I am indebted to Sutcliffe's book for explaining why the Owl disappeared from the Leeds shirts, and why the "Peacocks" nickname was dropped. Apparently, it was because birds were considered unlucky in the Revie household, and indeed there were no pictures or ornaments of birds anywhere in his home. I can, by the way, thoroughly recommend the book as a bloody good read. *"Revie, Revered and Reviled", Richard Sutcliffe, Great Northern Books, 2010.*

Maybe I should start blaming my wife for any Leeds defeats, as she has a fascination with owls and we have dozens and dozens of owl things in our house.

As was now my custom, I took the afternoon off to make sure I could get to Elland Road in good time to meet Mark, who got the bus from the city out to the ground. I met him in the Pavilion. It would quickly become almost a ritual, that we would both have a couple of pints of Beck's, and either a meat and potato pie with mushy peas and gravy, or the pork baguette! We generally try to read Ken Bates' programme notes, and skim through the rest of the programme to keep up to date with any news, although we do tend to look at the web most days anyway. Then we would decide on a couple of bets, before making our way over to the ground.

The team was the same that had started on Saturday against the Blades. We assumed that Snoddy would have started, had he not now been suspended, following his late sending off in that game. So it was Becchio and Somma up front again tonight.

I don't know what odds I would have got on Leeds losing this game 6 – 4, but I would guess that a) it would be under the "other prices on application" category, and b) it would have been several hundred to one! It was the most astonishing game I have ever been at, but by the end of it Mark and I were just plain angry. Angry that we didn't seem to have learned anything from that second half at Barnsley. Angry that the players' heads seemed to go down once the game had been levelled. Angry, that our defending was so poor yet again.

The game had started at a frenetic pace, just like so many of the Leeds games this season, and once again there was an early goal. The game was barely 5 minutes old when Preston took the lead. Keith Treacy loped into the box on the left and hit the ball straight across goal from the bye-line. Higgs got down at the near post but lamely parried it straight to big Jon "The Beast" Parkin, who tapped it in from a couple of yards. It was a soft, soft goal, and Higgs should have done better. I made a mental note that I no longer considered Higgs to have good hands. All around us the fans were angry. As it happens, the goal had gone in right in front of the Kop, so there was no hiding place for Higgs, and the replay on the big screen, at the opposite end of the ground, only confirmed what we had all initially felt. It was poor keeping.

There were chances galore throughout this game, but it took Leeds 10 minutes to get level, when George McCartney sent over a cross from the left that Becchio met at the near post to head into the bottom corner, past the diving Andy Lonergan in the visitors' goal. From that point Leeds built up a head of steam, and it started to look like we would run riot. I had gone for 4 - 0 again with my pre-match bet, so that was already toast, but 4 – 1 now looked a distinct possibility, as Preston were dire. It was only 5 minutes later that Leeds took the lead. Jonny Howson collected the ball wide on the left and put in a long cross to the back post. Two Preston defenders were there, under no pressure, but one of them headed the ball straight out to Alex Bruce who returned it first time with his head, over the keeper, into the top left corner. Another 7 minutes and it was 3 – 1 and we were coasting. Lloyd Sam took the ball into the box on the right and toe poked it across goal, where the unmarked Davide Somma just had to swing his right leg to smash the ball past Lonergan again. The Leeds fans by now were ready to party. There was a clear feeling that this game was already over, and it was going to be a Leeds goal fest. But at the same time some of the Leeds defending had again been very sloppy. We had got away with it so far, all bar Higgs' calamity, but time and time again Preston were able to break with pace and create chances, but they just hadn't managed to convert them. Leeds got their 4th on 39 minutes, when Somma went unchallenged to the edge of the box on the left, and his shot just ran straight along the ground inside the far post. Mark and I were bouncing up and down with everyone else, we were all going "f****** mental", but at the same time we just knew we were not solid at the back, and literally anything could happen. We had been a goal up at Barnsley remember, and we messed that up. It would not be impossible to mess this up. Sure enough, within a minute of being 4 – 1 up and cruising, Preston struck again, to reduce the deficit back to 2. Parkin was in a race with two Leeds defenders, down the inside left channel. For some reason neither Leeds man put in a challenge. Parkin toe-poked the ball towards goal with his left foot, and Higgs couldn't stop it going in with his "good hands". He ended up on his arse. Preston were now on a high, and for the remaining few minutes of the half it was like the Battle of the Alamo all over again, as the Lilywhites surged forward, winning umpteen corners, forcing a good save out of Higgs, and having another shot cleared off the line. Never has the half time whistle come as such a relief. As we cheered the Leeds team off at half time, everyone around us was saying "We can effin lose this you know" and "We did this at Barnsley the other night". I turned to Mark and said, "I have never been this nervous at 4 – 2 up before."

The second half was just a blur. It was all somehow inevitable and yet unbelievable, all at the same time. The players didn't look right; they looked nervous themselves and played tentatively, often having the ball, but then giving it away really cheaply. It was like watching your kids play on a Sunday morning when they have just gone 4 or 5 goals down, and you can tell they just want to go home, and have lost all interest. There was no passion; there was no obvious pride in the shirt. In short, it was unacceptable for players at this level to play like that.

PNE were putting us under loads of pressure; they were two goals down remember, but they were giving it their all. They could sense the nervousness of the players in white, and the crowd; they knew they could get something out of this game. They believed. Yes, that was it exactly. Preston "believed" they could still win this game. Leeds didn't "believe" they could hold on.

The goal avalanche started on 54 minutes. Keith Treacy took an in-swinging corner from the right, and the next thing we knew was that the Preston fans massed up there in the South East corner were going mental, as the ball had sailed straight into the roof of the net. Images of schoolboy football again came to mind. How can a keeper allow that to happen? The crowd was now urging Leeds to work, work and work again and to get a grip. I was doing the same, and my throat was sore from shouting, pleading with the players, but we all knew in our hearts that something was wrong here, and it was just inevitable that this was going to be another "what might have been" night. Sure enough, within 4 minutes the scores were level. "Gentle George" McCartney was marshalling Paul Coutts towards the bye-line at the right edge of the area, he was going nowhere. McCartney stuck out a needless leg and Coutts went down as if hit by a rifle shot, from a sniper somewhere in the South stand. The referee pointed at the spot. The Leeds fans began to sing "What the f*** is going on" again, just as they had at Barnsley the other night. Callum Davidson stepped up and hammered the ball past Higgs with his left foot.

On 64 minutes a high hopeful ball into the box fell between two Leeds defenders, and while they debated who should clear it, The Beast nipped in between them both and smacked the ball into the net for his hat trick goal. As the Leeds players turned to line up again there were no recriminations, there was no arguing with each other, no frantic waving of hands, and no sign of anger with themselves or anyone else, just resigned acceptance that they were unable to stop this inevitable comeback. We had all seen it at Barnsley two weeks ago. It was distressing to watch, and we deserved more from them than this.

In ten second half minutes, we had conceded three appalling goals, including a corner going straight in, a needless, pointless penalty, and a soft long ball that we failed to clear. If my lads had ever shown such a lack of passion and effort on a Sunday morning I would have gone absolutely berserk. But it wasn't over yet. On 79 minutes, Preston became the first away team to score 6 goals at Elland Road. It was another nothing long ball into the area from the right wing, and even though there were 4 Leeds players in the box, none was less than three yards from Iain Hume, who rose unchallenged to head in their 6th goal. In years to come, I am sure this match will be mentioned many times, and it will be something to be able to say "I was there", but as we trudged wearily away from the ground, Mark and I were just livid, angry that we could turn in such a poor display. We really started to think that we would be nearer the bottom of this division than the

top come next May, if we didn't start to tighten up and show some passion. In the distance we could still hear the Preston fans singing "4 - 1 and you f***** it up, 4 - 1 and you f***** it up!" and that hurt.
I dropped Mark back at his student house in Leeds, and then set off on the long journey back down the Motorway. It was an awful night that had started so magnificently. I didn't know it at the time of course, but that rollercoaster ride of ups and downs was to be an ever present feeling over the next few weeks and months, as we constantly got ourselves into winning positions in games, only to throw them away with naïve defending.
As our anthem "Marching on Together" tells us, "we've had our ups and downs..."
Next, was Ipswich Town away, which Mark and I were missing, and then it was the trip to the Riverside, on 16th October, which we were very much looking forward to.

The Ipswich game was always going to be a tricky encounter. Ipswich were doing OK under Roy Keane at the time we went there, though they would begin to self destruct not long afterwards, and Roy Keane would be on his bike shortly after Christmas. I for one have never had any time for Roy Keane, not since that day in 2001 when he injured Alf-Inge Haaland, then a Manchester City player, in a foul tackle that all but ended the Norwegian's career. When Keane subsequently revealed, in his autobiography, that he had harboured a grudge against Haaland since a similar foul tackle in 1997 when Alf-Inge was playing for Leeds, and that he had deliberately set out to harm Haaland in that Manchester Derby, I considered that Keane should then have been banned from taking up any role in football for life. For now though he was still the Ipswich manager and I could only wish defeat on him.

Leeds made four changes from the team that started the infamous Preston North End debacle, with Naylor, Kilkenny,

Faye, and Snodgrass, coming in for Hughes, Gradel, Sam, and Becchio. I watched the highlights of the game on the BBC's Football League Show on the night of the game, and on balance it looked like Ipswich just shaded it.

The opening Ipswich goal, on 19 minutes, once again highlighted our frailty down the centre of our defence. Jake Livermore collected the ball in his own half and played a one two. He then realised that the whole of the Leeds half had opened up in front of him like the Red Sea did for Moses. He ran on before poking the ball forward to Jason Scotland, who easily went round Higgs to slot the ball into the empty net. Ridiculously easy! I wasn't to know it then of course, but the same Jake Livermore, a Spurs player on loan to the Tractor Boys, would be taken on loan by Leeds for the last few games of the season, though he never again looked as good as he did that afternoon.

It took Leeds until the 77th minute to equalise, but it was a well-worked goal when it came. Lloyd Sam fed the ball to Watt down the inside left channel in the box, and despite being under pressure, he managed to slide the ball across the face of the goal with his right boot. The keeper was stranded at the near post, and Snoddy was on hand to side-foot the ball in from two yards. That should have been the signal to shut up shop and go home with a point...but this is Leeds United we are talking about here, and almost inevitably we contrived to throw away the point we had just spent the last hour working for. To make it slightly easier for the Portman Road outfit, Alex Bruce first got himself sent off for two very similar, poor tackles, out on the Ipswich left wing. Then with just 7 minutes left, Tommy Smith popped up to win it for the Tractor Boys. That win put Ipswich into 4th place, 4 points ahead of Leeds in 10th. No great damage done, but a feeling that the trip to the Riverside next week might not be very fruitful with Leeds in this very charitable mood. Whatever, Mark and I would be there to see it. There was a two-week international break between the Ipswich and Middlesbrough games, in which hopefully some of these defensive problems could be worked on.

The Bridge Inn

As soon as we received the e-mail from the club to say we had been successful in getting tickets for the 'Boro game, we began planning for a weekend away. Some good friends of ours live in Darlington, which is only a 20-minute drive from Middlesbrough, and they kindly offered that we could stop with them for the weekend in question. It was just Mark and I going to the game, but the wife came with us to Darlo' while Adam stopped at home, as he was playing rugby for the school on the Saturday morning. The missus and I had a good drive north on the Friday night and Mark had got the train to Darlo' from Leeds on Friday afternoon.

Our friends in Darlington are a story in themselves. We first met them whilst we were honeymooning in Korcula, in the then Yugoslavia in 1984. It was one of those hotel holidays – a two-centre holiday in fact, with Yugotours – where the waiters paired off couples to make sure that all the tables in the restaurant were filled. We had been taken to our seats first and were enjoying a starter when the waiter brought over the couple that we would be dining with for the rest of the week. As we recalled later and as Brian himself acknowledges, at that time he was the spitting image of Jasper Carrot, the Brummie comedian, who in those days you just couldn't get away from. Carrott was on TV back home almost every day on one show or another in the late 70's, and of course he had that big hit with Funky Moped in 1975. Brian and Sheila, as they introduced themselves to us, tried to get the conversation going by asking if we were married. We obviously told them that we had been married for just a couple of days and that this was our honeymoon. That seemed to unsettle them a bit and eventually they confessed that perhaps they were not the best choice of table mates for us, as they were both recently divorced, and this was their first holiday away together as a couple!

In fact they were the perfect tablemates, and have become great friends over the years. Brian and I have football in common. Despite living in the North East for many years, Brian is a life-long Chelsea supporter and season ticket holder. He makes the trip down to London every fortnight to watch the Blues, and is football mad. He was born and bred in London, but moved north with work many years ago. He goes to many away games and will also take in any game of any club if he is not at a Chelsea match. During the season he will quite often take in two or three games a week. He currently has both a Chelsea and a Darlington season ticket! Sheila is a lovely lady who would do anything for anyone, as would Brian. In 1991 they agreed to become godparents to Mark and that holiday in Korcula in '84 was the beginning of a friendship that lasted probably until they read this book. We had a great time sampling the local white wine that went by the name Grk (pronounced "Gurk"). God knows how many bottles of the stuff we got through, but we made sure we brought several home with us, just to keep the memory alive. We spent the second week on the island of Mlini, and we just continued on where we had begun in Korkula. When it was time to say our farewells, we swapped addresses in true "Corfu" manner, but we have enjoyed their company ever since. Incidentally, if the reference to Corfu here is lost on you, please Google "The Meaning of Liff" by Douglas Adams and John Lloyd, and you will find amongst other definitions:

CORFU (n.) The dullest person you met during the course of your holiday. Also the only one who failed to understand that the exchanging of addresses at the end of a holiday is merely a social ritual and is absolutely not an invitation to phone you up and turn up unannounced on your doorstep three months later. (The Meaning of Liff, Pan Books, 1983)

On 23rd December 1990, Brian and Sheila took us all to Roker Park, for the Division One game between Sunderland and Leeds. When I say, "us all", it was of course just my missus and me in those days, but the wife was pregnant with Mark at the time, so I guess that was officially his first Leeds United game! We had bought the tickets on the day at the ground, and were on the terraced standing area in the Clock Stand. Brian, had thoughtfully realised that Karen would not be comfortable standing in the cold for a couple of hours while 7 months pregnant, so he managed to smuggle into the ground, a small wooden stool under his coat. You would never get away with that today of course, as it would be considered a dangerous weapon that could be thrown at the players. It was ideal though for Karen, who was able to sit down when she got tired. As to the game, it was a dour affair on a difficult pitch. Leeds won it 1 – 0, with a fine goal from Mel Sterland, hit from distance in the goal to our left. Simon Grayson was in the Leeds squad around this time, but he only ever played twice for the Whites, and wasn't involved in the Sunderland game. Leeds ended that season in 4th place but the following season, Leeds would lift the Division One title, under Howard Wilkinson. That Sunderland game is just one of many we have been to with Brian and Sheila over the years. Another memorable one was the Leeds versus Chelsea game in December 2002. Brian and Sheila were in with the Chelsea fans, while we were in the South Stand, to watch James Milner score a memorable goal, his second in 3 days at the start of his career as a 16 year old. Karen, Mark, Adam and I, can all be seen clearly in the crowd behind the goal on the archive footage of Milner's goal.

After sharing a few bottles of beer with Brian and Sheila on Friday night, it was settled that we would all go to Middlesbrough on the Saturday afternoon. Mark and I would be dropped near the ground, while the others found something to do in the town centre. This game was a 5:20pm kick off, as it was on Sky TV as part of their Championship coverage. Apparently, the Northumbria Police in Middlesbrough had all leave cancelled and they had tried to move the kick off to mid-day, to avoid the possibility of fans spending all day in the boozers before going to the game. As we left Darlington and headed out on the A1150, we spotted the black Starliner Leeds United coach coming in the opposite direction, into Darlington. It was empty at this stage, so we assumed that the players had stopped in a hotel near there overnight, and that the coach was on its way to pick up the team to take them to the Riverside.

We arrived outside the ground very early. Mark and I had decided we would have a few beers before the game. Brian had another agenda, as he was determined to find a pub that was showing the 'Villa versus Chelsea game, that was also coincidentally kicking off around the same time as the 'Boro match. Brian would have been at Villa Park had we not been going up there for the weekend; that is just the sort of bloke he is, even prepared to give up his beloved Chelsea to accommodate us. We drove around the ground for a while, to see if there was a likely parking spot, but in the end decided that we would get dropped in town and we would walk back to the ground. That way, the car was well away from the crowds and any trouble, when we tried to get away later.

The two of us first tried Walkabout, the Australian themed bar on Corporation Street. It takes up the first two floors of the Centre North East Building, which is reputed to be the tallest building in the North East, at 19 storeys high. The Walkabout bar is massive, with huge bars and enormous TV screens up on the walls where they show live sports action. On October 16th at around 3pm, it was heaving, and packed out with 'Boro fans in their distinctive red shirts with the Ramsdens name across the front. Mark and I both had our Leeds shirts on underneath our jackets, with our collars turned up, despite the fact that it was a warm day, and inside Walkabout it felt like it was about 100 degrees! We queued at the bar for an age, and while standing there we spotted that they had a deal on, whereby if you showed your match ticket to the bar staff, you got a discount on your beer or food. Mark nudges me and tells me to get the tickets out, and I was on the point of doing so when I noticed that the lads currently at the bar showing their tickets had red ones; ours were edged blue to denote they were for the away end! We decided we would pass on the match day deal! After waiting for another fifteen minutes, we gave up, and decided to try to find a less busy boozer. I read later in the year, that the Walkabout Bar in Middlesbrough was up for sale, following Regents Inns going into administration at the end of 2009. I should have written to them with my idea as to how they could increase beer sales. GET MORE BLOODY BAR STAFF IN ON MATCH DAYS!

As we came out of the bar, I spotted a white police minibus full of Bobbies, parked up on the opposite side of the road. I had an idea. I asked the coppers where the Leeds fans would be drinking in town. They seemed very confident that it would be at a place called The Bridge. "It's a little pub just round the corner from the main railway station," they said. We thanked them, and set off towards the station which was about 15 minutes walk away. We found The Bridge, and discovered that it was a run-down, one room dive of a place, with a counter, a couple of hand pumps, and a few café type tables. It was unlikely to ever feature in the CAMRA Good Pub Guide. There were a few lads in there wearing Leeds shirts, and a TV in the corner was showing Gillette Soccer Saturday. Perfect, we thought, we could spend an hour or so here watching the scores come in from the 3 O'clock kick offs, before making our way out to the stadium. There were some decent games on in the Championship that day, QPR 0 Norwich 0, was one half time that came up while we were watching. We got a couple of pints and sat watching the TV, and all was good for about 10 minutes. Then, all of a sudden, about thirty young lads burst into the pub through a back door, and with them came about half a dozen uniformed coppers, including one with a little hand held Sony video camera! As Mark said later, "it was like a scene from the movie 'This is England'". All these lads were clearly in some sort of a gang, as they were mostly dressed the same, with several of them wearing Parkas, and white shirts with a red check pattern. Maybe this was some sort of modern day Mods gang. There was no trouble yet, but Mark had noticed that the Leeds fans that had been in there to start with had all gone out, and we could now see them through the window, finishing their beers outside, talking with another group of coppers! One of the 'Boro lads spotted my Leeds shirt and he lent over me saying something like "Leeds, Leeds, Leeds, you here for the game?" He had a mouthful of wire keeping his yellowed teeth together, and a broad Tyneside accent. It was not easy to understand him. I just said "yeah, you going?" He laughed and replied something like "Nah Leeds, I'm only here for the trouble". At that point Mark and I looked at each other and Mark quietly suggests "Time to go Zebedee?" and we both got up to make our way out. Several of the kids (they were all about 15 or 16 I reckoned) tried to push us about as we left, but they stopped short of any real contact, probably because Mark is six feet six, and I am six two. When we got outside I approached the gang of police waiting there, and I informed one of them that his mates up the road had told us this place would be OK, and that the Leeds fans would be fine in here. At first he just shrugged, but then, as we were walking away, he obviously overheard us talking about it, and he followed us. He told us that it should have been OK, but someone had obviously 'phoned through to these lads to tell them that Leeds fans were in here, and then they had made their way over to see if anything was going to go down. He seemed worried that I thought the police had set us up! We learned later in the day that there had been trouble in a few of the town centre pubs when the 'Boro and Leeds fans came upon one another.

We thought that was quite enough excitement for one day, and so we made our way out to the stadium. It was a pleasant, sunny day, and we were impressed when we saw the Riverside Stadium up close. We were not sure if they would be selling alcohol in the ground, so we asked at one of the turnstiles. They confirmed that they were, so we decided to go in, even though there was still over an hour to go 'til kick off. There were just over 4,000 Leeds fans at this game, with the Leeds allocation sold out, as it always is, and when we got into the area under the South Stand it was really rocking. The choice of beer was err, limited, to Carlsberg, Carlsberg, or Carlsberg, in plastic bottles, so we had a couple of Carlsberg's. The staff serving behind the bar were all good natured folk and one lady was even wearing a Leeds pin badge. She told us the score would be 4 – 0 Leeds, so I decided to put my normal 4 – 0 bet on. Mark went with Neil Collins for first goal. The atmosphere was building nicely, and all 4,075 Leeds fans now seemed to be crammed into the area under the stand. Every now and again a chant would break out, and every last fan was joining in. It was enough to make the hairs stand up on the back of your neck. At one point, a bloke came by us singing "Marching on Together" at the top of his voice and he threw his arms round me and gave me a big bear hug, like a long lost brother. It was shaping up to be a magic day out, and as a result of our little episode in The Bridge, it was certainly going to be unforgettable.

The 'Boro manager at this time was former Leeds man Gordon Strachan of course, and we knew he was under pressure, with 'Boro having only picked up 11 points from their first 10 games, despite them being pre-season favourites to go up. We didn't know it at the time of course, but Gordon was to resign immediately following this game, and I think it fair to say that the Leeds fans had something to do with that. Early in the game the Leeds fans were singing, "Gorrrr-don Strachan is a Leeds fan, is a Leeds fan" and Gordon gave us a little wave to acknowledge the chant. After the game, a lot of the 'Boro fans ringing into the local radio stations, commented on that, and felt Strachan was showing too much respect to Leeds.

The main shock in the team for this game was the first start for goalkeeper Jason Brown, who had come on when Higgs was injured in the Ipswich game. Paul Connolly was back at right back, and McCartney was on the left, with Collins and Naylor in the middle for this one. Amdy Faye was making his third consecutive start, with Howson, Watt, and Snodgrass, completing the midfield this time round. Somma partnered Becchio again up front.

23,550 were in the Riverside, its' biggest attendance of the season so far, and it was quite a spectacle. It seemed from where we were that it was only the Leeds fans making any noise, and boy, were we making some. 12 minutes into the game and we were in front. That was the 9th time this season, out of 13 Leeds games, that a goal had been scored in the first quarter of an hour, and it was usually Leeds that had scored first. It was all going on at the far end of the ground, so it was difficult to make out exactly what happened, but Snoddy and Watt combined before Watt hit a shot across the box. Somma latches onto it and fires it past Steele in the 'Boro goal. Cue Leeds fans to go mental. At half time, the home fans boo their team off, which can only be good for Leeds.

Strachan obviously got his boys fired up at half time, because they came out and gave it a real go, and it was no surprise when on 53 minutes Kris Boyd equalised for the 'Boro. Boyd was one of several Scottish players brought in by Strachan, and if the catering staff serving under the South Stand are representative of them all, that was not too popular with the 'Boro faithful. It was a tough tackling game, with plenty of heavy challenges going in, and it was after a couple of particularly robust tackles in the 'Boro half, that Leeds got the winner. First, Connolly was wrestled to the ground, but the ball broke forward to Becchio. He in turn took a crunching blow but got straight back up and the ball squirted out to the left wing, where substitute Bradley Johnson was lurking. He looked up, spotted Becchio now running in from the edge of the box, and clipped a delightful ball over to him. Becchio met it first time, on the volley, with his left foot, and he hammered it in off the far post. It was a tremendous strike to put Leeds 2 - 1 up. It was a nervy old last 25 minutes or so, but Leeds hung on for a hard won three points. Once again, the home fans vented their anger on their own team, but we were all bouncing in the South Stand, rejoicing at a magnificent result. It had come at a price though, as we lost Watt, Faye, and McCartney, to injury, all following heavy challenges. The momentum was back though, and we were off and running again after the recent disasters at Barnsley and Ipswich, and that pantomime performance against Preston a couple of weeks ago.

We made our way out of the ground, only to find all hell had broken out. There had clearly been little or no thought given to the fact that the massed ranks of Leeds fans were coming out of the South Stand to mingle with the 'Boro fans, in the dark, as everyone struggled to get along Dockside Road, back towards the town centre. At one point, everyone stopped, as a fight broke out and dozens of white police mini buses appeared from nowhere, trying to also make their way up the road, amongst the thousands of fans of both clubs that were walking along it. A couple of lads were walking in the middle of the road next to us when one of the mini buses screeched to a halt behind them. A couple of burly coppers, dressed in riot garb, threw back the door of the bus and jumped out, and then almost threw one of the lads out of the way. It was unnecessary and was no doubt fuelled by adrenalin. It was a very tense walk back, not least because it was so dark, and it was impossible to tell who was a Leeds fan and who was 'Boro. We rang the wife to find out where they had parked, and we tried to make our way to them as best we could, but every time we thought we were getting close, we ran into a police blockade and they would just tell us to go another way. In the end, we went into the railway station and out the other side, and eventually, with the sounds of sirens and shouting in the air, we jumped into the car and sped off out of the town. Mark and I were both hot and sweaty after the long jog, but as we sat back in the car, we contemplated a job well done at the Riverside. Brian was happy, in that they had found a pub showing the Chelsea game (0 – 0), and the girls had had a sleep in the last of the autumn sunshine. So, everyone was happy that night as we all enjoyed a wonderful evening meal prepared by Sheila, and copious amounts of alcohol. It was hard to tell if this win at the Riverside was a turning point, or whether it was just further proof that this season was going to be another rollercoaster ride like last year. We might have a better idea on Tuesday night, when Leicester City are back at Elland Road for a league game. It would be our 5th Tuesday night game of the season, and the record so far was, won 1, drawn 0, lost 3.

We Don't like Tuesdays...or Mondays

Another afternoon off work and another 100-mile trip up the M6 and M62 to Leeds, this time for the home league match against Sven-Goran Eriksson's Foxes. Sven had joined the Foxes before the Hull City game at the weekend, and saw his new charges gain a point from a one-all draw. That left Leicester in 20th spot in the table, on 12 points, only 5 points, but 10 places, behind Leeds. Paolo Souza had only been appointed manager at the Walkers Stadium in July, and his reign had lasted less than three months by the time he was sacked by owner Milan Mandaric. Now, Sven was at the helm. Following the excellent victory at the Riverside on Saturday, it was no surprise that Grayson gave that team another chance to show that they were perhaps the best line up he had at his disposal. That meant that big Jason Brown remained in goal, although that was due to continuing injuries to both Higgs and Schmeichel.

Within minutes of the start, Leeds were under tremendous pressure, as Leicester seemed determined to get Sven his first win. The Leeds team might have had the same names in it as on Saturday, but the performances were chalk and cheese. This performance was already looking like the last three Tuesday night efforts, lacklustre and weak. Somehow, we managed to get back into the dressing room at half time with no score on the board, but Leicester had been unlucky with a number of close efforts. The best of them saw Bruno Berner, despite being surrounded by four Leeds players, hit the bar with a long-range shot that had Brown clawing the air in front of the Kop. Grayson had already had to deploy Bradley Johnson from the bench, to try to change a system that clearly wasn't working, and it was Sanchez Watt that had to make way for him.

The Foxes scented victory, and came out for the second half to batter us again. It took them only 15 minutes of the second period to get their well-deserved lead. Kyle Naughton had the ball out on the right wing; it was no danger at all. However, he just waltzed into our box, skipping past first McCartney and then Somma, before poking the ball through Collins' legs, past Brown, into the corner of the net. It was yet another soft, soft goal. Grayson threw Gradel and Kilkenny on for Faye and Snoddy, but it was the defence that let us down again on 80 minutes. Andy King won a challenge just inside the Leeds half and was again allowed to run with the ball right to the edge of the Leeds box, without the remotest threat of a tackle. It was a run very similar to the one made by Adam Hammill against us up at Barnsley, when he scored, but this time King rolled the ball to his left and Steve Howard was able to gently steer the ball into the far corner of the net with Brown unable to get a hand to it. Howard had also scored in the Carling Cup game a few Tuesdays ago to help Leicester win that one 2 – 1 at Elland Road, and it looked like this one would go the same way. We did get one back a couple of minutes later when Gradel, only just off the bench, crossed a simple ball from the right wing, and Becchio out-jumped his marker to plant his header in the bottom right corner. 2 - 1 it finished, exactly the same as that Carling Cup game in August. After the match, Simon Grayson said that we "just didn't have that spark", which sums it up pretty accurately. He also noted that once again it was two mistakes that undid us, and that we must eradicate mistakes from our game. I'll drink to that. Five Tuesday night games had yielded just one win – against Lincoln City – and four defeats. I checked in the programme and found that we had at least seven more Tuesday night games to endure before the end of the season. In that book about Don Revie I am reading, it was noted that Revie, in the middle of one period of fixture congestion, refused to play a game on a Thursday, saying "Leeds United don't play on Thursdays" Well, I can now add to that, saying that they don't bloody well play on Tuesdays either! The next game though was on a Monday night, and it was against the highflying Bluebirds of Cardiff City.

I didn't go to the Cardiff game, but Mark was there. Adam and I watched the game live on Sky TV, as it was their Monday night game. Schmeichel was back in the side, after his injury, Johnson started in place of Watt, and Bruce came in for the injured Richard Naylor. The rest were the crew that disappointed us on Tuesday night, meaning that Becchio and Somma continued as the 2 up front in a 4 - 4 - 2 formation.

It was to prove another nightmare performance, littered with mistakes at the back starting as early as the 22nd minute. The Cardiff keeper, Tom Heaton, pumped a routine clearance downfield, and Bruce, for some reason known only to him, allowed the ball to bounce. When it came down the second time Bruce left the ball for Schmeichel, but he somehow fumbled it, and Jay Bothroyd was there to pounce on it and stab it into an empty net. I had lost count of the number of times a long ball down the middle had undone our defence, but this one was possibly the worst example so far. There was no further action in the first half, but after the break Cardiff had a devastating 10 minute spell in which they struck three times. First, Michael Chopra thumped one in from the right edge of the box; Schmeichel got a hand on it, but couldn't stop it. Then, 5 minutes later, a simple ball cut back from the bye-line on the right managed to slip through 4 Leeds players to Bothroyd, who lashed it into the net from 6 yards. Then, Lee Naylor tried a speculative shot from outside the area that somehow beat Schmeichel at his near post. Mark was regularly texting us to tell us how bad we were and all we could respond with was to tell him that Bothroyd should have been sent off early in the second half, when he clearly went over the ball and caught Becchio on the inside of his left calf. He was not even booked, but the TV replay showed it clearly, and it also showed Bothroyd puffing out his cheeks as he walked away, as if to acknowledge that he knew he was a lucky, lucky fellow, to still be on the pitch. Becchio had a header ruled out for offside late on, but this was another eminently forgettable display by a Leeds team that had begun to look well short of the standard needed to succeed at this level. What we didn't know though, was that we were about to embark on a run of games that would suggest that *au contraire,* this team did in fact have the quality to make a mark on the Championship. In fact, we would not taste defeat again until the next time we met the Bluebirds, in the New Year. As the man says, "It's a funny old game!"

Marching up the League

On the night of the Cardiff defeat, Leeds were in 16th position in the table, a full 12 points behind QPR and Cardiff at the top. We had won just 2 of our previous 7 games when we travelled to Glanford Park, the home of Scunthorpe United, on Saturday, October 30th.

The trip to Scunthorpe was slightly longer than our normal trip to Elland Road. The Leeds journey for us from Market Drayton is almost exactly 100 miles, but as it is almost all motorway it is possible to do that run in an hour and twenty minutes – OK, that is late at night coming back with no traffic hold-ups. Scunthorpe was 115 miles from home, and the AA route finder suggested it was a two and a quarter hour trip, which proved about right. At least the ground was easy to find, being almost right at the end of the M181. It was a clear day with a bright blue sky when we set off, but our mood didn't match it. We were still concerned at how easily teams were scoring past us, and those hidings we had received against Barnsley, Preston, and Cardiff, suggested this could be a difficult season after so much promise in the first few games. We watched the players emerge from the Eddie Brown Silverliner coach outside the little Glanford Park ground, and they all looked confident enough, as did Simon Grayson, looking the part in his grey suit. Over 2,000 Leeds fans were packed into the tidy little ground as part of a total crowd of just over 8,000. We were in the AMS Stand at the South end of the ground, while the rest of the Leeds contingent was to our right in the South end of the Grove Wharf Stand. All sides of this ground look identical though, as it resembles an open top box with the sides all the same height. The Iron, as the team is known, because of the importance of the metal to the history of the area, moved into this ground in 1988, and it was the first brand new football league ground to be built since the Second World War.

Having persisted with Becchio and Somma up top for the past few games, Grayson appeared to go conservative here, reverting to an obvious 4 - 5 - 1 with Becchio the lone striker, although both Davide Somma and Billy Paynter were on the bench. Gradel and Snodgrass provided the width, with Howson (now the only ever present this season), Faye and Kilkenny, in the centre of midfield. Schmeichel, having returned for the Cardiff game, looked settled again in goal, with Connolly and McCartney also now looking the first choice full backs, as long as McCartney's loan deal from Sunderland was allowed to continue. At centre back this time it was Bruce, together with Andy O'Brien who was making his Leeds debut, having come on loan from Bolton Wanderers the previous week.

As always the atmosphere amongst the Leeds fans was fantastic. Come rain or shine, ups or frequent downs, it is always the same with the Leeds faithful. True, there were some fans grumbling about the recent poor results, but when the game started they gave it their all as they always do. There was an awful moment in the opening minutes of the game when, just as against Cardiff the other night, Schmeichel and Bruce got into a tangle, but this time Andy O'Brien was on hand to clear the ball off the line, his first touch in a Leeds shirt! As so often this season, we had a goal in the first 15 minutes. This time it came on 8 minutes and it went to Leeds. Jonny Howson pushed the ball through three Scunny defenders and Mad Max Gradel ran onto it. He crisply drove the ball into the right hand corner with his left foot from the inside left channel, despite the close presence of a defender tugging at him. None of us were thinking this was going to be that easy though, we had seen leads given away and games lost throughout the season, and there had hardly been a Leeds game this year without one drama or another. We also knew we had seen 51 goals in just 15 games, so a 1 - 0 win here, was somewhat unlikely.

And so it was. On 27 minutes, Scunny won a corner on the right at the South end of the ground where we were all massed. The corner was met perfectly at the far post by Cliff Byrne, who planted his header in the top corner. For a moment, the Leeds players had that look of panic on their faces again, but this time they did then knuckle down to the task in hand. My 4 – 0 bet was already toast though.

In the second half, kicking towards the Leeds fans, it was a white tidal wave, and the match stats after the game would show we had a total of 20 shots, 15 of which were on target. 3 of those were from Jonny Howson and came in a 15-minute spell between the 60th and 75th minutes of the game. First, Paul Connolly crossed from the right wing, the ball bounced once in the box before arriving on Howson's left foot. He hit the ball crisply across the keeper, and the ball nestled in the far corner. Next, Mad Max swung in a long cross from the left wing with his right foot, over to the far post. Howson rose unchallenged to nod the ball over the keeper into the opposite corner. Finally, Becchio ran with the ball at speed in the inside left channel, passed inside to Howson who took one touch before unleashing a great right footer high to the keepers left. It was the so-called perfect hat trick; one right foot, one left foot, and one header. The Leeds fans broke into the obvious "There's only one Jonny Howson" and the less obvious "Leeds Calypso" but the sun was shining and with only 15 minutes left, surely we couldn't throw this one away! Johnson, Paynter, and Nunez, all got a run out in the latter stages, and this performance restored our faith that maybe, just maybe, we could force our way into the play offs by the end of the season. It was nice to have a relaxed end to a game with a 3-goal lead. We were already looking forward to another away trip next Saturday, to the slightly larger Ricoh Arena in Coventry.

Younger son Adam was playing rugby for the Newcastle under Lyme School First XV at King Edward VI School, Lichfield, on the morning of November 6th. His brother had suggested we drive to Lichfield to watch him play, before going on to the Ricoh in the afternoon. It was the day after Bonfire Night, and

Mark had been at a fireworks party the previous evening when a stray firework had shot through the crowd and ended up in some bushes. He was telling me this as we were driving to Lichfield, and then we heard on the radio that a 21 year-old man in Lewes in Sussex was fighting for his life, after a stray rocket hit him in the chest, during one of the biggest bonfire night celebrations in the country. There but for the grace of God etc. Some 40,000 people had attended the traditional Lewes event that is held in the narrow streets of the old town every year.

It was another decent bright day, but bitterly cold, as we arrived at the school in Lichfield in good time to see the game. A quick scan of the two teams told us that Lichfield were odds on to win this one. Two of their "lads" looked as if they were likely to be "picking their kids up from school after the game" as the old joke goes. They were huge! Sure enough, Lichfield raced into a 12 – 0 lead, with some fairly basic rugby. But then Newcastle got themselves a couple of penalties and pulled the score back to 12 – 6. Lichfield ended up winning the game easily, after scoring a couple more tries in the first half, and then three more in the second. Newcastle did have a spirited last twenty minutes though, and during that spell, Adam did make the trip worthwhile for us by running in a decent try. He has played first team rugby for the school for a couple of years already, even though he is only 17 now and has one more year to go after this at the school. He plays outside centre these days, and, like his brother, is well over six feet tall, and so is well suited to the game of rugby.

We said our farewells to Adam and headed off down the Toll Road. We didn't actually want to go on the Toll Road really, but after going round a traffic island three times we gave up trying to understand where the plain, ordinary, M6 sign was supposed to be pointing. So we had to fork out £4.50 for the privilege of going a couple of miles on the Toll. We hadn't realised quite how close we were to Coventry, and it was still only half eleven in the morning, so we decided to kill some time at Corley Service Area, as we had no idea what facilities would be available at the ground.

I thought the service area would be packed with Leeds fans doing the same, as it was reported that Leeds were taking over 6,000 this time. As it turned out, I think we were just so early that they hadn't got there yet. They were clearly expected though, as there were plenty of West Midlands Police around! Just one Leeds fan was sat alone in the Burger King Restaurant area as we arrived, and he acknowledged us with the Leeds salute. There were a few West Ham fans in there, obviously en route to St. Andrews for the game with Birmingham City. I initially mistook them for Villa fans, but Mark put me right muttering something like "Can't you see the bloody hammers on their shirt badge?" We then had a debate with the Burger King counter staff that concluded with us ordering a family meal deal for 4 at £12.99, even though there were only the two of us. We had worked out that this was in fact cheaper than two standard meals at £6.99 each! Hence, we worked our way through 4 burgers, 4 standard size Cokes, 4 lots of fries and a portion of Onion Rings! Having munched our way through that lot, we were both stuffed. Mark disappeared to the bogs for 10 minutes and on his return told me that he felt much better, having had a good dump, but as a result of his successful visit, I should now avoid trap 1 on the left if I was going in there, and I should certainly not light a match anywhere near the vicinity! I took his advice, having followed him into the bathroom at home on more than one occasion!

We set off again, and within 20 minutes we were in the traffic queue in front of the Ricoh Arena. The signs all helpfully proclaimed that there was no cash match-day parking in the stadium car parks. Just as we were wondering what the hell we were supposed to do now, Mark spotted another big yellow sign pointing down Winding House Lane to an "Official Car Park". I spotted some Leeds scarves in the car in front and it went that way, so we followed. Winding House Lane is a long straight road running to the West of the ground, and about a mile or two down there is the car parking. It didn't look too "Official" when we got there, it was just a rough bit of ground in a fenced off area, backing on to a school playing field, but someone on the gate in a Hi-Vis jacket took a fiver off us, and another bloke parked us up, so that was near enough. All the other vehicles in this car park seemed to be full of Leeds fans, and many of us set off together on the ten-minute walk back to the ground. As we walked back past the school field, we could see a line of Leeds lads having a much-needed pee against an old shed. Well, it's a long way from Leeds! As we approached the ground, this time on foot, we had a chance to have a good look at it. It looked tired, the little bits of greenery planted around were all overgrown, and it generally looked to have seen better days. At the turnstiles, we noticed that fans were being frisked before being let through. We both had plastic bottles of orange Lucozade in our pockets, so we decided to sit in the sun in the car park and drink those, and have a read of the programme. There was an article in it about Remembrance Day, which was the following weekend, and it explained that Coventry, like all other clubs, were wearing special shirts with a Poppy Appeal motif for their home game this week, and the shirts would then be auctioned off to raise funds for the appeal. Before the game, the photos and names of all the local soldiers who had lost their lives in the recent Afghanistan conflict were to be shown on the big screen in the ground. Leeds would do the same at the home game against Bristol City, next Saturday.

When we were in the ground, we got ourselves a couple of Carlsberg's and a betting slip. I decided to go for my usual 100/1 bet. This time it was for Leeds to win 4 – 2. It seemed a long shot at the time, but worth a quid just in case. Mark wanted to put a quid on Jonny Howson for first goal at 17/1, but I persuaded him that was mad, as Howson had already won him 16 quid at the Barnsley game, and he had scored a hat-trick at Scunny last week, so there was no way he was going to score again today...

The Leeds fans were as vocal as ever, and with 6,000 of them having made the trip, the noise below the stand was incredible. If you have never been to a Leeds away game, then have a look at some of the YouTube videos on the internet, there are usually several from each match, mostly taken on mobile phones, and they capture the atmosphere perfectly. We were in the concourse under the stand, watching the tail end of the Bolton Spurs game on a TV that was hardly fit for purpose. It was only a normal 26 inch domestic set, yet it was the only one, in a concourse that was now housing thousands of chanting, beer swilling, and rowdy Leeds fans. Anyway, cracking goal by Pavlyuchenko, but a very pleasing 4 – 2 victory for Bolton. Maybe an omen for my 100/1 bet?

We filled the whole of the South Stand. There was a big screen to our right, in the corner. The bulk of the hard-core Coventry support appeared to also be in that corner to our right, which would mean that, since we out numbered them, we could fit our words to their chants, which we did! The ground is very similar to the Riverside at Middlesbrough, except of course everything is light blue and not red! The pre-match entertainment included a brass band and a minute's applause for the fallen heroes of the Afghan war, and the Leeds fans behaved impeccably throughout, as did the home supporters.

On the team sheet, Jason Brown (unflatteringly christened The Flying Pig by some Leeds fans because of his ample girth) got another outing in goal for this one, as Kasper was at home following the birth of his first child last night, and Neil Collins was back in place of Alex Bruce. Apart from that it was the same line up as Scunthorpe, and again in 4 - 5 - 1 formation with Becchio on his own up front. In the Coventry team was one Gary McSheffrey, who had failed to do much for us last season during a loan spell. As he took the field, the Leeds fans broke into "You're too s**t to play for Leeds" which I thought was a fair summary of his time with us. Micky Doyle was also in their line up, but Mark and I, like the rest of the Leeds fans, thought he did a great job for us last season and so his chant was "McSheffrey's a **** but you were alright"! Doyle played 52 games for us while on loan last season and played a big part in our promotion push.

The game kicked off and once again the first goal went in very early. This time it was only 4 minutes, and it was that man Howson again. (Ooops! Sorry Mark!) It all happened right in front of us, at the South end, with Rob Snodgrass dinking the ball back into the 6 yard box to find the head of Howson, who nodded in from no more than three yards. Mark gave me a few choice words at that point to the effect of "Next time I need your advice, I will ask for it!" Not long after the goal went in a number of Leeds fans came out of one of the Coventry corporate hospitality areas to our left to take their seats behind a cordon of police. We all immediately broke into a chant of "You're just a town full of Leeds fans!" to great hilarity from all around. Marlon King was then introduced to the fray on the half hour when Clive Platt was injured, and that spurred a number of new chants that then went on most of the game. The main ones being "Marrr-lon King, you're a rapist, you're a rapist" and "She said no Marrr-lon, she said no. She said no Marrr-lon she said no" to the tune of "Kumbaya My Lord". This related to King's arrest and imprisonment for an alleged assault on a woman in a London nightclub, in December 2008.

Five minutes before half time, and the day got even better. Snoddy played a one-two on the right corner of the area, and when he got the ball back he clipped a curling left foot shot into the far corner. 2 - 0 and Leeds were in command, and more importantly we were well worth the lead, having played some fabulous football, with Gradel on the left, and Snoddy on the right, running the home defence ragged. Coventry had started this game in 4th place in the table, so we all knew that they were no mugs, but so far it was all Leeds.

At half time, ex Leeds and Coventry striker Noel Whelan was introduced to the crowd, and he delighted the 6,366 travelling Leeds fans by performing the Leeds salute, and waving to us as he left the pitch. This was turning into a perfect and unforgettable away day, and it confirmed that there is nothing quite like an away trip with the Mighty Whites, and their army of fans. The main half time entertainment was to watch a fan, chosen from the crowd, try to score from varying distances. They do it at Elland Road every game. It is more difficult there though, as the rule at Leeds is that the ball must go into the net on the full, without bouncing. At Coventry, the rule is that it just has to go into the net. They start from the penalty spot and this lad side foots the ball all along the ground and in it goes for £10. Then he is taken to about 30 yards from goal, and again he side foots the ball and it crawls in, this time for £100. Now it gets interesting. They move to the half way line and he could have chosen either to take the £100, or gamble on winning £1,000. This lad has clearly been in the boozer all day, and he hasn't just been supping J2O's. He is determined to go for the big one. But he knows there is no-way he can side foot it from half way with any chance that it will reach the net, so he has to take a big swing at it this time. Fair play to the lad, he makes a decent contact with his right foot, but it runs out of gas and curls away from the left hand post, coming to rest about a yard wide, just short of the goal line. The Leeds fans are not particularly charitable in helping him get over the fact he just blew £100! They start singing "A hundred quid and you f***** it up, a hundred quid and you f***** it up". It was a decent effort though, and it kept us amused for 10 minutes before the teams re-emerged for the second half.

If we all thought this was going to be plain sailing, we should have remembered that this was Leeds United we were watching. This was the Leeds United that never does anything the easy way, the Leeds United that took an early lead at Barnsley, and that went 4 – 1 up against Preston, only to end up on the wrong side of a thrashing in both games. To prove it, the game had been restarted for only 7 minutes, when Coventry reduced the arrears. A long cross came in from the right wing, our left, and found Ben Turner, unmarked in the centre of goal on the 6-yard line. He could have had a go at goal himself, but he had so much time that he just headed it across to Lucas Jutkjewicz, as if setting him up for a volley ball smash. Jutkjewicz, also unmarked, just had to nod it down into the unguarded corner of the net, with our man Brown stood, rooted to the spot. We hadn't heard the City faithful until now, but this brought them to life, and they really got behind their team. On this occasion though, Leeds kept doing the right things on the pitch, and suddenly Mad Max was given the ball on the left corner of their box, at the far end of the ground. Max went down, pole axed, and the referee was pointing to the spot. Penalty! Max dusted himself down to take the kick himself, and he made no mistake with a confident right foot strike, just inside the keeper's right hand post. 3 – 1 and we could relax again – couldn't we? There was still half an hour to go though and Leeds were no longer looking quite as assured. Amdy Faye succumbed to a heavy challenge and limped off, to be replaced by Bradley Johnson, and then just 2 minutes later the deficit was back to just one goal.

A long hopeful ball (how many times have we suffered this season from one of those?) was pumped into our box, and yet again our defenders all stood around making "After you Claude" gestures to each other, while Ben Turner got on with the job in hand and prodded the ball into our net. Now, the Leeds fans around us were getting very nervous, and even more vocal, demanding that the Leeds team "work, work, work" to hold on to this lead. Mark and I were doing our best to help get the lads going as well, but the phrase "not again" kept cropping up every few minutes. Time seemed to stand still, as the last half hour of the game unfolded, and the only good news was that I was now only 1 Leeds goal away from £100 with my 4 – 2 bet. Andy Hughes was brought on when Max was hurt in another strong challenge, and then Somma came on for Kilkenny. Leeds seemed to be unable to keep the ball for any period of time though, and we started giving away throw-ins and free kicks on the edge of the area. It looked like panic had set in, and maybe it was the players' demons from those big defeats earlier in the season revisiting them. Fans near us are muttering "This is f****** Barnsley and Preston all over again!" McSheffrey, thankfully, couldn't hit a cows arse with an oversized banjo, and so a couple of his free kicks were no problem, and Brown flew around the goal line a couple of times giving everyone a heart attack, but eventually grabbing the ball. Becchio had the chance to win me some money, but after rounding the keeper and shooting towards the unguarded net, a City defender gets to the ball on the line, and its' knocked out for a corner. Eventually, after 5 minutes of time added on, Mr Stroud finally blew his whistle to end the game, and relief washed over us like a tidal wave. The players came down to our end to thank us for our support, and we thanked the players for a very gritty performance, but also not forgetting some of the excellent football played in the first half, and particularly by Max and Snoddy, who were both in sparkling form today. As we struggled to get away from the Ricoh, stuck in traffic following an accident somewhere near the ground, we were listening to the scores and reports on the car radio. It had now got to that stage of the season where I was already looking at the other results to see whether we had gained or lost ground on the teams around us in the table. Today had seen us get back up to 8th in the table, but QPR, Swansea, Derby and Ipswich, had also all won, albeit the Swans at Cardiff, halting the Bluebirds good run. We were still 10 points behind QPR, who continued to lead the division as they had done all season. Next up, it was Hull City at Elland Road, and guess what day of the week that game was?

Tale of two Cities

I just couldn't face another Tuesday night disappointment, so I didn't go to the Hull City game at Elland Road, but Mark had got himself a ticket and went along on his own. He said he would text me with any goal news as it happened. We went into this game on the back of two decent away performances that gave us some hope that we were finally settling down, but we really needed a home win, to break a run of three straight defeats at Elland Road, to Preston, Leicester, and Cardiff. We hadn't had a home run like that since 2006, when we were last in the Championship, when we also lost three in a row during October of that year. It was also important that we stopped conceding goals. We had shipped twelve in those last three home games, and had now conceded 30 in the 17 games we had played so far this campaign. In fact, watching Leeds this season seemed to guarantee you goals. The tally now was 61 goals in those 17 games. So we had scored just one more than we had conceded!

Hull City was never going to be easy. Ken Bates, in his programme notes for the Hull game commented "This evening will be no pushover and the whole of our team – the whole 18 of them – will have to be ready to do battle." Couldn't argue with that Batesy! So it was important that we got off to a good start.

I was therefore somewhat startled when the mobile signalled the first text arrival of the night with just 14 minutes on the clock. For the 12th time in 17 games, a goal had been scored in the opening quarter of an hour. Sadly, it was not good news. The text read simply "Bloody screamer, 1 – 0 Hull".

In my research for this report, I have just watched the highlights of the game again, and the text says it all. John Bostock struck a free kick from all of 35 yards with the outside of his left boot and the ball hit the net in the top right corner, while Kasper was still rooted to the goal line. Most of the goals we had conceded, most of those 30 goals, had been the result of defensive errors or sloppy play. This one was just a class strike. As it said in the report in the next issue of the "Leeds, Leeds, Leeds" magazine, Bostock's shot "would still be rising now if the net hadn't got in its way..."

It was quiet on the text front until the 32nd minute when Mark wrote "Bradders, 1 - 1". Watching the replay, I have to say that it was a bit fortunate. Becchio tried to run across the edge of their box, right to left, with the ball, but instead it bounced off his left knee. Fortunately, it ran straight to Bradley Johnson, who struck it first time with his left foot into the bottom right corner. I noted the half time score on Sky at 1 – 1, and there was nothing more from Mark yet. Until the 71st minute in fact, when the mobile buzzed again. "O'Brien header" is all it said. That hardly does justice to the goal. Howson fed Snodgrass out on the right wing; Snoddy checked, got the ball on his trusted left foot and clipped a lovely ball into the middle where Andy O'Brien jumped to head home his first goal for the club. 20 minutes to go and Leeds should have shut up shop and got back in the dressing room with all three points, but I've written that before, and I would be writing it again throughout the season. That we didn't hang on this time is all the more ridiculous when you consider that Hull were down to 10 men, having had Bostock sent off in the 75th minute. But this is Leeds United.

I can do no better than repeat here the report from that "Leeds, Leeds, Leeds" magazine.

"Instead of trying to kill the game with a third goal the Whites' eased off and played back-four keep-ball. All momentum instantly evaporated. Attempting to clear a goal-bound near-post corner, Johnson merely sliced it into his own net for Hull's equaliser. It looked like the ultimate demonstration of Leeds' masochistic approach. It also jettisoned two points." Simon Grayson was stoical again after the game, saying that we had been naïve and should have been able to see the game off.

Marks final text of the night said simply, "F****** ridiculous, can't keep throwing away points like this." Little did we know at the time, but we would continue to throw points away many, many more times this season.

What Mark had failed to appreciate, was that there had in fact been some progress that night. It was Tuesday let's not forget, and we hadn't lost! We had not achieved that since early August.

Saturday came and I was heading for Elland Road again for the Bristol City game. I drove up on my own and got in the Pavilion early, to make sure we got a seat at one of the tables. Mark and Suzi arrived just after 1pm. Amdy Faye was interviewed by Peter Lorimer on the stage in the Pavilion, and he predicted a 3 – 1 win for Leeds. That was good enough for me and so I had a quid on it at 12/1. Mark got Amdy to autograph our programme, and he obligingly added his squad number, 17, to his name, which will help in a few years time if anyone ever looks at it because his signature is totally unintelligible!

Before the game, 25 members of the crew of the soon to be decommissioned Ark Royal paraded on the pitch. They stood in front of the big screen which was showing the magnificent aircraft-carrier in all its glory on the high sea. As fate would have it, we would be at the Portsmouth game in the New Year, on the day that the ship was actually decommissioned in Portsmouth, and we would have one more chance to wave farewell to this magnificent ship and its crew.

There was a big crowd in for this game, 27,567, and the atmosphere was excellent. The line up looked as if it could be a 4 – 3 – 3 for a change, in that Somma was up front supported closely with Snodgrass and Gradel, both of whom we knew would press on. Somma was in for Becchio, who had picked up a black eye from a stray elbow in the Hull game. Luciano was on the bench though, just in case he was needed…

Dodgy David James was in goal for Bristol, and he was keeping in front of the South Stand in the first half. He actually did quite well, at one point stopping a fine shot from

Davide Somma. The first half though was goalless, Leeds were looking pretty solid at the back for a change, with no major dramas, but up front it wasn't really working for us. Eventually, sensing how important three points was today, Grayson sent on the cavalry, in the shape of Becchio and Lloyd Sam for Gradel and Somma.

It took Luciano just 6 minutes to make his presence felt, and predictably it was in the air. Robert Snodgrass beat his man out on the right wing and as usual he checked back onto his left foot. He curled a cross over to the near post, where Becchio headed neatly in, with James stranded on his line. We were still bouncing when the wind was well and truly taken from our sails, as Bristol equalised within 2 minutes. They do say that a team is at its most vulnerable in the minutes immediately following the scoring of a goal and Leeds were to prove that on numerous occasions, throughout this frustrating season. Yet again, it was as if we were just not allowed an easy ride, according to some cosmic rule that orders the way a Leeds United game must be played out to keep everyone on the very edge of their seats, until the final whistle...every bloody week.

Gentle George McCartney got his feet tangled up in trying to tackle Albert Adomah out on the Bristol right wing, resulting in the winger getting to the bye-line in the box and jabbing the ball to the near post. John Stead just had to connect to score, which he did. Leeds fans all around us are disbelieving, the air is blue and it's like sharing the stand with 5,000 Victor Meldrew's all muttering, "I don't believe it, I just don't believe it!" We had been at the very summit of the rollercoaster ride just seconds ago, even daring to look out to the horizon, and seeing promotion dangling tantalisingly out there. Now we were right down as low as it gets, with our stomachs churning, despondent, and disbelieving. But wait, Leeds are on the attack again, the rollercoaster car is soaring skywards again, almost imitating the season we have had so far. Lloyd Sam, who has without doubt added some much needed spark to our forward play, is on the edge of the box and he unleashes a tremendous right foot shot that James can only parry out to Becchio. Luciano slips on his backside as he gets his left foot round the ball, but he gets enough on it to send the ball past James, who is still on his arse at the near post. 5,000 Victor Meldrew's are transformed again to become bouncing, delirious, jubilant believers once more. I turn to Mark and mouth something like "This is bloody crazy, I'm going to need oxygen in a minute" I hadn't even begun to think about the pre-match bet at this stage. We have just seen three goals in 5 minutes, and everyone is going mental. Things calm down for a few moments, and we try to catch our breath, but Lloyd Sam is causing all sorts of problems for the now overworked Bristol City defence. Then it is the turn of Gentle George, doing a passable impression of Snoddy, as he weaves in and out of defenders in the box just down in front of us. He then clips a delightful ball with his left foot over to the far stick, where Becchio rises to plant another header firmly inside the post. Absolute pandemonium all around! There was still life in this Bristol team though, and Schmeichel then pulls of an amazing one handed save in the top corner, to deny Stephen Caulker's header, and then he denies Brett Pittman.

The last half an hour of this game had to be seen to be believed, and when the final whistle went, Leeds fans all around the ground let out a positive wail of joy and relief. The team had yet again put us through the mill, and we had experienced highs and lows and "Ups and Downs" to match any we had endured so far in this frenetic season. At the end of it all, we had got the three points we wanted, and we were back in the play-off places in 5th. Still a long, long, way to go, but we didn't doubt this side had spirit and attacking flair in abundance. That defence was still a major doubt though, and it had chronic problems. As we made our way from the ground, we were both absolutely knackered, our emotions were in complete turmoil, and our voices were almost gone.

Next up, two tricky looking away games, at Norwich and Reading, but for now I was off to collect my £12 profit, from the good folk of Sportingbet.

Draw away, win at home

"Draw away and win at home", they say, is a recipe for football success. Before the two away games at Norwich and Reading, in late November, I would certainly have taken a draw in each game had it been on offer from some divine match fixer in the sky.

For the Norwich game, Leeds took 2,300 supporters, but Mark and I had missed out on the ticket allocation once again, so we didn't get to make the trip. This was the one that pretty much decided us on getting season tickets for next season, to try to ensure we got away tickets for the big games.

Leeds started the game with the same team that opened the Bristol City encounter, except Becchio was now fully recovered from his black eye, and so he started in place of Davide Somma. In all the papers, this was reported as a great game, with chances at both ends, and the Leeds defence at last earning some praise for a solid performance. Yet again there was a goal in the first 15 minutes, and again it was Mad Max getting in on the act. Becchio was felled from behind, on the edge of the penalty area, but the referee waved play on as the ball fell to Gradel. He struck a left foot shot from the inside left channel that somehow got through keeper Ruddy. The Norwich equaliser came in the 65th minute, and Leeds had some complaints that the goal was allowed to stand. As a corner was taken from the left wing, Norwich striker Chris Martin bundled Schmeichel into the net, so that it was an easy task for Norwich defender Barnett to head home from close range. Leeds protested, but referee Mike Russell apparently comes from the Arsene Wenger School of spotting off the ball incidents and he "saw nothing". At this stage of the season, a draw at Norwich, who were well in the hunt for a play off place themselves, was a decent effort. Delia Smith hadn't felt the need to rally her team as she famously did in 2005 with her "Let's be 'avin' you" rant, in a game against Manchester City.

The following Saturday, and the fixture computer had got us away again, this time in Reading. Over 4,000 fans made the trip south, despite snow falling in the north of England on the Friday night, which was to be the start of a prolonged spell of freezing weather in the UK. Leeds were unchanged from the team that took a point at Carrow Road last weekend, and in the Reading defence was one Ian Harte, the former Leeds favourite and dead ball specialist. Harte scored 28 goals in 213 appearances for Leeds between 1996 and 2004, and spent much of that time in a full back pairing with his uncle, Gary Kelly. How much would Leeds give to have those two at the back again?

The game was reported as another solid performance, with few scares for the visitors, but equally, few chances to steal the points. Harte had a free kick turned away by Kasper, while Jonny Howson could have won it for the visitors in the dying minutes, as his shot was well saved by Reading keeper, Frederici. The 0 – 0 draw saw Leeds gain their first clean sheet since the Sheffield United game in September, and it was only the 5th clean sheet in 21 games. It did maintain an unbeaten run that now stretched to 6 games, and it meant that Leeds had still only been beaten twice on the road in 10 games.

We all moved on to Elland Road, for the first game of December, the clash with Crystal Palace. The freezing weather was still causing all sorts of problems, with transport all across the country in chaos, and matches being postponed left, right, and centre. In Leeds, heavy snowfalls earlier in the week had left Elland Road under several inches of the white stuff. It was reported on the Leeds website, that Operation Buckingham (get the Palace game on), was well under way on the Thursday morning, and they were confident that the game would go ahead. So, I set out early on Saturday morning just in case of problems on the way, and the roads were pretty dodgy in certain areas, albeit the worst seemed to be on the Manchester side of the Pennines. When I got to Elland Road though, the evidence of the snow clearing operation was clear to see everywhere, especially on the car park, where the council had obviously had to get some heavy weight kit on the job, as they had scraped the top surface off along with the snow, which was now all piled up at the bottom end of the car park. I met up with Mark as usual in the Pavilion, and we were entertained by Peter Lorimer as normal who was interviewing Paul Connolly, who was suspended for today's game. Until I heard Paul speak, I hadn't realised that he was quite such a scouser, with a very broad scouse accent, and it didn't seem quite right for a Leeds player! He signed our match-day programme and thoughtfully added his squad number, as his signature, like that of Amdy Faye a few weeks ago, was also completely illegible! What has happened to the art of autograph scribing?

All the talk in the Pavilion was about the forthcoming FA Cup tie with Arsenal. The 3rd round draw had been made in London the previous Sunday evening, and had seen Serge Pizzorno, of the rock band Kasabian; pull out the ball for Arsenal, and then Noel Gallagher, pull out the ball with Leeds United's number on it. It would immediately evoke memories of the many previous FA Cup ties between the two sides. 7 times we had been paired since 1983, and often the ties had taken one or more replays to decide the outcome. Surely Leeds couldn't bring the Gunners back to Elland Road again, could they? Probably the greatest coincidence of this cup draw though, was that Pizzorno and Gallagher had joked before hand about their two respective teams, Leicester City and Manchester City. Amazingly, they then proceeded to draw the balls for those two teams, to pair them in a game at the Walkers Stadium. As they say, "It's a funny old game!" We all know it is just a coincidence, but it is so tempting to attribute such things to some other power!

Mark and I would try for tickets on Monday morning for the Arsenal game, but without much expectation of success, as we were sure the season ticket holders would snap them all up. Still, you never know, there might be a replay…

I spoke with a few folk who had travelled up from London for the Palace game, and it was clear that they were regulars. They were discussing travel arrangements for future games and the costs of hiring a minibus with a driver, which they reckoned was a couple of hundred quid. Consequently, they were drawing up a rota of who would drive to which game!

Ken Bates obviously mentioned the Arsenal game in his programme notes, and he also made a point of mentioning the recent contract negotiations with Bradley Johnson and his agent. Bates' comments were made against the background of an increasing number of clubs getting into financial difficulties, and how Bates believed this would have to impact on players wage demands eventually. The story was that Leeds had offered Johnson a big wage rise for his new contract, but that his agent had then turned it down. Bates noted that we'd had an enquiry from Hull City about a possible player swap, but that "Simon doesn't fancy any of their overpaid squad". Bates concluded, "It's tough out there and it is going to get even tougher".

In Simon Grayson's programme notes for the Palace game, he commented "...both Ross McCormack and Billy Paynter ended the game as our strikers at Reading last weekend..." and "you haven't had chance to see either player yet, but both are quality additions to our squad and you will see that in the coming weeks." I still wasn't sure about that, particularly in the case of Ross McCormack. In fact, the season would be all but over, before we saw the first McCormack goal for Leeds.

The Palace game produced the usual rollercoaster ride for the Leeds fans. Why wouldn't it? Every other game has! The first half was almost done and we were telling our bladders that relief was on its way when Nathaniel Clyne played a neat one-two on the right wing. He got to the bye-line and squared the ball across goal, where James Vaughan missed an opportunity at the near post, but Neil Danns was unopposed at the back post, to side foot the ball into the net in front of the Kop. It was a well-worked goal, and though you could argue we should have prevented Clyne getting through, it was not by any means the worst goal we had conceded this season. In the background of any video of the goal though, you can see Bradley Johnson just ambling back, as if too tired to give it a real go. It almost became even worse, as Schmeichel pulled off a superb save, to tip over a Darren Ambrose effort, just before the break. It was obviously disappointing though, to go in a goal down, as we had done much of the pressing in the first half, and indeed Howson had the ball in the net at one point, only for it to be ruled offside. TV replays would later prove that the officials got that one wrong, and the goal should have stood. Becchio and Gradel also had good chances, but couldn't take them. The sucker punch just before half time was therefore even harder to take.

Bladders duly relieved, we wondered what the second half would bring. It started to look as though our recent unbeaten run would come to an end, as Palace had further chances to extend their lead. There was no doubt that Schmeichel at least was up for this one, and he made two more first class saves from Ambrose and then Danns.

On 55 minutes Grayson had seen enough, and he made two changes. First, McCormack came on for Gradel, and then Lloyd Sam replaced Bradley Johnson. Neither Gradel nor Johnson had had particularly good games, but the response to Johnson being taken off was still surprising. Whether it was BJ's lack lustre performance in the first 45 minutes, or whether the fans on the Kop had been reading Ken Bates' programme notes, who knows? But as he jogged off, boos rang out, loud and clear, for Johnson, and then a chant of "There's only one greedy b*****d" filled the air, as he slipped away down the players' tunnel. Mark and I didn't join in the condemnation of Johnson, as we felt it would do nothing to help the team, either now or in the coming weeks. For now, it was time to get behind McCormack and Sam. Another 20 minutes went by, and there was still no break through. Not for the first time this season, Simon Grayson went for broke, by underlining his programme notes, and throwing Billy

Paynter on in place of the ever-popular Andy Hughes. At this point we were effectively playing 3 - 3 – 4, with Sam, Paynter, Becchio, and McCormack, all playing high up the field, and it was a case of twist or bust for the Leeds manager. Jonny Howson was actually playing at full back now! Fortunately, it worked to our advantage, and Palace came under wave after wave of Leeds pressure, with Lloyd Sam causing most of the havoc down the inside left channel, and the busy McCormack, with the distinctive "44" on his back, darting here, there, and everywhere.

On 81 minutes, Neil Kilkenny took a corner on the right wing that floated over to the back post. George McCartney, of all people, nodded it towards goal, Billy Paynter got his head to it to knock it even nearer, and there was Luciano Becchio, to swivel and smash the ball in from very close range with his left foot. Once again, it was right in front of the Kop, in the Don Revie Stand. We were still cheering that one when the ball was knocked forward to Robert Snodgrass. He helped the ball forward to McCormack who was pulled back by a defender, but the ball broke to his right, where Becchio was on hand to hit a left footer past fellow Argentine, Julian Speroni, in the Palace goal, to send the Kop into ecstasy. It was Becchio's 5th goal in two home games, and they had proved to be worth 6 points.

Leeds ended the day in 6th place in the table, on 32 points, 9 points behind the leaders QPR, and now on a run of 7 games unbeaten. Next Saturday we were off to Turf Moor, Burnley.

A trip back in time

Still in the grip of the freezing winter, I set off to Burnley on Saturday, 11th December, having been regularly checking the Leeds website for news that the game was still on. Mark was getting the train over from Leeds to Burnley's Manchester Road railway station, which I eventually found, after a few circuits around the centre of Burnley. Mark was going to come home with me after the game, as his University term had finished on the Friday. The town was busy with Christmas shopping traffic, and probably more so because the snow had thawed overnight, at least temporarily. I parked the car in a little side street, just above the station, and waited at the top of the narrow walkway that comes up to the main Manchester Road that gives the station its name, and that leads down into the town centre of Burnley. The station dates from 1866, and it looked to me as if it hadn't changed much in the last 150 years! It is, these days, an unmanned station, that is served by the Northern Rail, semi-fast services, from Blackpool North to Leeds and York, via the Caldervale line.

I waited with a number of the local police, who were on the look out for any trouble from the dozens of Leeds fans who would shortly be arriving at the station. From where I stood, I could look out over the town of Burnley, and it was easy to spot the claret and blue colours of Turf Moor, glinting in the winter sunshine in the distance. Eventually, one of the coppers asked me what I was waiting for, and I explained that my son was on his way from Leeds, on the train. They immediately asked if I was going to the game, and where I was heading for in town. I asked the police if there was anywhere in particular where the Leeds fans would be drinking before the game, and they suggested that most would probably park at the cricket ground next to Turf Moor, and then have a drink in the clubhouse. They pointed out the directions, and I thanked them and wished them a peaceful afternoon, mentioning that it hadn't been too peaceful at a recent game at Middlesbrough! One of them laughed and said, "Well, that's Middlesbrough for you!"

Eventually, a train arrived, and a steady stream of Leeds fans marched up the long ramp of a walkway. Most were carrying a plastic bag, with their shirts and scarves in. Mark later explained that he had got on the train with the Leeds fans at Leeds Central, and that virtually all of them had immediately unpacked a four-can pack of ale or lager from the plastic bag they carried, and then proceeded to drink them one after the other!

Mark appeared, and we said cheerio to the police, and walked back up the road to the car.

We followed the Bobbies instructions, and found the car park which was actually on and around the outfield of the Burnley Cricket Club ground, and sure enough, the Leeds fans were all gathered either in the old club house, or on the terraced area overlooking the cricket pitch. We made our way up the steps (presumably the same steps used by the cricketers when entering or leaving the pitch). Inside the clubhouse it was another world, and a very old world at that! Burnley Cricket Club's website proclaims; "Burnley is one of the most illustrious cricket clubs in Lancashire League history." The cricket club was founded in 1833, and they originally played their cricket at Turf Moor. They were one of the original 14 clubs that formed the Lancashire League in 1892, and they have won the Lancashire League title 14 times. In 1883, the cricket club invited the football club to join it at the Turf Moor site. Among several first class cricket stars that began their careers at Burnley, the most celebrated is without doubt the current England fast bowler, James Anderson, who has his photo liberally splashed around the walls.

There was a brilliant atmosphere in the bar of the pavilion, a pavilion so far removed from our own Centenary Pavilion that you would not believe! This was the heart of Victorian Northern England, the place was old, and it was battered and worn. The soles of your shoes stuck to the beer soaked carpet, the upholstered chairs were threadbare, and the locals spoke with that distinctive accent that Burnley, Bury, Bolton, and Blackburn folk, all have. But the hospitality was excellent. They were doing a roaring trade in the kitchen on the hot dogs and burgers, and each time an order was ready, a bloke would announce a number over the PA system by tapping the mike three times, loudly clearing his throat, and then telling the waiting customers "order 27 is ready, please collect it now at t' kitchen duwerr" in true "Wheel Tappers and Shunters" manner. We had a first class hot dog and a couple of pints of Thwaites Original bitter from the bar, which by now was heaving and about 6 deep all the way round. The bar maid serving us, was a fine Burnley wench, with long blonde hair, a bare midriff complete with interesting tattoo, and a pair of black jeans about three sizes too small for her. I spotted one of the Cockney guys I had been talking to at the Palace game, so they had obviously worked out their travel arrangements. As the bar area got even more crowded, we went outside to sup our second pint, sat on the old wooden seats overlooking the playing area. It is a strange cricket ground, with a factory wall running all along the boundary at the one end, no need for a sight screen over there I wouldn't think. There were now cars and minibuses parked all over the outfield and I wondered what damage that would do to the grass, as it was still very wet from the recent snow, but from what I could see of the grass it was full of weeds anyway! It was a brilliant, brilliant atmosphere though, and already the Leeds fans were starting to practise their chants for the afternoon. With about 30 minutes to go until kick off, and the light fading fast, Mark and I reluctantly left the quaint old cricket club and made our way to the, err, well, quaint old football club!

The football ground dates from 1883, and it looks it too! True, half of the ground, the James Hargreaves Stand, and the Jimmy McIlroy stand at the one end, were built as part of a redevelopment in the mid 1990's, and they are modern and well serviced areas.

We were housed in the ageing David Fishwick Stand, at the cricket ground end, and to our right, was the equally ancient Bob Lord Stand. Leeds had sold out their allocation as usual, and took 4,029 fans to Turf Moor, so we filled the Fishwick Stand.

Just going through the turnstiles, was like walking back in time. We should remember, I suppose, that Turf Moor is one of the oldest football stadiums in the country, only surpassed by Preston North End's Deepdale, and Sheffield United's Bramall Lane, both of which we were due to visit later in this Championship campaign. The turnstiles were so tight that anyone over 12 stone had to be pushed through from behind, and a girl in a little area by the turnstile had to tear off the bar code section of the ticket – I did wonder what the bar code was for! The Leeds fans queuing with us broke out into a spontaneous chant of "Premier League, you're having a laugh" referring to the fact that Burnley only recently got relegated from the Premier League. Quite how they managed to get their ground accepted beats me. We fought our way into the cramped concourse below the David Fishwick Stand, and tried to catch a glimpse of the Sky TV broadcast on the old tube TV set, that was perched precariously on top of a wall, high above our heads. Health and safety considerations are clearly not a priority here. We had to laugh when one Leeds fan commented that "at least Uncle Ken gets us decent tellies!" We then tried out the bogs and we nearly choked on the smoke! There were plenty of no smoking signs in evidence, but it appeared that the Leeds smokers had decided that this was the official smoking area! Thanks for that guys.

Having surely contracted lung cancer in the bogs, we then climbed the steep steps up to our seats to find the next shock. Our seats were numbered 43 and 44, in row R, and like all the other seats, they were small, individual, wooden benches, hinged at both ends. It is the first time I have seen such seats in many a long year. OK they were well spaced, and so there was plenty of legroom, but it was a good job that we would be standing up all through the game, or else we would have been having our haemorrhoids treated while in the oncology ward for our newly contracted lung cancer.

Leeds made two changes to the side that started against Crystal Palace, with Paul Connolly returning, after his one match suspension, so Andrew Hughes dropped back to the bench and Neil Collins was in at centre back after an injury to O'Brien.

In the notes, in the QPR programme the next Saturday, Simon Grayson would write "I saw a stat in the programme before the Burnley game saying how we had come from behind to win more games than anyone else in the Championship and, while that says a lot about the character and the belief of the players here, it isn't something I want to see happening every week!" Thanks for that Simon; after 27 minutes of today's game we were a goal down at Turf Moor.

Leeds looked lack lustre and short of ideas in the first half, and Burnley looked every bit a team that was unbeaten at home so far this season. In the 26th minute, Kasper Schmeichel saved well from Chris Iwelumo, but gave away a corner on the Burnley right. From the corner, Andre Bikey's header was blocked on the line by Schmeichel's left leg, but Brian Easton lifted the ball into the roof of the net with his left boot.

Just ten minutes later and it was 2 – 0 to the claret and blue outfit, and it was another shocker of a goal to give away, and so similar to several already conceded this season. Clark Carlisle, another Leeds old boy, lumped the ball clear from his own penalty box and it sailed into the Leeds half with Alex Bruce and Burnley's Jay Rodriguez both in hot pursuit. It looked for all the world as if Bruce had it covered, and he was just about to head it back to the advancing Schmeichel, when disaster struck. He just seemed to slide to the ground, leaving Rodriguez to hit a left foot shot low past the keeper. It was another long, aimless, ball over the top, and another calamity by a Leeds defender. It wasn't the first blot on Bruce's copybook this season, either. At half time, the mood in the

Fishwick Stand was decidedly flat. As flat, as those splinter ridden, wooden seats, in fact.

The second half though, was yet another example of the rollercoaster Leeds we have come to know and suffer heart attacks over. There was no doubting that Leeds had been given a good talking to at half time, as a different team emerged to do battle in the second half. From the off, Leeds tore into the home side, mounting wave after wave of attacks, and on 52 minutes, we got a foothold in the game. Snodgrass hooked a bouncing ball over to the far post where it was a simple task for Becchio to head down to Gradel, who smashed a right foot shot just inside the post, with the keeper marooned on his line. On 64 minutes, Ross McCormack was given another chance to live up to Simon Grayson's expectations, replacing the largely ineffectual Neil Kilkenny. Once again, McCormack did buzz here there and everywhere, like a bumble bee in an overstocked country garden. He seemed to cause confusion to the opposition as if what he was doing wasn't logical, which, truth be told, often it wasn't! But 2 minutes later, Leeds had levelled the scores. Jonny Howson slotted an inch perfect pass through to Paul Connolly, who knocked the ball across goal for Becchio to slide in at the far post on his backside, and toe-poke the ball inside the upright.

Leeds had scored both goals in front of the now delirious Whites fans, and all the noise was coming from us. We turned as one towards the Burnley fans in the Bob Lord Stand to our right, and started singing. "You should've gone Christmas shopping, you should've gone Christmas shopping!" We were urging the team on. I had been floored by the bloke to my right when we equalised, as he had fallen backwards and smashed his wooden seat with his full weight. He had grabbed me to try to break his fall. Somehow, I had taken a blow in the crown jewels that doubled me up, winded, but I managed to stagger back to my feet. Mark was wetting himself with laughter. It was complete delirium all around. We would have been happy with a point of course at this stage, but Leeds kept bombing forward towards us, and that momentum (yes, that word again) was back for the first time in a while. We all just knew the winner was coming. It had to be. Quite why we couldn't have played like this in the first half was a question to be answered by the coaching staff on Monday back at the training ground.

With 5 minutes of normal time left, it came. Jonny Howson collected the ball in the centre circle, and then just sort of ambled forward with the ball. Then, he spotted an opening to his right and he ran into it. No one challenged him, and then from about 25 yards, he just stroked the ball towards the right corner of the net as he looked at it, and somehow it crept in, leaving the keeper clawing nothing but the cold, damp, Burnley turf. Jonny Howson ran to the corner flag to celebrate with the rest of the team, and it was absolute bedlam everywhere. Fans were toppling over seats and crashing into each other, and complete strangers were grabbing and hugging each other like long lost lovers. All of the Leeds fans remained, applauding and chanting, until the last Leeds player had left the pitch, and as the manager walked off, last of all, we all sang, "There's only one Simon Grayson" with what was left of our voices. What a game. What a bloody trip that was. It was a long, long painful crawl out of the car park after the game, but we really didn't care. The Cockney bloke walked past as we sat in the car, and he beat his chest three times with the Leeds salute. Bring on Queens Park Rangers, the Championship leaders, at Elland Road next Saturday.

A Football Man

The Queens Park Rangers game fell on the Saturday before Christmas. With Mark already at home from University, and Adam having finished school for the term and therefore not having a rugby match, it was a chance for us three "boys" to have a day out together. We travelled up on the Saturday morning, once again having to carefully negotiate the local roads, due to another overnight snowfall in the Potteries. In fact, listening to the radio in the car, it was clear that the weather everywhere was a major problem. There was no football going to be played at Arsenal, Chelsea or Liverpool this weekend due to snow, but a bit of white stuff was no match for the team of volunteers and the ground staff at Elland Road.

On arrival at the ground I made my way to the Pavilion, while Adam and Mark made a dash to the club shop to get their last minute Christmas shopping done! Something for their Dad was on the list. (The gift was supposed to be a set of Leeds United cuff links, but when they saw the price tag of around £30 they opted instead for the Revie biography I keep referring to and one of those little Leeds kits that you hang up in your car window). It was Adam's first taste of the Pavilion today, and I think he was as impressed as any seventeen year old is with anything these days, you wouldn't exactly say he gets excited about much.

Johnny Giles was in town, publicising his new autobiography, "A Football Man". Johnny was a member of that Revie team of the early 70's, and so had been part of my Leeds United upbringing from day one, back in fact to that first game at the Hawthorns, all those years ago. Today, Johnny was on stage in the Pavilion with Peter Lorimer, and he was asked among other things, if the current Leeds United team was ready for the Premiership, or whether this season would perhaps be too soon to go up. He responded, that you have to take your chance when it's there, as the team might not be in a position to challenge for promotion the following season, although he did acknowledge that we were maybe a couple of players short of a really successful side. As a fan, I found it fascinating the way Lorimer and Giles clearly still got on so well with each other, and indeed how all of that great team Don Revie built, still seemed to be such good pals. Later this season, we would see the easy manner in which Paul Reaney and Lorimer interacted on the same stage in the Pavilion, and we had also seen Norman Hunter and Allan Clarke as frequent visitors to the club and Eddie Gray of course, doing his stuff for the radio. We knew Mick Jones had been there the day the Pavilion was opened although we missed seeing him. Richard Sutcliffe also mentioned this camaraderie in that Don Revie biography. Apparently, Revie was determined to ensure that he didn't bring any "troublemakers" into the camp, and he fostered a close-knit atmosphere among the players and backroom staff. Lorimer is quoted in the book as saying "Even now, we all hang out together as friends and enjoy spending time with each other, playing golf and the like." I can't imagine that the players of today from any club will be as close with their current teammates in 30 years time. I guess one big difference is that all the teams these days are made up of so many different nationalities that when players end their careers they will inevitably return to their home countries. Revie's great team were all from the home countries of course.

Mark went up to get Giles' autograph on the match day programme, and later on Richard Naylor was also in the Pavilion, so we got him to sign as well. Naylor was still injured and would be playing no part in any of the games over the Christmas period.

We made our way into the ground following the usual rituals of using exactly the same turnstile, joking about the fact that the poppy seller was absent again (a bloke selling Remembrance Day poppies had been stood by our turnstile on the day we beat Bristol City, so we joke that we ought to wear poppies for every game!) and me making sure that I followed Mark, rather than he follow me, into the ground. We also usually manage a pre-match ritual pee, once inside the ground, but that one is never guaranteed, as it depends on how many pints of Beck's Vier we have supped in the Pavilion.

The team had been announced in the Pavilion as unchanged from the victorious starting line up on the Burnley trip last week. So, it looked like a 4 - 5 - 1 to me again, with Becchio the lone striker, but with ample attacking options from Snoddy and Gradel on either side. QPR had lost only one league game all season, but that had come in a live televised game as recently as last Friday night, 3 – 1 at home to a Watford team that had given them a real run around. We didn't know though, whether that was a poor QPR performance, or whether Watford were really that good.

Nearly 30,000 fans were packed into Elland Road, on a bitterly cold afternoon, to witness a thoroughly professional performance by a Leeds team that would end the day second in the table. Unusually, there was no goal in the opening 15 minutes, and the only real worry, was that Alex Bruce hobbled off after just 11 minutes, to be replaced by Leigh Bromby, for only his second appearance of the season. In fact, Bromby had a fine game, and there were to be no dramas at the back today.

On 25 minutes, Leeds made the breakthrough their play had deserved.

In a move very reminiscent of the first Leeds goal last week at Burnley, Robert Snodgrass got the ball out on the Leeds right. As always, he tried to jink back on to his left foot, but this time he went back again and chipped the ball over to the back post with his right foot. Jonny Howson rose to head down to the corner of the 6 yard box, and Max Gradel, stretching, met the bouncing ball perfectly on the half-volley to rifle it past Paddy Kenny in the Rangers goal. It was 1 – 0 at the interval, and as we filed off to the bogs again (it had been a three pint lunchtime today, so we set off with some urgency!) we were well pleased with the first half display.

There was no particular half time nervousness as there had been so often this season.

The second half continued with more of the same, and watching this, a visitor from Mars could easily have thought that it was Leeds who headed the table, not the "R's".

In the 70th minute, Mad Max collected the ball in his own half on the left wing, and he ran straight at the visitors defence. As he got inside the box, he shaped first to come inside but then went to the outside of two defenders, and with his left foot he fired a shot in at the near post that Kenny should really have stopped. But he didn't, and that was 2 -0, and that was Leeds in Comfortable City. Gradel was able to take his bow in the 76th minute, when he came off to be replaced by Lloyd Sam, and then Billy Paynter got a couple of minutes at the end of the game, in place of Becchio, as Leeds marshalled the remaining minutes away safely.

The over-riding feeling at the end of the game was that Leeds had shown no signs of the defensive frailties that had plagued us all year, and we looked like a team that could do something special this season. The momentum was back with us, and as we drove home, we contemplated that automatic promotion was a real possibility. Tonight, we were second in the table, and only 3 points behind the leaders, who we had just seen off comprehensively. We looked forward to the three games over Christmas, starting at Leicester, and then at home to Portsmouth and the 'Boro. We reckoned 7 points was a distinct possibility. Could life get much better? For a few days we forgot we were Leeds. We should have known better, and we should have been preparing for the next rollercoaster ride. A prerequisite for supporting Leeds United is to be able to expect the unexpected at any time.

Christmas turkeys

What a wonderful Christmas! OK, there was still snow and ice all around, but Leeds United were second in the table, and all had had a fun time. We had not been away for Christmas, the wife's Mum and Dad came down from Scotland for a week, and the wife's brother and his family had come over for Christmas lunch. It seemed ages since the QPR game, and so by Boxing Day, Mark and I were ready for another fix of Championship football.

The fixture computer had dictated, that the first of our three Christmas games was at the Walkers Stadium in Leicester, no easy place to go, despite the Foxes languishing down in 16th place in the table. We could hardly forget, that Leicester had already been to Elland Road twice this season, and had come away each time with a 2 – 1 win, under two different managers. Paulo Sousa had been at the helm when they knocked us out of the Carling Cup, and then Sven had taken over by the time the league game came round in the middle of October. So, it was not without some concern that we set off on Sunday morning, once again braving the freezing weather. At least we were fairly sure that today's game would be played in better weather conditions than the Leicester game played at Portman Road, Ipswich, on the 18th of December. While Leeds were demolishing QPR, at a relatively green and pleasant Elland Road, the Foxes were battling their way through a blizzard at Ipswich. Their game was still going on when we got back to the car, well after our match had ended, as the referee at Portman Road had taken the players off to try to clear the lines of snow, and to find some orange footballs! Quite why they didn't abandon the game, no one understood, but Leicester complained bitterly (literally), not least I suspect because they got beaten 3 – 0. The front cover of the Leicester programme for the Leeds game was a superb picture of a Leicester player at Portman Road, peering through the blizzard conditions. It would have made a fantastic club Christmas card.

I was looking forward to my first trip to the Walkers Stadium, even though the "Leeds on Tour" notes, in the back of the QPR programme, had dismissed it as "a bowl that resembles the stadiums of Coventry and Southampton". We had already been to the Ricoh in Coventry this year, and I guessed it wouldn't be all that different to the Riverside in Middlesbrough, either; perhaps more blue paint than red though. I was expecting another cracking atmosphere, as we had once again sold all our allocation of tickets, meaning that over 3,000 of us would be there. In fact, it would not be until February, and the long trip to Swansea, that we would first fail to sell all of our ticket allocation for an away game. The Premiership needs Leeds United as much as Leeds United needs the Premiership.

We set off around 10:30am, with the temperature gauge in the car reading minus 4, and the display regularly flashing up the message "Risk of black ice" and beeping at us. We had no problems on the main roads, which were all clear, but when we got into Leicester we dived into the first football parking we spotted, which was just off the main Upperton Road on a piece of waste ground. There were a good couple of inches of snow on the ground here, and I was a tad concerned when I missed the fact that there was a bit of a ditch running along the fence that I was reversing up to. Mark had to rock the car to help me pull out of that, and I then used the shovel from the boot to clear the snow from in front of the car, just in case it had frozen by the time we came back after the game. It was perishing cold, and we were in the full winter woollies, including gloves and hats, as we made the 15 minute walk to the ground, passing much safer looking, and snow free, car parks on the way! As we were walking along, someone behind us mentioned that the old Filbert Street ground, the Foxes home from 1891 to 2002, had been located somewhere off to the left, and that it had been demolished and the area was now a student accommodation village for the local university. Apparently, the new ground was for a brief time known as Filbert Way, until a lucrative sponsorship deal was struck with Walkers Crisps and the ground took their name. We also heard that the first idea Walkers had, was for the stadium to be known as the Walkers Bowl, but that due to the fans antipathy, it was changed to the Walkers Stadium. They didn't apparently like the idea of playing in a crisp bowl. The stadium is plastered with giant posters for Walkers crisps, most of them featuring the Foxes famous son, potato crisp connoisseur, and good friend of Noddy, Gary Lineker.

When we got to the ground, there were notices up on the entrance doors explaining that a very limited catering service was available today, due to the freezing conditions. We didn't know if that meant they had suffered any burst pipes, or if the staff hadn't managed to get in. We decided not to risk it too early, and so headed for a posh looking burger caravan, just opposite the away corner of the stadium, over the roundabout where Eastern Boulevard meets Burnmoor Street. The name on the caravan proclaimed it as Gillies Burgers. We ordered a cheeseburger, and a bacon cheeseburger with onions, both with chips, and I have to say it was bloody excellent. We stood eating and shivering, in equal measure, next to the burger van with a few other Leeds fans, and took in the view of the stadium. The view from the outside, it has to be said, is not that impressive. It didn't look very big, even though we knew it held up to 32,000 fans, when full. I guess impressive to us, is the massive East stand back at Elland Road. We finished the burgers, thanked Gillies staff, and made our way back over the road and into the ground. The concourse under the stand was pretty normal, but, unbeknown to us at this time, the Leeds fans had access to two different areas, separated by a locked metal door. The one we were in, had a food stall (no alcohol on sale today) and a TV showing Sky, but no betting point. We only discovered the other side at half time, when we noticed people going down a different stairway, so we followed and discovered the error of our ways. The other area did have a betting point. We failed to have our usual pre-match bet therefore, and just stood watching the TV, with a Coke and a coffee.

The Leeds fans were just as noisy as ever, and were in good voice despite the Christmas festivities and the cold, and many had come still wearing their novelty headgear, flashing antlers, in the main. When we got up to the seats, the ground looked much more impressive than from outside. The Leeds programme from last week, had said that it still had a new feel to it, and that is very true – it was all very bright and clean. We had one corner, and most of the one end, and the majority of the core home fans were to our left. We had been warned that there was usually a drummer amongst the home fans, and he was indeed there and he would take plenty of stick from the Leeds fans as the game went on. He was a big fellow who we guessed was probably Gillies best customer.

It was an unusual group of fans that we were seated with today. In front of us was a couple of old dears, one of whom we reckoned must have been well into her eighties. If you are reading this, lady, then all power to you, because we noticed that like everyone else, you were on your feet the whole way through the game! Next to us was a family, including a teenage girl who was clearly just as mad keen a fan as was her Dad. She wore a blue away shirt, with 'Kisnorbo' emblazoned on the back, and she was swinging her scarf like a whirling dervish during the "Champions" chant, and nearly took my eye out a couple of times! I am pretty sure that the chap and his daughter were stood near us later in the season at Fratton Park, for the Portsmouth away game, when the daughter was doing another passable imitation of a small helicopter, and again nearly sliced my retina a few times. The same pair would also be right in front of us at the Liberty Stadium in Swansea. It would not be until the home game against Reading that I would find out who they were, and introduce myself to them.

The team sent out to do battle today, was the same that started against QPR, except O'Brien was in for Bruce. So, it was that 4 - 5 - 1 formation yet again, that had proved so successful over the last 9 games.

This game was typical of so many already this season, with an early goal, albeit just missing that first 15-minute slot. It was actually 19 minutes, when an early ball across from Kilkenny on the right wing, at the far end of the ground, found Max Gradel lurking in the centre of goal, about 6 yards out. He banged a header seemingly straight through their keeper, largely thanks to his marker slipping, just as the ball arrived to him! Leeds played some decent stuff early doors, and Leicester didn't look to have much in response, at this stage. The drummer was very quiet. Half time and we retreated down to that other catering area to sup our concealed Lucozades, and to get out of the cold for a few minutes. It was only as the second half got underway, that I noticed three Leeds lads, a few rows behind us, who had no tops on, despite the sub-zero temperatures. Again, respect to you guys for that!

Second half and it looked all over in the 55th minute, when Snoddy rattled in the second goal with a swerving left footer. The ball had come back to him following a corner he took himself from the left wing. From where we were stood, the ball appeared to rifle straight through the keeper again. It was some shot. The Leeds fans thought the drummer had left at this point, and started singing various humorous ditties about him having gone home, and that he was probably cooking himself a few burgers and doing unspeakable things with his wife. Or words to that effect!

With the fans going "f****** mental" all around us, it was hard to see how we could throw this one away, but as we have now come to expect, yet again, we managed it! Even at 2 – 0 up, we were all nervous, and yet still clinging to the hope that today would be a QPR moment, and not a Barnsley or Preston moment. Snoddy was the first culprit who hadn't read his script properly. This time he was caught dawdling over the ball just inside their half, and got caught in possession. On TV later, it did look like he was fouled as he was bundled over, but anyway, the ball was poked forward to Vassell, who caught Connolly napping, and Kasper had little option but to trip him, once he had pushed the ball past him. That Kasper only got a booking, was a blessing, but the penalty was duly dispatched and we all knew it was going to be a nervy last quarter of an hour.

Point to note here though about the penalty. Paul Gallagher drilled it straight down the middle of the goal, about waist height. Had Kasper just stood his ground, he couldn't fail to stop it, but Kasper was already committed to diving to his left, so the ball flew in the net unobstructed. Worth keeping in mind in case he faces another penalty later in the season? I thought so.

None of us, and especially Kasper Schmeichel, would have expected Andy King's thunderbolt from the blue though a few minutes later. It crashed in off the underside of the bar, just 4 minutes after the penalty, and from then on we could easily have lost the game. Had we been offered a draw at 3pm, we would have taken it, so it was a point gained away from home, and at least we had stopped that run of 5 consecutive defeats at the hands of the Foxes. Nevertheless it was hard to accept that we had thrown away a solid 2 goal lead, and that for 70 minutes we had played some half decent stuff. Yet at the end of the day, we only shared the spoils. There were two home games to come in the next week, and both were winnable. Surely the drama couldn't keep coming every game...could it? We wouldn't have long to wait to find out, as we were back at Elland Road on Tuesday afternoon for the visit of Portsmouth. I for one couldn't wait.

Oh, bugger, did I say Tuesday?

So, soon after that exciting, yet ultimately disappointing trip to the Walkers Stadium, we were all hoping for, or even expecting, three points from what on paper, or even on grass, should have been a none too difficult home game against struggling Portsmouth. The weather had at last warmed up a bit; it was 3 or 4 degrees as we left the car in the Hoxton

Mount car park, where we always try to park. It is the first car park you come to on leaving the M621, and is where the away coaches are always parked. That does mean that sometimes it gets a bit hairy if any Leeds fans decide to approach the away fans, as they board their transport, but if you get the timing right and can get out before the away coaches, you can generally be back on the motorway in around 10 or 15 minutes from getting into your car. It does take a lot longer, if there are a lot of away coaches and the police have begun to escort them away, as they will let them all go together, before letting the private cars go.

Probably the scariest encounter we have seen in the car park was after the Liverpool League Cup game, last season, when for some reason dozens of Leeds hooligans started charging the visitors buses, and throwing stones at them, despite the best efforts of the mounted police and the dog handlers.

We made straight for the Pavilion today, and got in there about 12:45pm, so we were lucky to get three seats together, at a table in the first row from the entrance, just below one of the big screens that was showing the QPR match at the Ricoh. We all thought QPR might stumble at that one, but our hopes were dashed, as a couple of very poor goalkeeping errors let QPR in for a 2 – 0 win, that put them temporarily 8 points clear of us at the top. The only muted cheer, was for a booking for our old friend Gary "You're too sh** to play for Leeds" McSheffrey.

Both my lads were again with me today, Adam deciding that he "could be arsed" on this occasion, to join us. We dined on meat and potato pies and mushy peas, and washed that down with a couple of pints of Beck's Vier as per usual. The first guest of Peter Lorimer today was Leigh Bromby. That was a blow straight away, as we felt Brombs deserved a start after his performance against QPR last week, when he came on after the early injury to Alex Bruce. We knew also that Becchio was a doubt, after he had limped off at Leicester, and so when Brombs suggested Ross McCormack as likely first scorer, we guessed that Becchio was unlikely to be starting.

We also guessed that both McCormack and Billy Paynter would start with full debuts, as Grayson had played those two together on a few substitute appearances. Sure enough, that was the line up, the same team as at Leicester, but with Ross and Billy, instead of Kilkenny (due to go away with the Aussie squad to the Asia Cup in Qatar in a few days time) and Becchio. That was as close to 4 - 4 - 2 that Grayson had come in several weeks, we reckoned.

Today's second guest was little Brian Flynn. His main thrust was that Leeds were an absolute certainty for promotion this season, he didn't specify by which route.

Brian Flynn is one of the shortest professional footballers of all time at just 63 inches tall...or short. In the history of Leeds United though, he is a giant, as a result of the goal he scored to beat the Scum at Old Trafford, in 1981. That was the last time we had beaten them at Old Trafford, before Jermaine Beckford replicated Flynn's feat, last year.

Some great news in the programme today, was that Luciano Becchio had just signed a new three and a half year contract that would commit him to Leeds until at least 2014, unless anyone came in with a can't resist offer. Having lost Beckford in the summer to a Bosman, everyone naturally assumed that Becchio would continue to perform the role of work horse, rather than prolific goal scorer. But with the early season injuries and suspensions, and with Grayson persisting with the lone striker formation, Luciano had proved a revelation so far this season, with 12 goals, and he now needed only 2 more for his half century in a Leeds shirt.

We went through all the usual superstitions – same turnstile, same jokes about the poppy seller and the bloke doing the fan survey not being there, and when we got to our seats I gave my usual little wave to Kop Cat when he walked by. It was drizzling a bit, but it was nowhere near as cold as it had been of late.

What a start! Max just can't stop scoring! This time he poached a goal from close range, in front of the South Stand, after Billy Paynter had used his muscle in the box. Minutes later, Jonny Howson made it 2 – 0, skipping past a couple of defenders to slot the ball home. I was already getting excited because I had got a quid on Leeds for a 5 - 0 victory at 100/1! We were two goals up and only ten minutes gone on the clock. It was that first 15 minutes phenomenon again. It was all going to plan.

I should have known better of course. We should all have known better. Every last Leeds fan in the ground, should have bloody well known better. This is Leeds United remember. Chances came and went, with McCormack and Snoddy both going close, but Portsmouth were starting to knock the ball about and were gaining confidence, in much the same way that Leicester did once they got their chance last Sunday. Eventually, it was David Nugent – well it was going to be wasn't it as another former Leeds player? - who latched on to a ball about 10 yards out, in the inside right channel, and he fired an unstoppable shot across Kasper, and into the far top corner. 2 - 1 at half time.

The half time chat in the bogs was all about the missed opportunities to bag full points. Preston, Leicester the other day, and Hull, were all mentioned, and we just knew this wasn't going to be a straight forward win today. The feeling of momentum we had sensed a few times during the season, and for twenty minutes today, had ebbed away again, and you could tell that the fans were twitchy as we all manoeuvred for position in the familiarly crowded Gents under the Kop.

It looked as if it might be OK after all, when on the hour; Bradley Johnson lashed home a volley, following a corner on the left. Bradley celebrated with some feeling, right in front of us, giving the Leeds salute to the Kop, and we couldn't make up our minds if that meant he would be signing soon, or if that was his parting gift. Watch this space. It at least guaranteed that he wouldn't be booed off today.

As if the football Gods were having a laugh at our expense, that newly restored 2-goal lead lasted only one minute at most. There is absolutely nothing worse, than still being in the middle of celebrating a goal, when the opposition sticks one in at the other end. The recent substitute, Kanu, ex of Arsenal fame, pulled the ball back for Hughes, whose shot took a big deflection from O'Brien, and flew past Kasper for 3 - 2. Nerves all of a jangle again, and pleas from the Kop to "sort it out Leeds!" and "get a bloody grip!" I wonder how many heart attacks they get at Leeds games. Has anyone ever done that study? An ageing chap in a flat cap in the front row of the Kop looked a prime candidate for the emergency services.

The Kop was then jumping for joy again on 67 minutes, when following a corner on the Leeds right wing; the ball fell for McCormack who, with his back to goal, and the Pompey keeper Jamie Ashdown at his back, managed to flick the ball in at the far post for his debut goal. But he hadn't scored. The joy was short lived, as the referee had blown for a dubious foul on the keeper and we all reverted to status "nervous" again.

It has to be said that the Leeds defending in the last 10 minutes left a lot to be desired. It was down right amateurish at times, with clearances being hacked anywhere; needless back passes going astray, and wasted possession. The fans sensed that this was one of those days that Leeds have frequently put us through in the last couple of years, and sure enough, after another needless throw-in was given away by Collins, somehow O'Brien and Schmeichel contrived to give Pompey an equalizer and we could only agree with the Pompey faithful, as they jubilantly sang "2 -0, and you f***** it up" for the last couple of minutes. That equalising goal was later recorded as an own goal, in the 93rd minute. It was a real choker. The fans bravely saluted our lads off at full time, but it was a dismal drive back down the M62 and M6, with the news that Cardiff had been thrashed at Watford 4 – 1, but that Swansea had scraped past Barnsley to push us down to fourth, which is where we would be, as 2010 came to a close. That the strength of feeling was so muted at the end of the game, is probably due to the fact that, had we been told on January 1st 2010, that we would be 4th in the Championship come the end of the year, I think every Leeds fan in the country would have jumped at that!

I have just one last comment on this game, concerning the referee David Webb. It is a sad irony that the Webb name has a history for all Leeds fans that remember the Cup Final replay against Chelsea all those years ago. That particular David Webb, cost us the FA Cup. This one cost us 2 points, with a series of completely unfathomable decisions that went against us, including that disallowed "goal" from McCormack. Many YouTube video posts on the internet clearly show that there was nothing untoward going on at all and it was a perfectly good goal. It had sparked a long period of chanting by the Leeds faithful of "You're not fit to referee!" that is also captured on those YouTube postings. It has to be said, that we have seen some appalling refereeing in the Championship this year. Mr Bates, at Leicester last Sunday, was poor, but this bloke took poor to new extremes of poorness. He was so dire, that the entire Leeds fan base joined the chant at the end of the game – "S*** refs, we always get s*** refs" and then even more telling, the single word "cheat" echoed around the ground, so loud that it could be heard hundreds of yards away, outside Elland Road. We know this because a friend of ours, who met us in the car park after the game, told us about it. We were giving her a lift home to the Potteries. If we didn't know better, we would have thought there was some sort of conspiracy against us, being coordinated by some football Beelzebub – but then we would also have to accept, that we are often the cause of our own difficulties. Whatever; it was another 2 points tossed away in the wind, and we had just one more chance over this Christmas period, to take all three points. Surely we could sort things out for the visit of lowly Middlesbrough, on New Year's Day? I wondered what that game would bring us. A Christmas cracker? Or yet another Christmas turkey?

New Year – Same Old Leeds

Around the Christmas and New Year period each year, we pick one home game where we all go along as a family. This tradition has gone on since the boys were first old enough to sit through a whole game without causing havoc and annoying other fans in the vicinity. When the fixtures came out for this season, we quickly spotted that Leeds were at home on New Years Day, and that was the game we chose. Back in the summer – in fact back as far as the Middlesbrough away game in the middle of October – the match was scheduled as a normal 3pm kick off, and that was going to give us enough time to get our heads together after the inevitable excesses of New Years Eve. On the 19th of October though, immediately after that game at the Riverside where there had been some ugly scenes outside the ground as Leeds and 'Boro fans clashed, it was announced on the Leeds website that, at the request of the police, the game had been moved to a 1pm kick off. That wasn't going to be quite so straightforward. I worked back from 1pm, to allow our normal three hours at the ground before kick off. That allows time to get parked, spend a couple of hours in the Pavilion soaking up the atmosphere, and wandering over to the ground in good time. I then added on another 2 hours for the journey from the Potteries to Leeds. That meant setting off at 8am in the morning! Now on any normal morning that isn't a problem, but on New Years Day that was a tad early. The missus and I, and Adam, were spending New Years Eve at a party being thrown in a village not far from home, which was sure to be a boozy affair. Mark was also bound to be out and about with his mates getting pie-eyed. We all knew Saturday morning was going to be a struggle.

In the event, all of our New Years Eve celebrations were sufficiently sensible, and I was probably just about fit to drive the 100 miles to Leeds, by the time 8.30am on the Saturday morning came round. We just needed that extra half hour in bed! Fortunately, because of the time, the motorways were as quiet as I could ever remember, with some stretches being completely deserted apart from our old Peugeot, eating up the miles on the M6, M62 and M621. In fact, we did the trip in an hour and a quarter, so we were pulling onto the car park at 9:45am, and we were only the 5th car in there. We handed over our £6 (It had gone up by a whole pound due to the VAT change and a price increase since the last game) to the guys on the gate, and we were spoilt for choice as to where to park.

Everywhere was really quiet. We popped into the club superstore to see what was on offer in the sale, and came out with a very fetching, pink woolly bobble hat with the Leeds crest on the front – for the missus I hasten to add. She also spotted a big pile of Leeds garden gnomes, that were on sale at £14 each and she set her heart on having one of those as well. I think she had read something about the forthcoming animated film "Gnomeo and Juliet" featuring the voices of Emily Blunt, Michael Caine, Matt Lucas and Ozzy Osbourne, amongst myriad others, and decided it was the new must have garden accessory! In fact our Leeds Gnome, Gordon, is not unlike the Gnomeo in the film.

The boys walked down to the pavilion, while the wife and I went back to the car to drop off Gordon. As we then wandered down the road to the Pavilion ourselves, we commented on how few people were about. It was so quiet, that the steward in the Pavilion car park shouted good morning as we went by, and almost scared us to death. It was similar in the Pavilion, and we could have sat almost anywhere. We did a quick check on what food was being offered today, and the sausage or bacon rolls looked spot on to help sort out the lingering hang over. Mark and I decided to try the "hair of the dog that bit me" theory and we each had a couple of pints of lager, as usual.

Eventually the Pavilion began to fill up, and there didn't seem to be any shortage of customers at the bars, all seeking the dog's hair remedy to their overnight excesses. One person who was very, very, bright, was Paul Reaney, another member of that Revie super team. He was Peter Lorimer's first guest today, and was in very jovial mood. Peter first announced that a young lady in the Pavilion was 16 today, and Reaney immediately asked her to come forward for a photograph, and a birthday kiss. Just as that girl was making her way back to her seat, another pretty, young lass, walked across in front of the little Pavilion stage. Quick as a flash, Reaney called out to her. "It's not your birthday as well is it love?" I guess he was eager to double his kiss tally for the day. She gave him a "keep away you pervert" look, and walked on, to the great amusement of the many Pavilion fans that all cheered and applauded loudly. Reaney was clearly on good form, and none the worse for any late night revelling. This is more than can be said for Peter Lorimer. At one point, our former hotshot was clearly miles away, while Reaney was speaking to the audience, and then he asked the question that Reaney had just been answering! It was all good knock about stuff.

There was a lot of talk about the upcoming Arsenal FA Cup tie next Saturday of course, and the general feeling was that, as long as we did ourselves proud, we didn't really mind whether it was win, lose, or draw down there at the Emirates. A draw would be good though, as we had missed out on tickets for the trip to London, but would be able to secure them for any home replay. We were keeping the replay week clear in our diaries just in case. For now though, it was vital to get back to winning ways against Middlesbrough, another team arriving for the return fixture under a different manager from the first game. Leicester City being the other so far and many more would follow, before the end of the season, including Preston, Ipswich, Sheffield United and Burnley who had all recently jettisoned their managers! Gordon, (that's Strachan, not Gordon the gnome) had resigned almost immediately after our victory up at the Riverside, and now the 'Boro were led by Tony Mowbray, sacked by Celtic earlier in the year. Mowbray is 'Boro through and through, having been born in the North East. He played 348 games for them in the 1980's. He had already moved them up the table, and they had picked up a useful 3 – 1 win at Preston just a few days ago, while we were gifting points to Portsmouth.

Leeds were now unbeaten in 11 games, but 5 of those had ended in draws. The team was announced as usual in the Pavilion just after midday, an hour before kick off, and there were two changes from the side that had started against Pompey in midweek. Becchio started in place of Billy Paynter, who had still looked well short of being match fit on Tuesday, while Andy Hughes started in place of the temporarily departed George McCartney, who had returned to Sunderland, prior to arranging a second loan spell for us that would then go to the end of the season. That meant it was another go at 4 – 4 - 2 in my book, with Becchio and McCormack up front. I did note though, that in the following home programme, "We are Leeds" were listing Gradel, Becchio and Snodgrass as "ST" for striker and McCormack as "CM" for central midfield, but it didn't look like that out on the pitch. I was also starting to think that McCormack was not equipped for this league. He came with a reputation as a goal scorer having scored 25 in 74 games at Cardiff, but he had now featured in 11 games (mostly as a substitute admittedly) for us, and he had not looked like scoring. Indeed he had missed a few decent chances. There were a few murmurs around the Pavilion when Hughes' name was announced, but we knew it was coming as Ben Parker had been starring in the Pavilion earlier. He got a rousing reception, and Lorimer himself commented that Ben was unlucky not to be starting today.

We all pulled on our several layers of clothing, and the wife put her new pink bobble hat on, and we made our way out into the cold. By this time, Elland Road was bustling again, and a second consecutive crowd of over 30,000 was expected today. Indeed, had another 574 fans turned up for the QPR match, it would have been three on the trot.

From the start Leeds seemed to be playing with a hangover, as we just didn't look as if we were up for this one. We had been involved in some very hectic games in recent weeks, and we looked like we needed a break. It was vital to get something though, as the top two in the table – QPR and Norwich - were playing each other at Carrow Road today. So it was a great opportunity to gain on at least one of them, if not both.

In the 20th minute of the game, that looked a tall order, as we fell a goal behind. Once again, you had to point a finger at the very dodgy nature of the defending. Julio Arca took a corner on the 'Boro right, and he whipped it into the near post at the Kop end. The giant beanpole of a man, David Wheater, jumped, together with both Collins and Becchio, but it was the 'Boro man who got a touch. The ball flew across goal and bounced into the net with Schmeichel doing a star jump on the line, trying to stop four imaginary footballs, before ending up on his arse again. Jonny Howson was simultaneously doing the Can-Can at the back post, and he missed it too.

Leeds huffed and puffed, but 'Boro looked a much better team than the one we saw at the Riverside a few weeks ago, and at half time there was a sombre mood around Elland Road. In the Gents, at half time, it was the moaners who were in the ascendancy, believing that we were going to get beat, and that the defence just wasn't up to the job. The optimists were keeping quiet, if indeed there were any in there.

The second half though saw a brighter Leeds for the first few minutes, but without really looking like scoring. On 56 minutes, Grayson had seen enough, and he made a double substitution. Lloyd Sam came on for Mad Max, who had looked as if he had been partying well into the wee small hours, and Kilkenny came on for Hughes. Hughes, to be fair, had done nothing wrong, and this was just an attempt to go for broke, with Bradders filling in at left back as well as pushing on into midfield. In the words of my late Dad, "It was sh** or bust time" again.

Whenever the mercurial Lloyd Sam comes into a game, there is always a buzz, and today was no different. He is a different type of player to Gradel, doesn't come from as deep, and will cross much earlier if he gets the chance. He began raiding down his preferred inside left channel, and had a couple of decent efforts on goal. With a quarter of an hour left on the clock, Grayson made his final roll of the dice, sending on Sanchez Watt, for the overworked and under achieving Robert Snodgrass. The game was getting a bit feisty now, as 'Boro sniffed the sweet scent of victory at Elland Road, and a few rash tackles had gone in on Snods before he left the field. McCormack then had a couple of efforts, but fans around us were starting to mutter about him "not scoring before Hell freezes over", much as I had thought myself, in several recent games. Watt was also making himself a nuisance now, and there was a bit of that old momentum just starting to appear. Leeds then suddenly found top gear, and they went for it all guns blazing. Even big Neil Collins was piling forward at every opportunity as a central target man for the others to feed off. 5 minutes of stoppage time was announced, to a huge roar from the Kop, and there was a belief now that we could nick a draw from the jaws of this likely defeat. And so it was. A long ball was pumped up field from the Leeds right full back position, aiming for the head of the marauding Collins, who looked like he was enjoying his spell up front. He rose majestically on the edge of the box to knock the ball into clear space, just right of the penalty spot. It was a race now, between goalkeeper Jason Steele, and Ross McCormack, and both arrived on the same piece of grass at the same time, with a clatter. Steele though had got most on the ball, which rebounded back to Becchio who was following the play just to the right of McCormack. The ball bounced up, hit Becchio in the midriff, and as it came down on his left boot, he volleyed it straight back past the keeper's left hand, just inside the post. Mayhem all around us! This already felt like a victory, so out of sorts had we been all afternoon. But almost as soon as the teams had lined up again, we were back on the attack.

Why couldn't we have played with this passion earlier on? Now it was the team in white that was pushing forward at every opportunity. Within 60 seconds of levelling, Leeds should have been in front. The ball was out on the Leeds right wing, it came to Watt in the inside right slot and he jinked back and forth a couple of times before delivering an inch perfect cross with his left foot, on to the head of Ross McCormack. McCormack had got in front of his marker, and he met the ball perfectly in the centre of goal, 6 yards out. He seemed to have done everything right, as he twisted his neck muscles and sent his powerful header well to the right of the keeper. Sadly, it was also well to the right of the far post. It was a bad miss, and until he eventually scores for Leeds, assuming he eventually does, this will be the abiding memory of McCormack's ability in front of goal. The final whistle went, and we were all caught up in that rollercoaster feeling again. We were down and out 6 minutes ago, yet we thought we were about to win the game as that ball left McCormack's head. Once again the emotions had taken a right walloping. But that's why we watch football, and it's what more often than not you get watching Leeds United. It was a New Year, but it was the same old Leeds United.

So it was now 12 games unbeaten, and to extend that run it would take a great performance at Cardiff, our next opponents, on Tuesday night. Sadly, I was unable to go to the Cardiff game due to work commitments. It was of course the Bluebirds who were the last team to beat us, on that dismal Monday night in October. It was with some foreboding therefore, that we would await the result of the Cardiff game, as we still hadn't won a game on a Tuesday since August 10th, – and that was only Lincoln City. In 6 Tuesday games since then, the best we had managed was a couple of draws. There was also the small matter of the Arsenal FA Cup game next Saturday, which was bound to be in the mind of any Leeds player going in for a 50-50 challenge. I tried to think if I would have been able to put the Arsenal game completely out of my mind if I had a chance of playing, and came to the obvious conclusion that it was impossible! We couldn't expect any Leeds player to be winning any 50 – 50 balls on Tuesday night.

More "Ups and Downs"

I had started back to work on the 4th January, and working as a Company Accountant this was the start of my busiest week of the year. It was the time for getting the year-end accounts completed, and submitted to the Group. The good news for me though, was that this was to be my last ever year end. I had given notice of my intention to resign and "retire" at the end of March this year. For now though, I was stuck with the usual long hours that were necessary to get everything done in time.

Consequently, the Cardiff game had already started by the time I arrived home, at 8:30pm that evening. The news was not good. We were already a goal down, scored in the 11th minute (yes, inside 15 minutes yet again) by Craig Bellamy. When I saw the highlights on Sky, later that night, I had to cringe at the Bellamy goal. He started outside our box on the left, played a one-two, receiving the ball back well inside the box and to the left of goal, and somehow he managed to side foot the ball inside the near post, through Schmeichel's legs, and past the despairing efforts of a Leeds defender on the line. It was another poor goal to concede.

Grayson had started with Paynter and McCormack tonight, with Becchio on the bench, possibly to ensure Luciano was fit for the big Cup game on Saturday. The only other change from last Saturday, was that Ben Parker did finally get a start in place of Andrew Hughes, which I was sure would have pleased the 1,800 Leeds fans who had made the trip to the Cardiff Stadium. Whether the Paynter and McCormack partnership would provide a goal was uncertain in my mind. Paynter is undoubtedly a goal scorer – look how many he got last year for Swindon Town, including 4 against Leeds! In his 122 games for Swindon Town, Billy scored 45 goals. In the few games we have seen him play since his injury though, he just looked sluggish of mind and body, and not yet on the same wavelength as his new team mates. It was still early days though, as apart from a few substitute appearances, this was only his second start.

McCormack, on the other hand, was always busy, busy, busy, when he was on the pitch, but you had to doubt his ability as a goal scorer having seen his wasted efforts in recent matches, and most notably that last minute, wayward header against Middlesbrough. Still, similar to Paynter, McCormack scored plenty when he was with Cardiff.

At half time Leeds trailed 1 - 0 and no further news came through until the 57th minute. Just as at the Middlesbrough game on New Years Day, Grayson made his main changes at exactly the same time. This time he brought Lloyd Sam on for Gradel, as he had done on Saturday, and at the same time Sanchez Watt came on for McCormack, who clearly wouldn't be breaking his Leeds duck tonight. Within 2 minutes of the change, Leeds had levelled, and Simon Grayson must have thought he had the Midas touch. It was a goal from Robert Snodgrass, and it was classic Snoddy. His left foot is a magical thing on a football pitch. The ball arrived to him with his back to goal, a few yards outside the box, just to the right of goal. He took one touch, and then turned to curl a perfect shot into the far corner, similar to his effort at Coventry.

The Leeds momentum on the pitch though was then halted, as the next report we got, was that of Sam now limping away, and Becchio being forced into the fray. Then came the news we feared most; Cardiff had struck again. The description of the goal by the Sky news team sent shudders through me, as it sounded like our long ball malaise again. Sure enough, when we all saw it on the highlights programme later, it was just that. As we saw so many times in the early games this season, this time Peter Whittingham cleared a long ball down field from inside his own half and it sailed into our box, bouncing about 8 yards out and to the right of goal. Three Leeds defenders were running back watching the ball, presumably expecting Schmeichel to come and claim it, but while they were doing their "After you Claude" party piece again, Michael Chopra pounced, and his outstretched right boot just got enough on the ball to guide it into the unguarded net. One long ball, one bounce, 2 - 1, game over. Not good enough. Cardiff leapt up from 6th to 2nd in the table, passing us in the process, and the table was now led by QPR on 48 points, with the Bluebirds now second on 43, as were Swansea and Norwich, with Leeds 5th on 41 points. Watford and Forest were handily placed behind us, with games in hand. OK, not so bad, but we went to bed once again thinking what might have been had we been able to deal with a simple long ball. One thing was certain though, on Saturday, the Arsenal were unlikely to use the long ball, so who knows what might happen down there. We would be taking our places on the sofa for the 12:45pm kick off.

It all felt very much like 3rd round day this time last year. Last year it was "January 3rd" of course, so we were a week later and we were playing on the Saturday this time, not the Sunday. But the setting was similar. A full house at a top Premiership ground, and Leeds sitting handily placed near the top of their division and on a pretty good recent run of results, apart from the 2 Cardiff defeats. Mark and I took up our places in front of the TV, and settled down with a couple of beers. "He That Can't Be Arsed" was still in bed, and would only turn up a few minutes before the final whistle.

Arsenal had sent out a decent line up, although you could argue it wasn't their strongest possible side. In the line up were Andrey Arshavin, Rosicky, Song, Eboue and Bendtner. We have always had a bit of a soft spot for the Gunners in our house – in stark contrast to our feelings about the team from Old Trafford. We have never understood though, what Arsene Wenger sees in Nicklas Bendtner. Time and time again we have watched him play, and we are constantly amazed at his lack of ability in front of goal. Hence seeing him on the pitch gave us some comfort. Basically, if he scored, we deserved to lose. We were not too enamoured by the late change of referee, Chris Foy had dropped out for "personal reasons" and Phil Dowd took his place. To be fair though, I don't rate any of the current crop of Premiership referees, so it didn't really matter who was in charge. I am sick of watching referees who are clearly too full of their own self importance, playing to the TV cameras, and strutting around as if all the world wants to see them every two minutes. Still, in terms of getting decisions right, they are generally better than the shower of s*** we get in the Championship every week. Without knowing how this season would turn out yet, I was already convinced, that come the end of May, one of the major features of this season will be the appalling quality of referees we have seen, particularly at Elland Road.

8,500 Leeds fans were part of a total attendance of 59,520, and it was mentioned on the Leeds website after the game that it may well have been the all-time record away following at the Emirates Stadium. The Leeds contingent was certainly making plenty of noise, singing all the usual anthems.

The first half was steady. There were several glimpses of Arsenal's class and speed, but at the same time there were few moments of panic in the Leeds defence, where Alex Bruce, recalled in place of Neil Collins, and partnered by Andy O'Brien in the middle, was having a storming game. Sanchez Watt, an Arsenal registered player of course, had been given permission to play in this one against his parent team, and he was clearly enjoying the opportunity to show Arsene what he was missing. In commentary, it was mentioned that Arsene had said before the game, probably tongue-in-cheek, that he hoped Sanchez would not play.

On chances, Arsenal had a big lead at half time and Schmeichel had pulled off a few good stops. On one occasion the ball was slipped through the centre of the Leeds defence and Arshavin was clear through. Somehow, the ball wouldn't run kindly at his feet and he ended up scuffing a shot into Schmeichel who had raced out to the edge of the box to meet the little Russian. Equally, Becchio found himself in a similar position at the other end, but the result was the same with Arsenal keeper, Szczesny, blocking.

Jonny Howson cleared one off the line and Becchio did the same, in one spell of constant Arsenal pressure that also included a Denilson shot that swerved all over the place, but Kasper watched it all the way and tipped it around the foot of his right hand post.

Overall, it was so far, so good. The main thing was we hadn't looked out of place in a Premiership setting. In the grandstands, it was the Leeds fans that won the battle, as it was the Leeds songs coming out of the TV speakers. At one point, I am sure I heard "ITV is f****** s****" coming from the Leeds end of the ground. The Leeds fans have a habit of singing something like this regardless as to which broadcaster it is! Often, if it goes on long enough, the broadcaster will turn down the volume from the Leeds end of the ground "to avoid any offence to the listeners". The other great news was that we hadn't noticed referee Phil Dowd, so we reckoned he was having a good game.

We poured ourselves another beer, and waited for the second half to begin, content that there was still the possibility of getting at least a replay out of this game. As the cameras panned round the Emirates at half time, the commentators reminded us that it was nearly 15 years since Arsenal had lost a home tie in the FA Cup. Who was that to? We wondered. "Leeds United" says the commentator "in February 1997, when Rod Wallace got the only goal of the game".

On 54 minutes it started to look as if football was about to provide another one of those weird coincidences, whereby maybe Leeds could beat the Gunners again, 1 – 0. Robert Snodgrass was hemmed in on the left wing with his back to goal but he managed to push the ball inside to Max Gradel. Max skips into the box, shapes to go past Denilson to his left, but then pushes the ball past him to his right. As Mad Max goes after the ball, Denilson sticks out a leg and Max is felled in the box. "Leeds have a penalty" shouts the commentator, Peter Drury, and then "Opportunity knocks". It seemed to take an age before Phil Dowd was ready for the kick to be taken, but eventually Rob Snodgrass runs up to the ball and smashes it to the keeper's left, he gets something on it, but the power is too great and it strikes the back of the net in front of nearly 9,000 Leeds fans. "Leeds are at it again," shouts Drury, only just audible over the bouncing Leeds army. "We are Leeds" is the chant ringing round London. Fabregas, almost immediately came on for Song, and then 10 minutes later, Theo Walcott joined the fray, as Arsenal started to up the pace. On 79 minutes, Arsene Wenger made his final change, bringing on Vela to replace Rosicky. Walcott immediately caused problems with his pace, and he was clean through at one point only to lob the ball harmlessly to Schmeichel. Then on 87 minutes, Arshavin put Bendtner through (though that was never going to cause a problem) but then Walcott ran onto the ball in the box and tumbles over. Peter Drury, for the second time in the game shouts "Penalty" and then, "after consultation". The camera is darting all over the place at the liner and then the ref' and then on to the face of Alex Bruce who is suddenly smiling! He is smiling! "And then a change of mind" says the confused Drury. After speaking with the linesman, the decision is that Walcott was offside. So we carry on, as you were. But within a minute, the ball is being pushed into the Leeds box again, and again it is Theo Walcott after it. He had left Ben Parker flat footed and thinking Walcott was through, Parker just grabbed Walcott's arm for a second. It was enough to pull Walcott back just enough to be clearly visible, and in that moment of lack of thought, the chance of a win at the Emirates was lost. It was still possible that Fabregas would miss of course, and for some reason my mind went back to that penalty at Leicester on Boxing Day. I said to Mark "Kasper should just stay big in the middle of goal for this one, remember that one at Leicester?" Fabregas steps up and buries the spot kick right down the middle of the goal. Kasper meanwhile, is diving to his left seeking an imaginary ball placed just inside the post. I shook my head and Mark just mumbled, "You were right, good call".

There was still one more chance for Nicklas Bendtner, put clear on goal in the inside left slot, but it would have been a miracle too far if he'd suddenly remembered where the net was at this stage of his career, and sure enough he smashes it into the netting on the wrong side of the left hand post. Denilson then rasped a shot towards goal but Schmeichel launched himself to his right, and just got a palm on it to turn it away for a corner. Walcott did a Bendtner on the other side of goal, and then Phil Dowd brought the game to an end. Peter Drury closed his commentary saying "and what's more we are going to see it all again, on what's going to be a loud old night at Elland Road". It certainly would be, and the best thing of all was that we would be there.

On the Sunday evening we watched the draw for the 4th round being made by 3 members of the armed forces representing the Navy, the Army, and the RAF. 4th tie out of the bag was "Arsenal or Leeds United, versus Huddersfield Town". So the prize for beating the Gunners would be a home tie against our Yorkshire neighbours from Leeds Road.

Bread and Butter

On the Monday morning after the cup-tie, Mark sent me a text at work to say he had managed to get tickets for the Arsenal replay. The wife had decided she was going with Mark and I, and it was just "He That Can't Be Arsed" that was not going. To be fair to HTCBA, the replay had been set for a school day, so it would have been a rush if we had had to wait for him. So, as it was, I could take another afternoon off work, and we could get up to Leeds in good time to beat the crowds.

Before that game though was the arguably more important home game with Scunthorpe, as we all got back to the real bread and butter of our season, trying to get promotion. It was not that long ago that we had started off our 12 match unbeaten run with a 4 – 1 demolition of Scunny at their Glanford Park ground, with captain Jonny Howson bagging that perfect hat-trick. It would be good to get another run going with a similar score line. It was also important that we could exorcise the demons from this time last year when, following the "January 3rd remember the date" win, over the Old Trafford Reds, we had a seemingly easy home league game against Wycombe Wanderers. On that occasion, we had scored in the first minutes of the game, only to eventually draw 1 – 1, and then went on a dreadful run of 4 more games without winning. That Wycombe game was also an embarrassment to Mark and me, as we had provided tickets to a couple of Wycombe fans we know, who joined us at the game. They are also season ticket holders at Old Trafford, and had got Mark his ticket for the Old Trafford cup game. It was our thank you to them for that, but we really did want to prove to them how good we were, and on that score we failed miserably. We really couldn't afford a similar stutter this year, so a thumping win was demanded.

Although the programme for the Scunny game was packed full of reports and comment on the Arsenal tie, and previews a plenty for the upcoming replay, Simon Grayson made it clear in his "Simon Says..." piece "that today's game is far more important in the scheme of things than the Arsenal cup tie". He went on. "The league is our bread and butter, it's what we do come rain, hail or shine, and it is our main priority."

Another great piece of news in Simon's programme notes was that Paddy Kisnorbo was back home after a spell in America doing some rehab on his injury. Mark and I are both huge fans of Paddy, we felt that promotion would have been much easier last year had Paddy not got injured when he did, and although after such a long time on the sidelines there must be a doubt he will ever be the same again, it was at least good that there was a possibility.

We were in the Pavilion early for the Scunthorpe game, as we had dropped Mark's stuff at his student house, ready for his return to University next week. As we sat pondering what the team might be today, who should come along and start chatting to us, but one Duncan McKenzie. He said he was doing a spot of hosting today in the Pavilion, while Terry Yorath was also around doing the restaurants over the road at the ground. I was surprised how old McKenzie looked as he always had such a boyish, cheeky face when he was playing. It was only when I was able to Google him, when we got back home, that I realised he was now 60 years old. Brian Clough signed him for Leeds of course, during the infamous 44 days of his reign at Elland Road, but unlike the rest of Clough's signings, McKenzie became a firm favourite with the fans. We had spotted him earlier on as he was sat at another table, and I was chatting with the guys on our table reminding them about Super Mac's claims to fame, such as being able to leap over a Mini car, and being able to throw a golf ball the length of the Elland Road pitch!

In all, he made 66 appearances for Leeds, and scored 27 goals. He was telling us that he now spends a lot of his time doing pre-match hosting at Goodison Park, for Everton, who he also played for in the '70's. Everton were at Liverpool tomorrow and hence his availability for Leeds today. While we were talking, a fan came up and asked me to take a photo of him and McKenzie on a mobile 'phone, and as he shook hands with the former star, he said how he had been gutted when McKenzie had been left out of the European Cup Final side in 1975. McKenzie just replied, "So was I", and he grinned that cheeky grin of his. It was the controversy surrounding the defeat by Bayern Munich in 1975, and the many dubious refereeing decisions in the game by the appalling French referee, Michel Kitabdjian, that is still remembered at every Leeds game with the chant of "We are the Champions, Champions of Europe".

I keep meaning to dig out some old programmes to take to the Pavilion, and to get some of the autographs of these Leeds legends, but I keep forgetting. So it was again on this occasion, we didn't get Duncan's autograph.

In his interview with Peter Lorimer, McKenzie offered his forecast of a 3 -1 win for Leeds. That has become a pretty standard forecast that most pundits go for, and I thought it would, indeed it should, be easier than that today. I looked down the odds on one of the betting forms lying on our table, and decided I would go for a 5 – 0 Leeds win, at 100/1.

The team was announced at just after 2pm, and Simon Grayson had only made one change to his starting line up from Saturday at the Emirates, and it was the unfortunate Ben Parker who had to make way for George McCartney, now returned on loan again. Apart from the silly foul on Walcott that resulted in the Gunners penalty, Mark and I thought Parker had done OK.

The Scunthorpe game started slowly, almost as if everyone was re-acclimatising to league football, after the hype of the FA Cup, and this time we got through the first quarter of an hour with no goals...but only just. In the 16th minute, a clearance from Schmeichel was pumped up field to Snodgrass who niftily headed it inside to Sanchez Watt.

Watt had his back to goal, but he turned cleverly, leaving his marker on his arse. Shifting the ball to his favoured left foot;

he took aim and struck a lovely shot firmly into the right corner of the net at the South Stand end. That was Sanchez's first goal in a competitive game for Leeds, and how he enjoyed celebrating it, tugging at the badge on his chest as he raced to the South-west corner of the ground. That image made a great front cover for the Arsenal replay programme, a few days later. Scunthorpe were doing a passable impression of Celtic away, in their striking black and green hoops, but the similarity ended there. Within 4 minutes of Watt's strike, Mad Max was in on the act. Snodgrass bundled Sanchez Watt out of the way, before slotting the perfect ball through the middle of the Scunny defence where Mad Max was racing through. As the keeper came racing out, Max gave a little shimmy that sent Joe Murphy off to the left and the defender behind Max off to the right, leaving the goal unmanned as Max stroked the ball over the goal line. It was a typical little cameo performance from Gradel. 2 – 0 up after 20 minutes and I am thinking that my pre match bet is a distinct possibility. Having said that, I was also conscious that we had been two goals to the good at both Leicester, and at home to Pompey recently, and screwed both of those up. Not this time though.

10 minutes later and it is 3 – 0! Snodgrass again was at the centre of things, first collecting a loose clearance from the Scunny defence, and then working his way right to left across the edge of the penalty area. He played a one-two with Max and when he got the ball back he was clattered to the ground, but the ball rebounded backwards where Bradley Johnson was waiting to hit the ball first time with his left foot. He didn't catch it that well (he was saving the perfect strike for next week) but on the bounce it evaded the clutches of Murphy, and nestled in the corner of the net.

Becchio didn't come out for the second half, unsurprisingly in light of the upcoming Arsenal game, and Billy Paynter was given another 45 minutes to show us what he was all about. 13 minutes into the half, and he was joined by the other man trying to find his way in a Leeds shirt, namely, Ross

McCormack. He came on for Snoddy again, in a fairly obvious move to ensure Snoddy was fit for Wednesday night. As so often happens when a team gets a big half time lead, it started to look as though there would be no further additions to the score-line. The changes Leeds made were more to do with the Gunners than the Iron, and Scunthorpe had clearly been read the Riot Act at half time so they looked more organised now. Paynter and McCormack continued to work hard, but truth be told, no one around us in the Kop was really expecting either to register anything on the score-sheet. In fact one passage of play, right in front of the Kop, seemed to sum up the efforts of Paynter and McCormack perfectly. The ball arrived with Paynter, just 6 yards out in the centre of goal, and his well struck shot was blocked a foot from the goal line by McCormack, who just couldn't get himself out of the way! It was a shame. We were convinced Billy just needed a goal to get himself going.

In the 81st minute, Grayson gave Davide Somma another chance to show his wares, and the fact that it was Sanchez Watt who came off, suggested to me that the Arsenal loanee was a shoe in for Wednesday night as well. Somma, in stark contrast to the chuckle brothers, Paynter and McCormack, always looks likely to score, and in the 89th minute he was in the right place at the right time once again. Max Gradel did what Max does best, by skipping past three defenders as he skated down the right wing, and then he just stroked the ball through to Somma who was now in the clear in the box to the right of goal. Without breaking his stride, he swung his right foot at the ball, and it flew across the keeper inside the far post like an exocet missile finding its target.

4 – 0 with four minutes of added time to go and I did wonder if I would be queuing at the bookies on the way out. Sadly, it was not to be, and I couldn't help thinking about that Paynter shot that clouted McCormack on the line – it would have been good for both Billy and me!

Leeds had been efficient today, not brilliant like the Millwall game, for example, but clinically efficient in seeing off a team that was not unused to winning on the road this season. Scunny were matched only by Cardiff and Watford in having 6 away wins under their belts prior to today's games. Leeds ended the day in 5th spot, with QPR still heading the table with 5 points more and a game in hand. Everything was still to play for.

Our Big Night Out

It was hard to concentrate on anything much over the next four days, as all our thoughts turned once again to the Arsenal. Our tickets had arrived safely, and our plans were in place. I left work at lunchtime, and drove home to pick up Mark and the missus, and we set off at 3:15pm. HTCBA would sort himself out, getting the bus home from school and getting his own dinner, which we all knew would be a pizza. It always was.

We drove onto the car park at exactly 4:45pm, with over three hours to go before kick off, and there were only a handful of cars in there at the time.

We wandered down to the Pavilion and had no trouble getting a seat. We had heard several fans at the weekend saying how they probably wouldn't make it to the Pavilion tonight, as they would be coming straight after work and wouldn't have time. So that explained why it wasn't particularly busy yet, even though a near 40,000 crowd would be inside Elland Road, with the top tier of the East Stand open for only the second time this season. The previous time was for the Yorkshire derby against the Blades of Sheffield.

We were particularly pleased that one of the pre-match guests on the Pavilion stage was Paddy Kisnorbo. He got a standing ovation from the fans, as Peter Lorimer introduced him. The interview was not that encouraging though, as they were still saying it was going to be another 3 or 4 months before he would be playing again, and he would be turning 30 years old in March. Nevertheless, it was great to see him, and the crowd all clearly loved him. Mark queued up and got his autograph in the match day programme. Interestingly, on the page he signed across, the playing squad's page, I noticed that the match ball sponsor today was none other than the Morgan Motor Company. Now that will not be of any great significance to most fans, but for me it is. I grew up in the town of Great Malvern in Worcestershire in the shadow of the Malvern Hills. It is Elgar country, and it is also the home of the Morgan car factory that is located on Pickersleigh Road, in Malvern Link. I lived in Malvern from birth, until I went to University in '75, and my Mum and Dad lived just 50 yards from the Morgan Motors factory, from 1995, until Dad passed away in 2006. You can often see them road testing the new cars around the roads of Worcestershire. The waiting list for a new Morgan was always several years, although Wikipedia says it is currently down to between one and two years. If true, I guess that is the recession for you. Quite why Morgan was sponsoring the match ball for this game, I have no idea, and there was no clue in the programme. Maybe all will be explained in the Coventry home game programme, in a few weeks time.

As if one connection with my town of birth wasn't enough, I then came across another one. We were sat at a table with a couple of guys and three young lads belonging to one of them. We were chatting away, as you do, discussing various players, and the possible line up for the game. Eventually, the one bloke, Martin, he introduced himself as, asked where I was from. I told him we were living in the Potteries these days, but I originally came from Worcester. He casually remarked that his grand parents hailed from near Worcester, and when I said that I actually came from a place called Great Malvern, his face lit up and he said that's where his grand parents used to live. He then asked me what road I lived in when I was in Malvern, and I told him it was Madresfield Road, just down from Great Malvern town centre. At that point he then jumped up and disappeared with his mobile to his ear. A few minutes later he returned, to say that he had just called his Dad to ask him where he had grown up in Malvern, and the reply was Madresfield Road! How spooky is that? Martin was now getting quite excited and he asked me all sorts of questions about when I was there, and what it was like, and what the local landmarks around where we lived were, and he rang his Dad again. This time he came back and said his Dad could remember a girl who lived nearby who had the same family name as me – by this time I had told him my surname. He then said that his Dad remembered the name as Gillian. I looked at my missus, who was taking all this in, and we both said "spooky" at the same time. I have a sister named Gillian, and she would have lived in that road in Malvern exactly at the time Martin was saying his Dad would have been there, and by our calculations his Dad was just three years older than my sister. Martin gave me his Dad's telephone number and details, and asked that I pass them on to my sister in case she remembered him. Unfortunately, I had the conversation with Gill a couple of days later, and though the name rang a bell with her, she couldn't come up with any concrete connections. But if proof were ever needed that it is a small world, this was it! Chatting with Martin in the Pavilion, before each home game, would become a regular feature of our fortnightly visits to Leeds.

The Leeds team was announced, and it was the same starting eleven that began the original tie, with the exception that Luciano Becchio hadn't recovered from a knock he picked up against Scunthorpe, and Billy Paynter got another chance to impress. I thought that was a snub for Davide Somma, who had shown much more goal scoring ability so far this season, but you could argue that Paynter was a better battering ram up front than Somma.

Martin and his lads left to make their way over to the ground, and as they were leaving one of his boys asked what I thought the score would be. I explained that I expected Leeds to lose, but as long as they put up a good performance, I would be happy. I actually bet on a 3 - 1 Leeds win, at 66/1, which I thought were decent odds. Mark, ever the opportunist, was going 4 – 1 Arsenal! I joked with him that he would have to keep that quiet if he came up trumps and was picking up his winnings at the ground after the game! It reminded me of him collecting his winnings for that Howson first goal at the Barnsley disaster, when a passing Leeds fan had asked him if he had got 5 - 2 Barnsley!

We made our way out of the Pavilion, not really knowing what was going to transpire in the game, but as long as it was a good match, and we didn't get stuffed, we would all go home happy. After all, we had to keep in mind this was a side show, not the main event. The main event was promotion.

The noise in Elland Road was amazing, with over 38,000 packed in the ground. As the game kicked off, the Kop volume went a notch higher, and Leeds responded by trying to take the game to the Premiership outfit. On 5 minutes though, the dream that we could actually beat the high-flying aristocrats from North London, took a body blow. The ball was played forward to Chamakh, who tried to play a one-two with Arshavin, but when the ball came back he obviously had a shout from the football wizard that is Samir Nasri. Nasri took the ball under pressure from two Leeds defenders, but was able to coolly slot the ball into the corner, past Schmeichel, in front of the Kop. There was no great angst from the Kop, there was just admiration for the finish, and looking round, many were nodding silent approval for a typical Arsenal goal. Chamakh nearly made it 2 – 0 with a point blank header from a free kick on the Arsenal right, but Kasper did brilliantly to beat it out at full stretch to his right, before then getting up in time to collect the headed rebound. Kasper was then down to his left to stop a low, speculative, Arshavin shot.

Half an hour later and it was 2 - 0. Sagna got the ball inside the box on the right edge, and just smashed the ball diagonally into the far top corner. On the big screen replay, the ball did appear to go straight through Schmeichel's hands, but there was no doubt about the power in the shot, and it was not dissimilar to the first goal of the season at Elland Road, scored by Rob Hulse for Derby.

For a couple of minutes we were all a bit nervous as to just how many Arsenal would get tonight, as they were playing like only Arsenal can play, with fast, sharp passing, and great movement off the ball. But suddenly, out of nowhere, we were back in it. "Who needs Fabregas, we've got Rob Snodgrass" was the chant that had been coming from the

Leeds Kop, and on 37 minutes it was Snodgrass battling in the right corner, in front of the South Stand, who won the ball and gave it inside to Mad Max. Gradel struck it across goal, where an Arsenal toe managed to poke it out to Howson. Howson spotted Bradley Johnson to his left, and just rolled it across to him. If he had of shouted anything at that moment, it would have been "Go on Bradders, make a name for yourself mate". BJ did just that, as he stepped towards the ball and took a measured aim with his head down. From all of 28 yards he smashed the ball into the top right corner; with the Arsenal keeper making a magnificent dive high to his left, clawing only fresh air as the ball hit the net. It was as good a shot as that Bostock rocket of a free kick, earlier in the season at Elland Road, and the description would be the same; "If the net had not been in the way, it would still be rising even now". The goal came at a great time, just before half time, and was the talking point in the Gents below the Kop. No one particularly cared that we were a goal down and likely to be going out of the cup, it was a goal for the memory banks of 38,000 fans, who could all say they were there to see it.

In the second half, Arsenal continued to have chancs, but Schmeichel was equal to them. Leigh Bromby had to come on for the injured Andy O'Brien, and a couple of minutes later, Davide Somma deservedly got his chance, replacing Paynter. Paynter had one chance when he failed to connect with a Gradel cross shot, but again, he didn't really stand out on a night where he had the eyes of millions on him, live on TV. I for one, thought again that maybe, just maybe, he would never be as good at this level as he was in League One with Swindon. Within minutes of arriving on the pitch, Somma had a chance, but he blazed over, and then on 71 minutes Wenger sent on Van Persie and Fabregas, for Arshavin and Chamakh, as if he intended to try to finish us off. It worked. Within minutes of being on the field, Cesc Fabregas took control of the ball in his own half, out on the right. He played the ball forward to "He that will not score this millennium", but Bendtner did manage to put over the most perfect right foot cross on to the head of Robin Van Persie, who nodded the ball back over Kasper and into the far corner of the net. It was a very precise, again typical, Arsenal move, and again, once we had all seen it replayed on the big screen, we could only appreciate that we were watching a class act.

With a comfortable 3 – 1 lead, Wenger allowed Nasri to take the applause he deserved, by bringing him off to be replaced by Gael Clichy, and the three of us, and everyone around us, joined in the applause, showing appreciation for a truly great player.

Bentner continued to go close to increasing the Arsenal lead, but each time he missed, the Kop would heartily sing out "That's why you're 52, that's why you're 52" referring to the squad number on his back. The final whistle brought our latest FA Cup adventure to an end.

The last word must go to Simon Grayson, who, after the game said of Bradley Johnson's goal, "Bradley shoots like that in training and most of them end up in Wetherby but he hit that one so sweetly and it was a goal worthy of winning a match". Well-said Simon.

Now, where to next? Well, Leeds were at Portsmouth on Saturday, but Mark and I had failed to secure tickets, due to our not applying quickly enough, as I had stupidly said at first that it was too far to go. By the time I had changed my mind it was too late, and the Leeds website was now proclaiming that they had sold out all of their allocation of tickets, as we had done for every single away game so far this season. Driving home after the Arsenal game, I pondered how on earth we could get to see the Portsmouth match. I decided to explore the Internet, to see if I could find anyone wanting to sell his or her ticket. Mark said he had already tried, but I thought it worth one more go…

Pay - up Pompey, Pompey Pay – up

Thursday lunchtime at work, I was just idly looking at the web and went into the Pompey site. I had also tried to put "any spare tickets for Portsmouth Leeds game" into Google. A few other people were doing the same, but no one seemed to have any tickets they were trying to get rid of. Anyway, on the Pompey site, I spotted a statement to the effect that for the Leeds game some new "ticket pods" would be in action for the first time. These are little "pods" or prefabricated plastic sheds, from where they sell match day tickets. They had just invested in four new pods, which would free up the main ticket office on match days. The interesting bit for me though, was that one pod was said to be for "away fans tickets". Now I thought that was an odd thing to post, since a) Leeds had sold all of their allocation, and b) I didn't think any clubs were allowed to sell Leeds tickets on the day of the game. But what the hell, nothing ventured, etc. I e-mailed the Pompey website, and explained that I was a Leeds supporter and had read this bit on their site, and did they indeed have any tickets and were they intending to sell them on the day of the game? Almost by return, I got an e-mail from the Portsmouth FC ticket office, telling me they did have a handful of tickets available in the Leeds end, and I was to ring the ticket office if I was interested. I rang. They confirmed that they had just a few tickets, "a handful" they said, for the away end, how many did I want? And the rest, as they say, is history! I bought two adult tickets, paid by credit card, and then just double-checked. "These tickets are definitely in the Leeds end are they?" I asked. "Yes Sir, they are" came the answer, and that was good enough for me. I sent a text to Mark saying "We are both off to Portsmouth on Saturday!"

We set off on Saturday morning at 8am, and were in Portsmouth by mid-day having stopped just once, for a pee, on the way. On the Pompey website, it had mentioned there was parking available at the Milton Cross School. We were following signs to Portsmouth FC when, as luck had it, Mark spotted the sign for the school while we sat at a red traffic light. We turned left at the lights and then right onto the school car park, and quickly noticed that most of the dozen or so cars parked in there had some Leeds flags or other obvious signs, such as tax disc holders carrying the Leeds crest or scarves. There was no one collecting any money, even though the website had advertised that there would be a £6 charge. I checked with the school caretaker, who was there washing three school mini-buses that were parked in front of the school, and he said it was fine. Apparently, they were often late getting there, and usually didn't bother about any cars that had already arrived. (And that proved to be the case, as there was still no-one there after the game, so that was a result!). I checked that the gates wouldn't be locked or the car clamped when we got back, and the caretaker assured me it wouldn't be, and it was quite OK to park there.

First of all we walked to the ground to pick up our tickets, as there was obviously still a small doubt in my mind that this caper was going to go to plan. We walked down the rows of terraced housing that surround Fratton Park. Some of the houses looked a bit rough, but then we noticed that many of the cars parked outside them were expensive new motors, so it wasn't that bad an area of Portsmouth. We stopped at a programme seller to buy the match-day mag', and to ask the way to the main ticket office. Unbelievably, the lad had no idea, which was a tad strange, so we continued our walk around the perimeter of the ground and eventually found some more stewards who we tasked with the same question. They pointed out one of the new "pods", but when we asked there we were told that we definitely had to go to the main ticket office in Frogmore Road. We asked directions again and they said to walk down the side of the ground and we would find an alleyway leading through to the main entrance and the ticket office. As we passed the group of stewards again, they asked us if we were sorted, we explained that we still had to go to the main ticket office. They asked us where that was! We could only conclude that they had got a load of extra staff on today, for the bumper crowd expected!

Eventually, after negotiating a very dodgy alley way that you wouldn't want to go down late at night on your own, we finally discovered the ticket office, set in a brick wall, right next to what was obviously the main hospitality area as there were a few folks waiting there in jackets and suits. Above the entrance next to the ticket office, was the famous mock Tudor façade with its black and white architecture. It was still only about 12:15pm, so there were not that many folk about, and there was only one couple at the ticket office window collecting their tickets. We got ours without a problem and quickly opened up the envelope to check the tickets. "Milton End", Row X, Seats 42 and 43. That looked just the business.

Next objective was to get some food. We had passed a set of three burger vans as we had turned down towards the ground on our walk from the car park, so we made our way back there.

There was a lad in the first van, right on the corner, wearing an old yellow Leeds shirt, and he spotted Mark's Leeds scarf straight away. Funnily enough, in the Leeds programme for the Coventry game a couple of weeks later, there was a photo of the very same burger van, with this lad in his Leeds shirt clearly visible serving behind the counter. It turned out that his Dad owned the burger van, one of three that were all pitched on the walk to the ground. He asked where we had come from, and then regaled us of several stories about trips up to Elland Road when he was younger. His Dad, who was also in the van serving, was a big Leeds fan, and he told us that they used to drive up to Leeds from Portsmouth the night before a game in his Mercedes, and they would sleep in the car on a bit of waste ground on the Industrial Estate that used to be behind Elland Road. He also told us, that on one memorable trip, he drove up to Middlesbrough for a game and it took just 4 hours! We worked out that it could be done, just, but it was only possible at very illegal speeds! The burgers and chips they served up were possibly the best of the year so far, and we noted that they wouldn't serve the chap behind us with his chips until they were absolutely ready. In most places they just don't care if the chips aren't ready, they just serve them anyway. The son was going to the game after he had done his stint on the stall.

We then made our way to the Good Companion pub, recommended by the lad at the burger stall and the local Police, who were dotted along the main Milton Road. We had in mind the problem we had encountered up at Middlesbrough, but still thought it worth risking again! We made the short walk up Velder Avenue, and were pleased to spot several cars in the pub car park with Leeds flags in the back windows. There was also a huge "Darlo Whites" flag flying outside, with a group of the lads from the branch. Another photo in the "Away Days" section of the Coventry programme showed them all with their pints in front of the flag.

Inside it was jam-packed with dozens of Leeds fans, and a few Pompey, and the main bar was serving draught Speckled Hen! Another result! We bought a couple of pints, and then made our way round towards a second bar where we found some very comfy old brown leather sofas. Luxury at a football pub, unheard of! We got talking to three folk from Essex, and spent a very pleasant hour and a half in there with them. We swapped stories about some of the away games we had been to, and they were very similar to ourselves, being members who couldn't always get tickets, if the allocations were only small. They also had very similar views on the current team, believing, like us, that the defence was still not strong enough, and we had just made too many silly mistakes this season. The banter between the fans in the pub was excellent, and the Leeds fans would break into "Marching On Together" every now and again. Mark went off to the bar for refills and came back a good twenty minutes later, commenting that the staff were serving the Pompey faithful regardless of the fact they might have been behind Leeds fans in the queue, but that was a minor complaint on what was turning into another fantastic away trip. Eventually, we made our way back down the road to the ground, and noted that it was starting to get a bit chilly again. Mark noticed it was just 4 degrees, according to a neon display on one building we passed.

When we got to the entrance of the away stand, the Milton End, it was clear that this was a very old part of the stadium. In fact, the Milton End had been the last open terracing in the Premiership, until a roof was erected over it in time for the start of the 2007/8 season. It is clear that the seats have just been bolted onto the original terracing, which means the legroom is dire – not that any of the Leeds contingent would be sitting. I had read during the week, on one of the stadium guides on the web, that Fratton Park was the first ground in English football to host a league match under floodlights, when Pompey played Newcastle United, in 1956. I wondered if they had installed any upgrades to said lights over the years...

Before entering the ground, we had to pass through a gauntlet of stewards searching bags and frisking suspicious looking fans. For some reason no one made any effort to search either of us, possibly because we are both well over 6 feet tall. One irate Leeds fan vented his spleen with a torrent of abuse aimed at one hapless steward who had just searched his bag, and then he rapidly disappeared up the ramp to the stand, when other stewards started to become interested. To get up to the seats in the stand meant quite a feat of mountaineering up a steep concrete slope. Near the top we got our first experience of the Pompey toilets. The first one you come to, has a sign proclaiming "Urinals Only", but in fact on entering the brick built sh** house, it was just a black painted wall, with a small kerbed channel at shoe level. This is in no way suitable for a Premiership club, and the Leeds fans came up with many a quip about the state of these particular bogs. The most damning statement came from Mark, as he proclaimed them to be "Worse than bloody Burnley!" as he watered his brand new, size 14 trainers!

As we came out and continued our climb up the Everest that was the walkway to the top of the stand, we passed the next set of bogs that we assumed had sitting facilities. Thankfully, neither of us had the need.

There was a food stall at the very top, handily placed by the second bog block, and we got a couple of plastic bottles of Coke, (without tops of course in case we wanted to throw them at the players), before walking along the back of the stand. Below us, and to our left, were the back yards of a row of terraced houses, and all that was keeping us from toppling down into them, was a very dodgy looking chain link fence. Again, Premiership? You are having a laugh.

I did expect our seats to be crap, having seemingly got the very last of the tickets in this area, but in fact they were OK - right at the very back of the Milton End Stand, but only just to the right of the goal. Great view! And, as they were at the back, no problem in messing anyone else's view, as everyone stands up all the time of course.

We watched the Leeds team warming up down below us on the pitch, and each acknowledged our chants with a wave as their turn came.

Just before the teams came out, some of the crew of HMS Ark Royal were paraded on the pitch, in front of a magnificent image of the great aircraft carrier up on the big screen to our right. The Ark Royal was being de-commissioned today, in Portsmouth, and of course we had already paid our tributes to the ship and her crew up at Elland Road at the Bristol City game, last November. Some of the crew looked familiar from that day. As they left the pitch down in front of us, many of them bowed to us with their arms aloft, signifying that they were Leeds, and that spurred us to start singing "You are Leeds, and you know you are!" and several of them nodded furiously and gave us the thumbs up or the Leeds salute.

Before kick off there was a minute's applause, for a former Pompey Director and long time supporter, Jim Sloane, who had died over the Christmas period. It was observed perfectly by the Leeds and Pompey fans alike.

The Leeds team had a familiar look about it, with Becchio back up front in place of Billy Paynter, and George McCartney replacing Ben Parker again. Leigh Bromby was partnering Alex Bruce at the back, in the absence of the injured Andy O'Brien, who had picked up a hamstring injury against the Gunners in mid-week.

So far, the day had been just about the perfect away trip. Within a few minutes of the start though, it looked as though we were in for a difficult 90 minutes. Pompey, being roared on by their fans, chanting "Play up Pompey", surged towards the Leeds goal below us, at every opportunity.

The experienced Kanu was first to cause us problems, just missing out on a ball fired across goal. Kanu then had a shot deflected for a corner, and when it came over, Greg Halford smashed a header against the bar. We collectively urged the Leeds defence to hold firm, and were almost trying to blow the ball away from the Milton End, but Pompey kept coming, at one point winning corner after corner in a prolonged spell of pressure and Greg Halford went close with a couple more headers. Liam Lawrence, ex of Stoke City, was tormenting Leeds on both flanks, and it was from one of his runs on the left that Pompey finally breached the Whites goal. He got the ball wide on the left but managed to jink his way into the box; he shaped to have a shot at goal but instead intelligently rolled the ball back to Joel Ward who cracked the ball into the net at Schmeichel's near post.

For the rest of the first half, Leeds were clearly second best, we looked out on our feet, and all the talk at half time was about how we desperately needed some time off. It was hard to see how we could get anything out of this game, if we didn't up our performance in the second half. The bottles of Coke meant that we had no choice but to brave those prehistoric bogs again. First though, we had to fight our way along the back of the stand. The walkway between the back of the stand and that flimsy wire fence was about three yards wide at most, and about 2,000 Leeds fans, all desperate for a pee, were trying to make their way along it. There were police every couple of yards taking up room as well, and when the advance party began to return, to meet the stragglers who had only just started out on their short trip, it was total chaos, and tempers were getting a bit fraught to say the least, as we all jostled for position. We did get there eventually, and by leaning your head against the wall, and keeping your body at an angle of 45 degrees to the wall, you could just about avoid soaking your trainers with pee. Whether you escaped your neighbour's splash back was just a matter of luck though, and depended more on his accuracy and strength of flow!

Back along the alley of terror we went, to return to our seats just in time to see a huge group of scantily dressed, Pompey University Cheerleaders, leaving the pitch. Bloody marvellous, we even missed the half time talent.

The Leeds players came out early for the second half, and the body language seemed to suggest they had been given a right ear bashing during the interval. It did the trick. Within 2 minutes of the restart, Rob Snodgrass had floated a free kick to the back post, Jonny Howson had got there first to side foot the ball across goal, and there was Becchio to sweep in his 14th goal of the season with his left foot, his 50th goal in a Leeds shirt.

We looked a completely different outfit now, and Snodgrass was marauding down the right wing towards us much as Liam Lawrence had done for the home team in the first half. Leeds were awarded a free kick just outside the box, and immediately Bradley Johnson was interested. We all waited with baited breath to see if he could find a shot similar to his Arsenal rocket. He found the power, but the ball flew high wide and not too handsome. Grayson's comment about most of his training shots ending up in Wetherby, came to mind. Then, momentarily, those famous old floodlights flickered, and then failed, and I guessed that they might actually have been the same set that was used in 1956! It was still reasonably light, so play continued, and the lights eventually flickered back on. On 61 minutes and against the run of play, Pompey struck again. It was that old chestnut, the hopeful long ball into the box, which once again undid us. The keeper kicked the ball downfield, and this time Kanu was there just inside our box to head it towards goal. Then, somehow, the old Kasper and Brucey comedy show was with us again, and that allowed John Utaka to sneak in and steer the ball into the net. Grayson immediately sent on Davide Somma, in place of Sanchez Watt, who, to be honest, had not had much of a game today. He was conspicuous by his absence most of the time, and was either dog tired, or just out of sorts. Somma though, looked as keen as the mustard that is the same colour as the Leeds shirts, and with his first touch, he had levelled the game again. Becchio slotted a perfect ball through for Somma to run onto, and he hit a fine shot, low into the corner. Leeds then had the upper hand, and were pressing for a winner, when those pesky lights failed again, 15 minutes from the end. This time, they didn't come straight back on, and the game was stopped. The Public Address system told us that it was a problem all over the city, but the Leeds fans were pointing out that the street lights behind our stand were on, as were many of the lights in the ground, and the big screen was unaffected too! Later, we learned from some Pompey fans, that the B & Q and McDonald's behind the Fratton End stand were also ablaze with light throughout the afternoon. The players tried to stay warm by knocking balls to each other, while we filled the time with various chants of "Pay-Up Pompey, Pompey Pay-Up" suggesting that with their recent financial problems, someone had not paid the electricity bill. Then "Sh** ground, no lights" was the Leeds fans summary of the situation. After quite a break, the lights were back on, at least until 5 minutes from the end, when the same thing happened again. Once more the tannoy told us that it was a local problem, not a problem in the ground, but once again the big screen continued to glare out across the dusky pitch. Finally, the lights returned, and the last few minutes were played out, but by this time both teams had lost all momentum. A draw was a fair result overall. We had been poor in the first half, but much the better team in the second, and it was another point away from home. We now had a decent break, courtesy of the Arsenal cup defeat, and were not in action again until the game at Hull City in ten days time. We walked back to the Milton Cross School car park, and were pleased to note that no one had turned up to collect the parking fee, so that was £6 saved! We worked our way out of Portsmouth, and eventually back onto the M40, and we had a great journey back, doing the trip to the Potteries in just over 3 hours. In the car we reflected on what had been another excellent day out, and our thoughts immediately turned to the trip North to Hull on the 1st of February. Tuesday, 1st of February!

Sharpen up lads

We took a while to decide how to travel to the KC Stadium for the Hull game; it was yet another Tuesday night game, and it would have been a long drive for me, something like 150 miles, and at least 3 hours. Eventually, I decided to take the afternoon off work again, and drive up to meet Mark in Leeds. We would then make the trip to Hull together by train.
I arrived at Mark's house in Leeds at about 4:30pm after an uneventful trip up the motorways. The weather had warmed up a few degrees over the last 48 hours, and the temperature reading in the car was plus 7, so conditions were fine. That was not the case on the other side of the globe, in and around Cairns, in Queensland, Australia, as the car radio reported the imminent arrival of Cyclone Yasi. We had stopped in Cairns three years ago, as one part of a three-week holiday in Australia, joining Mark, who was out there on a School rugby tour. I then remembered that we also had a few days in Brisbane, on the same trip, which had also recently suffered at the hands of the weather, with terrible flooding. My mind couldn't help wandering back to an excellent afternoon spent at the Castlemaine Brewery in Brisbane, and the plentiful samples we were given. When anywhere you have actually been to is reported in the news, it makes it so much more real somehow.
Mark and I walked into Leeds to the station and we boarded the 5:38pm, First TransPennine Express, to make the hour or so journey to Hull .The train was packed, mostly with commuters presumably returning home to Hull after a day spent working in Leeds. There were a few Leeds fans, and they were equipped with the standard supermarket carrier bag, and a 4 or 6 pack of beer.
On arrival at Hull's Paragon station, we were told the stadium was just a 20-minute walk away straight down Anlaby Road, and we could see the lights of the KC as soon as we were out in the open. Most of the walk to the ground was on a narrow

walkway, not dissimilar to the walkway built to cater for fans at the Britannia Stadium, home of Stoke City. That one runs from the waste processing plant and incinerator, up to the ground. In the dark after the match, with thousands of fans making their way back to the station, this one would be potentially quite dodgy we thought. Dockside Road in Middlesbrough came to mind, and the hassle we had there.

I had not seen the KC Stadium before tonight, but from the pictures on the web it looked something special, set as it is, in Hull's West Park. It is said to be the first newly built stadium in England to be located in parkland. The initials KC come from Kingston Communications, the original name of KC, the telecommunications giant that sponsors the stadium. It is comparatively new – only completed at the end of 2002, at a cost of approximately £44 million. Sadly, it was dark when we arrived there at around 7:15pm, so we didn't get to see it in all its glory. The correct technical description of the structure is an asymmetrical bowl, and the capacity currently stands at just over 25,000, with 5,000 accommodated in the second tier of the West Stand. The other three sides are single tier. In a 2005 poll of football fans across the country, the KC Stadium was given the highest rating for comfort, services, and view. Quite a difference then from Fratton Park last Saturday, where the bogs were a disgrace and the floodlights packed up! There were plenty of Leeds fans around to enjoy the KC's facilities, as we had yet again sold out our allocation, this time of 3,163 tickets, and we would therefore definitely make ourselves heard in the sell-out crowd.

There was the usual buzz before the game among the Leeds fans, as there is at every away game, and, as we munched our burgers (no alcohol on sale to away fans) in the concourse under the North Stand, I tried not to think about today being Tuesday, and the fact that we still hadn't won on a Tuesday night since that Lincoln City, Carling Cup game, several light years ago. Mark had a bet on 3 – 1 Leeds with Jonny Howson to score first at a potential 165 /1 if it came up.

When we got to our seats, we started to see what all the fuss was about with this stadium, as we had to admit this was no ordinary football venue. We were in the North Stand at one end of the pitch, with the enormous video screen above and behind us to our right, and the view of the pitch was magnificent. The additional tier on the West side of the ground was over to our right. The hard-core Tigers fans (Cod Heads as Leeds fans know them) appeared to be gathered to our left.

Hull City had been on a good run recently. In the 12 league games since our 2 – 2 draw with them at Elland Road in November, they had only lost once, on New Year's Day, at home to Leicester City. They had only conceded 6 goals all season in league games at the KC, whereas we shipped that many in that one disastrous home game against Preston! As recently as last Saturday, Hull had battled out a creditable 0 – 0 draw with the leaders, QPR, here at the KC, so it was going to be another titanic battle tonight – we hoped though that we wouldn't be going down, and that we wouldn't get that sinking feeling.

Andy O'Brien was passed fit again, and so he returned in place of Leigh Bromby who stepped down to the bench, while up front, Simon Grayson turned to Davide Somma to partner Luciano, with Sanchez Watt missing out through injury. It looked like 4 – 4 - 2.

The North Stand was rocking, with over 3,000 Leeds fans giving it their all, but the team didn't start that well, and the Tigers missed a glorious opportunity in the first 30 seconds. Aaron McLean missed from close range when he somehow put the ball in the stand, despite it looking easier to put it in the Leeds net. Leeds did settle after that, and started to play some decent football in spells. Hull though, looked the most dangerous, and that frail defence of ours was giving the fans little confidence that it would be going home with a clean sheet. We had now conceded 43 goals so far this season, though we had also thankfully scored 50 in our 28 league games. That is an average score of not far off 1.8 to 1.5 in our favour! Shall we call that 2 –2?

Obviously there is a rivalry between Hull and Leeds, as we are Yorkshire neighbours, but the Leeds fans were trying very much to play that down with the chant of "You mean f*** all to us" that blasted out during the early exchanges. The home fans were not making much noise at all at this stage, there only appeared to be around 500 of them who were actually singing.

Schmeichel had to make several great saves in the early minutes of the game, as Hull really went for it, but then on 33 minutes our defence was sliced open yet again, with the simplest of passes, and this time Kasper was helpless to keep the Tigers out.

The ball was side footed from inside the Hull half down the centre of the pitch, arriving with McLean who suddenly found himself completely on his own, in the middle of the Leeds half. He controlled the ball with his back to goal and had plenty of time to turn, and then slot another identical side-footed pass straight through the centre of the Leeds defence to Matty Fryatt, who wasted no time in spearing the ball past Schmeichel. It was another case of the Leeds defence just not being up to the job. In an interview on BBC radio prior to the game, the interviewer had picked out McLean and Fryatt as the men to watch, Grayson had agreed. He must have had his head in his hands though now, as the whole move was just so simple. Any under 8's team would have dealt with it in the park on a Sunday morning.

Just 7 minutes later, and it got a whole lot worse, and all we could do was pretend it was Burnley all over again, and that the second half would be different! This time, Andy Dawson sent over a corner from the Hull right, and James Chester knocked a header into the net unchallenged. The ball had missed out the man on the front post who had three Leeds defenders challenging him. It was heads in hands time yet again. How the hell could we be in the top six in this division, and yet have such a crap defence? It just didn't make sense.

Just 4 minutes later, and 1 minute before the break, we started to make some sense of it, the answer being, we might be crap at the back, but we are more than half decent going forward! We were awarded a free kick just outside the box, and just right of centre. Snodgrass made it clear he was taking it. Sadly Mark, me, and the rest of the Leeds fans in the right hand end of our stand, missed what happened next. We were all involved in a bit of tasteless banter with a Hull supporter just down to our right. Someone had spotted the unfortunate fan, sat with a young boy, and considered that his thick black rimmed specs and oversized red anorak gave him the appearance of the archetypal comic paedophile! So while we were still ridiculing "Paedo", suddenly the Leeds fans to our left gave out that unmistakable roar, the one that says a goal has just been scored. On the TV recording, when we eventually got to see it later in the week, Snoddy waits patiently for the referee to blow his whistle, and then the Scotsman curls a fantastic left foot shot over the defensive wall, and into the right hand corner of the net. Game on.

Half time came and we were all getting ourselves strapped into that old Leeds rollercoaster carriage again! There was no longer any doubt at all that we could once again rescue a result from this game, even though only a couple of minutes ago it looked like we were out of it. But equally, there was no doubt that we could also ship more goals in the second half, and the spectre of another Barnsley, Preston or Cardiff, was never far away.

We came out for the second half in positive mood, as we had done so many times this season after poor first half performances. On 56 minutes we were level. George McCartney took a longish throw from the left hand touchline, about level with the penalty spot. Becchio challenged for the ball, and it just looped off his head on to Somma's left foot. Somma was just about 6 yards out in the centre of goal, and his left foot half volley crashed off the bar and bounced down over the line. Just in case the officials had a Geoff Hurst, Russian linesman moment, Snoddy bundled it further into the net, just to make sure. It was with relief that the Leeds faithful could now wave at the Cod Heads and sing "2-0 and you f***** it up" with appropriate gusto.

Sam, McCormack, and Billy Paynter all got a brief run out before the final whistle, but the game ended, probably fairly so, in that 2 –2 draw that our season's average goal tally had predicted, and exactly the same as the Elland Road game between these two Yorkshire giants had finished.

Near the end of the game an aerial challenge between Lloyd Sam and Liam Rosenior, left Rosenior prostrate on the ground for several minutes. Eventually, he was stretchered off, but it meant that the game didn't finish until 9:55pm, which was not good news, as the last train out of Hull left at 10:20pm! So we ran, as did about a couple of dozen fellow Leeds fans, back to the station. It was quite comical actually, as we all tried to encourage each other along! If anyone started to flag, someone else would chirp up "Come on mate keep going!" We were forced to go the long way around the stadium by the police, who were trying to keep the two sets of fans apart, and at one point we found ourselves running in the wake of the ambulance that was now taking Rosenior to the hospital – it made a great "front door" for our "convoy". We just made the train, but it was a train to Doncaster, and then we had to get a train from Doncaster to York where we had a one hour wait before finally, finally, getting on a train bound for Leeds. It was 3am by the time we got back to Mark's house. That is dedication to football for you.

After the game, Mark's analysis was that Rob Snodgrass hadn't really performed tonight, apart from his free kick, and it was Mark's considered opinion that "No Snoddy, means No Leeds". Simon Grayson again pointed out that it was a hard won point away from home, against a team that had been on a good recent run. He alluded to the defensive mistakes and commented that we had to eliminate them in future games. Ken Bates also commented in the Coventry programme the following Saturday that "We must tighten up our defence, only two clubs have conceded more in the division and they are both in the relegation fight. Come on lads, sharpen up at the back!" It was hard to think what we could do though, without a change of personnel at the back.

I have just one final memory from the Hull game. Towards the end Neil Kilkenny was warming up just in front of us when one Leeds wag shouts out "Killa, can you play in defence mate?" Kilkenny nodded vigorously, as if to say he could play anywhere, he just wanted to get on the pitch. The Leeds wag responds "Good, get yourself on then 'cos our defence is f****** s****!" Everyone around us guffawed loudly.

Margate

The evening before our home game with Coventry City, we had visitors. Our very good friends Brian and Sheila had travelled down from Darlington to stay with us for the weekend. The reason for the visit was that Brian was on a football double header. On Saturday afternoon, Darlington were at Telford for an FA Trophy, 3rd Round Proper tie, and then on Sunday, he was getting the train down to London for the Chelsea versus Liverpool Premier League game, the debut game for Fernando Torres. We all went out for a meal and a few beers at a local pub on Friday night, to reminisce over many happy past gatherings and to plan the logistics for the weekend.

I will put the fact that I forgot to return my Leeds United membership card into my wallet, before setting out for Leeds on Saturday morning, down to the third pint of Courage Directors ale I supped the previous evening. Strangely, I remembered that it was not in my wallet as I journeyed over the Thelwall Viaduct on the M6, but I decided that I was too far into the trip to even consider turning back at that stage. In any case, I reasoned to myself, that nice man on the door of the Pavilion will let me in, he is bound to remember me, I have spoken with him every fortnight for the last 6 months, and in any case, my membership number is printed on my match ticket, which thankfully I *did* have in my wallet

This trip to Leeds was a real nightmare. When I left home it was dry, but as soon as I got onto the M6 it started to chuck it down with rain. Within a few miles the road was awash, and I kept thinking it would have been a good idea to have replaced that nearly bald, nearside rear tyre. The traffic slowed to no more than 60 mph, as the visibility was down to around one hundred metres because of the spray, and traction was minimal, particularly at that left rear corner. On the way up I was listening to the Christian O'Connell programme on Five Live, with Brian Blessed talking about his mountaineering exploits and also some unlikely story about how he played in a match for an under 8's team against the Red team from Old Trafford one time when their team bus stopped for a break. He reckoned they beat the Reds 26 – 0! Apparently, these days he's a Scum supporter. At 11am, Fighting Talk came on the radio, and I passed another hour listening to Bob Mills, John Rawling, Matt Dawson and Perry Groves doing battle for points with some entertaining sports conversation under the supervision of programme host, Colin Murray. At least it took my mind off the danger of me slewing off the road at any minute. I arrived at the car park and paid my £6, parked up and was then attacked from the rear by Mark, as I got out of the car. He had just this minute walked down the road to the ground, having taken the bus from the city centre.

I mentioned to him that I had forgotten my membership card and he shook his head slowly and muttered something like "Dick". I repeated out loud my earlier thought that, "I am sure that nice bloke on the door will let me in, he will recognise me, and in any case my membership number is printed on the face of my match ticket!" We walked down towards the Pavilion, I more in hope than expectation.

I didn't notice the A3 size posters that had appeared in the windows of the Pavilion at first, but when I approached the nice man on the door with my match ticket in my hand and began to explain that my membership card was nestling on the bedside table in my home in the Potteries, Nice Man just shook his head slowly and kept repeating the words "Sorry Mate, no card, no entry" before I had even finished my story! He then pointed out the posters that had gone up since the last home game that explained quite clearly, "Entry to the Pavilion is strictly upon presentation of a valid membership card at the door. No card, no entry".

I tried to appeal to Nice Man, along the lines that I had been going into the Pavilion every fortnight since it opened, but the response was basically "It's more than my job's worth mate" which of course is where the phrase "Jobsworth" comes from, to describe these people in minor positions of authority.

I was distraught, not least because I had remembered, at long last, to bring some of those old Leeds programmes to get Peter Lorimer to autograph. Mark was surprisingly sanguine about the situation though, and he just suggested we adjourn to Billy's Bar, so we trudged off back up Lowfields Road. Fortunately, the rule in Billy's Bar is that anyone can now get in there up to 90 minutes before kick-off, when it then switches to members only, again by membership card. There were still two and a half hours 'til kick off, so we were welcomed into Billy's bar by a different Nice Man on the door. Billy's Bar is decent enough, after all, it was our preferred pre-match location prior to the advent of the Centenary Pavilion, but it in no way matches the facilities the Pavilion has to offer. For a start, the food choice is very limited. They have a few pies in a warm cabinet on the bar, and a few sandwiches behind the bar, and basically that's your lot. We chose a couple of meat and potato pies to go with a couple of pints of Stella. But then of course the next disappointment is that there is no cutlery and there are no plates! One of the best things about the Pavilion is that they trust you with real metal cutlery and proper china plates! In Billy's Bar you have to replicate your student days of being able to eat a crusty pie by carefully nibbling around the crust, and then peeling back your lips to work your way into the boiling hot centre of the pie, without ending up with a foil dish, or worse, a lap full, of gravy. Mark and I did a passable job on our pies today, despite having been out of practice for a few months.

One advantage that Billy's Bar does have is that you can get a pint of draught Stella in there, even though it will set you back £3-50 a pint. In the Pavilion they only have Beck's Vier, and Boddingtons.

There is a bookies counter in Billy's, and I had two bets today – I went for a combination bet of 3 –1 Leeds with Snodgrass scoring first at 55/1, and a straight 5 – 2 Leeds win at 100/1.

Mark had already placed one of his accumulator bets, with a number of games, including the Newcastle v Arsenal league game, that he had got down as an away win...

Since we had only had a solitary meat and potato pie each, we decided to pay a visit to McDonald's for old time's sake, where we both had a McChicken Sandwich, before making our way into the ground.

We had to wait until the team was announced in the stadium to find out who was playing today, but there were no surprises, with Davide Somma named up front with Becchio, in the same line up that began the Hull game on Tuesday night.

More than 27,000 were in Elland Road today, but the Leeds faithful seemed quieter than usual. Mark mentioned this and we could only think that it was nerves, this was a must win game, not least because once again several of the top ten Championship teams were paired with each other in "6 pointers" this weekend, including Forest with Watford today, and Swansea with Cardiff tomorrow.

Leeds started brightly enough, and had Coventry on the back foot in the early stages. In the 18th minute, we should have taken the lead. Snodgrass worked his magic out on the right wing, floated a cross to the back post, and found Becchio unmarked. Somehow he tried to shift feet at the same time as trying to kick the ball, and he ended up just scuffing it wide, right in front of the South Stand. It was a bad miss, and was, from my memory, his first bad miss of the season. Leeds were in command for most of the first half, but we did miss a few good chances, and there was a slight feeling at half-time that it could be another "one of those days".

Having only had two pints before the game, we didn't have need of a trip to the bogs today, so we stayed put to watch a lad mess up the half time scoring challenge. Ben Fry, the Leeds United half time compare, picked out a lad from the north-east corner of the Kop who looked as if he might do the business. He was kitted out in an England football shirt and matching tracksuit bottoms. He wasted no time at all and clipped the ball in nicely from the penalty spot to win his £50. But then, gambling his £50 for £100, he miss-kicked horribly from the edge of the box, and the ball bounced well before the goal line. They gave him another chance, just for fun, and he did exactly the same. I think we have only seen one fan this season walk off with any money. The rest of today's half time interval is spent watching the highlights of the first half on the big screen, at the opposite end of the ground, and then we get our 15 seconds of fame as the camera pans across the fans in the Kop, and we spot ourselves there clearly in the middle of the picture, with Mark waving both arms in the air.

The half time scores from around the country are then put up, and Mark notes happily that Arsenal are already 4 – 0 up at St James' Park, Newcastle. At least that result is certain for his accumulator...

The second half started in much the same vein as the first, but the Coventry defence held out until the 55th minute. Mad Max Gradel got the ball wide on the left wing, and then he jinked first one way and then the other as he made his way into the box. He swung the ball over with his left foot, way past the far post, but found Howson, who volleyed the ball, side-foot, back across goal. Somma was there a couple of yards out to smash it into the net. It was similar to several previous Leeds goals this season, when Howson has found himself unmarked at the back post. For several minutes after the Leeds goal, we did look a bit frail at the back again, and we started that annoying trait of giving the ball away too easily. With 10 minutes left, Grayson withdrew Somma, and put Kilkenny on to stiffen up the midfield, and it did the trick. Killa was involved in much of the Leeds possession, and most of it was good. Bromby had to deputise for Connolly, when the lanky full back was injured, and a couple of minutes from the end, Billy Paynter came on for Becchio, who had suffered a head injury. Just prior to going off, Luciano gave the West Stand ladies an eye full when he unceremoniously stripped off his blood stained shirt and shorts to change them for a new set, without any regard to his own modesty!

The last few minutes were inevitably a bit nervy, but eventually the whistle went and the Kop saluted the players for quite some time. Max Gradel was last down the tunnel, to a chorus of "He's here, he's there, he's every f****** where, Max Gradel"! And how he loved it!

It was a job well done – a thoroughly professional performance. The other Championship scores came up on the big screen, informing us that Forest had beaten Watford 1 – 0, and Burnley had beaten Norwich City 2 – 1. Those results confirmed Leeds in the top 6, with the Swansea versus Cardiff game still to come tomorrow. Oh, and the Premier League results came up showing the score from St James' Park. Newcastle 4 Arsenal 4! "How the f*** did that happen?" asks Mark, tearing up his accumulator slip. Another score to take the eye was Everton 5, Blackpool 3. Driving back home listening to Sports Report, I learned that Jermaine Beckford had scored the 4th Everton goal, and it was a "well taken volley". He is starting to pop one or two in up there, and is maybe finding his Premiership feet at last.

When I got home, Brian had already made it back from Telford, and he was well pleased with a 3 – 0 Darlington victory, that saw the Quakers progress into the quarter-final stages of the Trophy. They were subsequently to progress all the way to the Wembley final this year. Sadly for Brian, on Sunday, his trip down to London didn't give him quite so much satisfaction, as his beloved Chelsea lost 1 – 0 to a resurgent Liverpool team, despite the Blues playing with their new £50 million Torres, up front. We commiserated with a few beers as we watched the first quarter of the Super Bowl on TV, later.

I am indebted to Brian for reminding me about another entry in the Meaning of Liff book. He was enthralled about my tale of the missing membership card, and how Mr Nice Man wouldn't entertain letting me into the Pavilion, even though he had greeted me cheerfully for almost every home game this season. The relevant entry this time was:

MARGATE(n.)
A Margate is a particular kind of commissionaire who sees you every day and is on cheerful Christian-name terms with you, then one day refuses to let you in because you've forgotten your identity card. (The Meaning of Liff, Pan Books, 1983)

Next up for Leeds, is a tricky trip to Ashton Gate, home of Bristol City. I would be watching this one from a seat right in the middle of the home fans!

Glory, Glory Leeds United

Not for the first time this season, we failed in our bid to get tickets for an away game, and at one point it looked like I wouldn't be going to Bristol at all. Mark had decided that he was going to Newcastle for the weekend, to a mate's birthday party. I decided to check on the Bristol City website to see what was available there, and I went on the Internet from work, on Monday morning. They still had tickets available in some of the home sections, but there was a clear statement that all away tickets had been sold out. Leeds had only been given 2,000 tickets for this match – just one half of the Wedlock Stand, at one end of the ground. The ground capacity is around 20,000, and at that moment they were saying they had just 1,000 tickets left unsold. I decided that I didn't want to miss the game, as I had missed a few this season already, and it made writing this bloody book much more difficult if I wasn't even at the game! I registered on the Bristol City website (which means I am now getting regular reminders from them, telling me that their flipping season tickets are on sale!) and then clicked on the online ticket sales. I didn't really know where to try for a seat of course, but I reasoned that I didn't want to be right next to where the Leeds fans would be, as that would be too much of a temptation to join in the banter! There were quite a few seats left in the corner of the Williams stand, next to the Leeds end, probably because the home fans were fearful of being too close. I eventually spotted one solitary free seat, right near the half way line in the Williams Stand near the front, just behind the dugouts. Now I do understand that it probably didn't make too much sense buying a ticket like that when it was the only one free in a whole section, as you might guess that there was a problem with it...but I did anyway! I couldn't see that there were any posts in that section, and I couldn't think of any other reason why the home fans would have left just a single seat free...

During the week, a few of the Leeds players had been away on International duty with various national teams. Davide Somma scored his debut goal for South Africa, in their 2 – 0 victory over Kenya, scoring in the 2nd minute of the game and later hitting the post as well, in a display reported in the press as "outstanding". Robert Snodgrass was a second half substitute for Scotland in their demolition of Northern Ireland in Dublin, in the new Carling Nations Cup and Ramon Nunez, who we hadn't seen much of this season, despite him regularly being included amongst the substitutes, played for Honduras against Ecuador. The other news was that Simon Grayson had signed the 22-year-old, Aston Villa defender, Eric Lichaj, on loan, and Grayson told the Leeds website that Eric would definitely start in the Bristol City game, as Paul Connolly was still out injured.

Saturday arrived after a seemingly endless week, (I think I am starting to get a football addiction, as the days between matches now seem very tedious!) and I set off from home at 9:30am on the 137-mile journey down the M6 and M5, aiming to arrive in good time to find a parking spot at Bedminster Cricket Club, as recommended on the Bristol City website. The sun was shining so brightly that I got the sunglasses out of the glove box for the first time this year; it was a truly gorgeous, almost spring like, morning. There was a lot going on in the world this weekend, so there was plenty to listen to on the journey. The car radio had regular reports from Egypt, following the story about Mubarak resigning as their President yesterday, and there were previews of loads of big sporting events going on this weekend in the UK. It was the second round of the Six Nations Rugby Union Championship, with England playing Italy and Wales taking on Scotland. And it was the opening weekend of the Super League XVI season, with a 7 game "magic" event at the Millennium Stadium, including the Leeds Rhinos against Bradford, on Sunday. It was also Manchester derby day, with City taking on the Old Trafford Mob, in a lunch time kick off.

The only disappointment was Radio Five Live's Fighting Talk programme. It usually makes great listening on match days, but was poor today. I can't even remember who was on it. I remember one of the guests was droning on and on about the Super Bowl, and even host Colin Murray seemed bored by it all.

The sat nav took me onto the M32, and past the famous landmark, Dower House, perched on top of a hill, on the right hand side as you go towards Bristol city centre. The building stands out because it is bright yellow, and today in the brilliant sunshine, it seemed even brighter than usual. Sir Richard Berkeley built the house, as long ago as 1553, and though it has variously been a hospital and a mental institution, it is now divided up into private housing. It is a very distinctive landmark.

The sat nav then took me on the A4, Anchor Road, along the harbour side in the centre of Bristol, and I had a great view of the S.S. Great Britain, Isambard Kingdom Brunel's magnificent Iron ship. The S.S. Great Britain was built in 1843 and at the time was by far the largest sea going vessel in the world. It was the first iron passenger ship with a screw propeller to cross the Atlantic, and it did it in just 14 days, a new record at the time. After a very chequered history, the ship was eventually scuttled off the coast of the Falkland Islands, in 1937, and was then salvaged and returned to her birthplace in Bristol, in 1970, where she has been restored and is now a major visitor attraction in the Great Western Dockyard. She looked magnificent today as I drove past.

The river Avon, sparkling in the winter sunshine, was quite a sight, and there were several jet skis skimming along the harbour. The sight I was really hoping I would see though, I couldn't find – the Clifton suspension bridge. I had seen many photos of Ashton Gate with the famous suspension bridge in the background, so I knew it was around here somewhere, but thus far I hadn't spotted it today. I remembered it from family holidays when I was a kid, sat in the back of the car as we drove down to seaside resorts in the South. We always seemed to have to go across the bridge, regardless of exactly where we were heading.

I had some trouble finding Bedminster Cricket Club, and wasted twenty minutes going up and down various roads in the area of Ashton Gate, before eventually spotting the 'Public Parking' signs at the entrance to the Club. In fact when I did spot them, I think they had only just been put up. I had probably driven past there a few times already without knowing it. Anyway, I paid my £4 to a very cheerful West Country lady, on the gate, and carefully negotiated the rough field next to the cricket pitch that was doubling as the car park. I followed everyone else, as I assumed they were all walking to the ground, and it was just a few minutes before I arrived at the main entrance of Ashton Gate. Another sign that spring is just around the corner, apart from the bright sunshine, was a garden full of purple crocuses that we walked past on the way to the ground.

I bought a programme and had a wander around the club shop – a very small shop compared to the Leeds Superstore – flicking through a couple of the books on the history of the club. In one of the books, it was mentioned that the main stand at Ashton Gate was bombed during the Second World War, in 1941, and it was completely destroyed. There were some great black and white photos of the stadium at various points in its history.

Going back outside into the sun, I thought about putting a bet on at the betting office, just at the corner of the stadium. I fancied Leeds 2 – 0, but on the big board outside it was only 15/2, so it wasn't really worth bothering with. I gave it a miss and went and queued for a burger instead. Once again, the burgers here were first class. In fact, my cheeseburger was so good, that I went back for another one, before making my way into the ground. I can't remember the last time I had a disappointing burger at a football ground.

At 2:30pm, I made my way into the Lancer Scott Williams Stand, through turnstile 12, having to squeeze past a number of police dressed in full riot gear, including crash helmets with visors. Quite what they were expecting, God only knows, but there were dozens of them, dotted around the outside of the ground.

I went straight to my seat, eager to see what the view was like, and I was pleasantly surprised. I was effectively on the front row, just to the left, and to the rear, of the away dugout. The 4 rows in front had all been covered in black plastic netting, and were clearly not being used today. The view was excellent, albeit quite low down, and effectively I was at about the player's head height. I would get a great view of what was going on in the Leeds dug out, as you could see straight through the clear perspex shelters. I took a few photographs and later on that night, when I watched the BBC Football League highlights programme, I was clearly visible with camera in hand, in the first few frames of the coverage, as the camera tracked City manager Keith Millen walking across in front of the dugouts!

As the ground began to fill up, I soon became aware just why my seat had been the only one not sold in this section. The chap, who arrived to sit on my left, was the fattest bloke in the West Country, and his wife, taking her seat two seats to his left, was the fattest woman I have ever clapped eyes on. The bloke was wearing a battered old England cap on his gargantuan head, and I could only assume he was something like a former England Sumo Wrestling Champion. They looked as though they had bought three seats between them, as the one between Sumo and his wife was empty. Well, no one else was sat on it, but it was hardly vacant, since the overflow of their arses completely obscured it. The woman's arse was so huge that I considered it must have its own gravitational pull, so I clung on to my seat as best I could, for fear of being dragged into the unknown. Fortunately, a small boy occupied the seat to my right, and by encroaching on his personal space, I could just about fit one bum cheek on the edge of my seat next to Sumo. I guessed that, since everyone in this section seemed to know each other, they all knew not to ever purchase seat 19, Row F, section J, in the Lancer Scott Williams Stand.

The teams were announced, and as promised by Simon Grayson earlier in the week; Eric Lichaj was indeed in the starting line up. The rest of the team was the normal 4 – 5 – 1 crew with Kilkenny, Howson, Johnson, Snodgrass and Gradel across the middle, with Luciano Bechio on his own up front. Bruce, O'Brien and McCartney completed the back four with Lichaj, and Schmeichel was in goal, as normal.

The teams were welcomed onto the pitch by a local under 8's team; waving huge Npower Championship flags either side of the tunnel that emerged from under the Atyeo Stand, at the end of the ground to my left. The PA blasted out "Drink up thy zider", by the Wurzels, obviously the Bristol City anthem! This just has to be the most inappropriate football anthem of all time. The Leeds players looked bemused, as the home fans joined in the chorus each time, and they went through the whole bloody record with it at full volume.

There were then various safety announcements and tests before the game kicked off, something I hadn't heard at any other grounds. They went round each stand in turn, testing the evacuation alarm, and then the PA announcer asked us to refrain from swearing. I would realise later, that the home fans didn't take much notice of that request.

Finally, the game kicked off, and immediately Leeds pushed forward. I could actually understand why "We are Leeds" does show ST (Striker) against Gradel and Snodgrass when Leeds play this line up, as both were playing high up the pitch, and even Jonny Howson was spending much of his time up around the City box.

The Leeds fans away to my right were making all the noise – the noisiest section of the home fans also appeared to be in the Wedlock Stand, at the opposite side to the Leeds fans, and separated by a whole section that was left empty.

After just 17 minutes, Leeds had the lead, and what a goal it was! Max Gradel pushed the ball through to Snoddy, who dug the ball out from under his feet on the edge of the box. He then bamboozled a City defender with those magical feet, before slotting the ball just inside the right hand post, with Dodgy James unable to get across to it. I couldn't help thinking again, how much like Eddie Gray, Snodgrass was playing these days. Snodds seemed to enjoy this one even more than usual, and one Leeds fan also enjoyed it way more than he should have. The fans around me suddenly started pointing and mouthing off towards the top corner of the Dolan Stand opposite, and judging by the scuffle that was going on there, it was clear that a Leeds fan in amongst the Bristol fans had given his identity away by celebrating the goal. Some stewards, and the police, started wading in to get the Leeds fan out, and the Bristol folk around me were effing and blinding to the effect that the home fans should give the Leeds lad a good kicking, for having the nerve to be in their stand. I put up with the language for a while, but then I just couldn't help myself, and I turned round to one bloke sat just behind me and said, "mind your language mate, there are kids sat all round here". Thankfully, Foul Mouth said "sorry mate" and shut up. I managed to pull my mobile 'phone out from under Sumo's right buttock, and sent a text to Mark, "1 – 0, Snodgrass" it read. I had to make sure no one around could see the screen, for fear of suffering the same fate as that lad over in the Dolan Stand.

Leeds continued to press forward, and Snoddy had a pile driver turned away for a corner by James, and numerous other half chances fell to Leeds. At the other end, Marvin Elliot had a shot that he put into the side netting from close range, right in front of the Leeds fans. Half time, 1 – 0, and Leeds look comfortable.

Mr and Mrs Sumo got their flask of coffee out and poured themselves a couple of cups. They had to bring their own refreshments, as there was no way they could make it through the crowd to the concourse behind us without squashing several small children on the way.

The second half started much the same as the first, with Leeds doing most of the attacking, although Bret Pitman should have done better with a strike from the left corner of the box that curled the wrong side of the near post with Schmeichel looking beaten.

In the 50th minute, it was 2 – 0 and I was thinking that maybe I should have put that bet on after all. Kilkenny exchanged passes with Snodgrass and Lichaj on the right wing, before Snoddy skinned Jamie McAllister and got into the box, almost to the corner of the 6-yard area. He tried a shot that cannoned back off Liam Fontaine straight to Max Gradel who took a couple of touches. Then he lashed the ball straight through James' open legs from a couple of yards out and on the angle. Max wheeled away to celebrate in front of the Leeds fans, and he held up two hands to signal it was his 10th goal of the season. That would be the front cover picture on the next Leeds programme, for the Norwich City game.

It has to be said, that for the remainder of the game, most of the possession was with City. Their right-winger, Albert Adamah, led us a merry dance, frequently getting past McCartney and crossing, but no one could put the finishing touch to his good work. There was one spell when Leeds defenders were throwing themselves at the ball to keep out a number of attempts following a couple of corners, but somehow the ball was repelled. It came back off the cross bar from one attempt, before Becchio hacked it clear. At the other end Dodgy James lived up to his name, when he contrived to clear the ball straight to Somma, but the South African striker, recently on for Kilkenny, snatched at his shot, and put the ball wide of an open goal. The Bristol fans sat near me, including Sumo and his wife, had long since given up supporting their team, and were constantly moaning about the manager, the players, the formation, the ground, and basically anything else they could think of. There was a genuine fear amongst them that relegation was a distinct possibility. As for the Leeds contingent, they broke into a rousing rendition of "Glory, Glory, Leeds United" as the players milked the applause in front of the Wedlock Stand, before walking jauntily away down the tunnel at the opposite end.

Sumo and his missus levered themselves out of their over burdened seats, and made their way slowly along Row F, scattering the unwary as they went.

It was still light as I made my way back to the Bedminster Cricket Club, and then, in the car, going back along Anchor Road, I passed the wonderful S.S. Great Britain again, still glistening in the evening sunshine. Then, to my left, I saw the iconic Clifton Suspension Bridge, another creation from the mind of Isambard Brunel. The history of the bridge is a story in itself. A Bristol wine merchant left a legacy to build the bridge in 1754, and Brunel won the commission when only 24 years old, to build it. Due to various political and financial difficulties, the bridge was not finally completed and opened until 1864, 5 years after the death of Brunel, at the age of just 53. The bridge is today the symbol of Bristol, and rightly so. I tried to take a photo of it one handed through the car windscreen, but failed miserably. I will be back to see it again sometime, but hopefully not next season, as I fully expect to be at least one division higher than the cider swillers from Bristol.

Isambard Kingdom Brunel cropped up in another book I am in the middle of reading, Ian Marchant's 'The Longest Crawl'. It is the diary of Ian, and his drinking mate Perry, as they undertake a month long pub crawl, taking them from the Scilly Isles in the South, to the Shetlands in the North, and visiting as many of Britain's 60,000 pubs as they can manage. The reference to Brunel comes early in the book, as they visit Kensal Green Cemetery, in London, to view the great man's grave, while trying to sober up between pubs in the area. The grave is simply inscribed, Isambard Kingdom Brunel, Engineer. The book incidentally is another excellent read, particularly, if like me, pubs and beer is your specialist subject!

The Longest Crawl, Ian Marchant, Bloomsbury Publishing Plc, 2006.

The big sports news on the radio, as I motored back up the M5 and M6, was that very strange affair at Newbury Racecourse earlier in the day, when 2 horses died, having apparently been electrocuted in the parade ring. In the following few days, it would become clear that an old cable had leaked electricity through the ground, following some routine maintenance work that had disturbed the cable. The two horses, Fenix Two and Marching Song, suffered a surge of electricity picked up from their steel shoes. Although it was said to be a freak, one-off accident, the history books soon 'unearthed' (sorry!), that an almost identical episode had occurred in the USA in 2008.

The other football news was that nothing much had changed at the top of the Championship today. It was spooky, and not a little disappointing, that 3 of the other top 6 sides had managed to secure wins today, with either very late, or even injury time, goals. Norwich City did this for about the eighth time this season, in their 2 – 1 victory over Reading. Similarly, Cardiff City only beat lowly Scunthorpe 1 – 0, with a goal in the 85th minute. Swansea, managed an amazing comeback at the Riverside, to beat 'Boro 4 – 3 with an injury time goal, despite having been 3 – 1 down at one point. Forest would draw at QPR on Sunday. So, QPR would end the weekend top, with 60 points. Just 2 points, with second placed Cardiff on 54, and 6th placed Leeds on 52, separated the next 5 teams.

In the next few days, other results would help keep the top of the Championship boiling nicely, as several clubs caught up with their games in hand. On Tuesday night, Burnley got a point at Cardiff, while bottom club Preston got a draw at Watford. Then on Wednesday night, there was a real shock, as Scunthorpe beat Forest 1 – 0 at Glanford Park, showing that their performance at Cardiff at the weekend was perhaps no fluke.

Everything was still to play for then, and for Leeds, two home games coming up on the trot. OK, we faced a tough game against the Canaries from Norwich next Saturday, and then another Tuesday night game against Barnsley, but hey, anything could happen.

I tried to count the Leeds coaches I passed, as I made my way home, and could picture the Leeds fans on board still singing "Glory, Glory, Leeds United". I counted about a dozen before giving up. Safe journey home lads, see you at Elland Road on Saturday.

Super Sub

The Leeds website was telling everyone to go early for the Norwich game as the road works on the M621 were still causing chaos, and the game was just about a sell out, with the Canaries having sold all of their 3,000 allocation and Leeds having less than a thousand tickets left, when I checked on the web on Friday lunch time. The annual Valentine's Fair was also occupying a large part of the Fullerton Road car park, to make things possibly even more chaotic around the ground. So I was all set to allow an extra half an hour when Mark sent me a text at 9am saying that there had been snow overnight in Leeds! I eventually set off at 9:45am, and had a really good trip, right up until I got to the famous White Rose boundary marker on the M62. It was almost as if its creator, Harry Yeadon, had set it there today, specifically to mark the boundary of the Yorkshire snow, and not back in 1976, when the motorway was opened. As soon as I crossed into Yorkshire, it started snowing, and the ground was already white with about an inch of the stuff. Driving conditions were appalling for a few miles, as it was also very foggy up there, and then we lost the outside lane of the motorway, as the snow was just too thick to risk. I still hadn't replaced that rear, offside tyre, so I definitely wasn't venturing onto the slippery stuff! Thankfully, it did improve as I got onto the M621, and as usual I was one of the first cars to get parked on the car park. I texted Mark to let him know I had arrived, and he texted back to say he and girlfriend Suzi would meet me at the car at about 12:15pm, so I just sat listening to the radio. The Chelsea versus Everton, FA Cup 4th round replay, had just kicked off when they knocked on the window.

I had remembered my membership card and loaned the wife's to Suzi, so we all got into the Centenary Pavilion, and I gave the "Margate" on the door a knowing smile as we flashed our cards. He smiled back cheerfully and said "Ow do".

The Chelsea game was now well under way, and was being shown on the screens in the Pavilion. There seemed to be plenty of interest in Jermaine Beckford, who was in the Everton starting line up. Martin, (the bloke who I spoke to at the 'Boro game who told me his Dad had lived in Great Malvern near my parents) and his lads were in there, and we passed a few minutes chatting with them.

I had remembered to take some old Leeds programmes again this week, and was hoping one of the Leeds legends would put in an appearance. I had the Chelsea Leeds FA Cup Final Replay programme, from 1970, that Jack Charlton had signed for me many years ago, at a Sportsman's Evening in Birmingham; an Arsenal Leeds Division One programme, from 1969; and the Leeds West Brom programme, from the opening day of the 1976/77 season – the season I eventually got to see Leeds in that disappointing Cup Semi final, against the Old Trafford lot, at Hillsborough.

The first guest in the pavilion today, was Terry Yorath, and after he had finished being interviewed by Peter Lorimer, Mark went and got both Lorimer and Yorath to autograph the team photo in the centre of the Leeds West Brom programme. Coincidentally, Yorath and Lorimer were sat side by side in the front row of the picture, although Mark said he had to point out to Lorimer exactly where he was, as he couldn't spot himself! I made a mental note to keep bringing that programme, to see if we could get any more of the players' autographs. Paul Reaney was bound to put in another appearance at some point, and he was on the photo.

Terry Yorath is probably better known to young Leeds fans these days, as the father of TV sports presenter Gaby Logan, (married to ex Scottish rugby union player, Kenny Logan) than as the tough tackling midfielder, who starred for Leeds in the 1970's. I asked Mark if he knew of Yorath, and just got a shake of the head. Yorath's prediction for the score was 2 – 0 Leeds, with Snodgrass to score first. Mark commented that no one had ever predicted anything other than a Leeds victory, not even a draw! Sanchez Watt was next up on the stage, and he also predicted 2 – 0 Leeds, but he had Becchio as his first goal scorer. Sanchez said that he had been training this week, following his hamstring injury, but Simon Grayson considered today to be too soon for the Arsenal loanee to make his return. He hoped to be back in the squad for the Barnsley game, next Tuesday, (yes, sadly, we were days away from another go at a Tuesday night fixture – might that one finally see our first mid-week league win this season?).

I couldn't see Leeds not conceding today, so I plumped for 2 – 1 Leeds. It was only priced at 15/2, so I wouldn't get rich on that one. I also did a 3 – 0 Leeds, paired with Snodgrass as first scorer, which would pay out a handsome 100/1 if it came up.

The team was announced as the same line up that started against Bristol City last Saturday, which meant 4 – 5 – 1 again, with new boy Eric Lichaj keeping his place with Connolly still injured, and Kilkenny keeping his place among the 5 in midfield. The programme continues to list Gradel and Snoddy as strikers though.

Flicking through today's programme, I was impressed that the centrefold picture was a snowy scene of volunteers clearing the Elland Road pitch in 1969 with the caption beginning "With rumours of an imminent return to wintry weather persisting…" Well done programme editor, spot on for today!

As we left the Pavilion, the Chelsea Everton game was still deadlocked at 0 – 0, but Everton would eventually go through 4 – 3 on penalties. Beckford was taken off just before the end of normal time, so David Moyes, the Everton manager, clearly didn't have any faith in him for the pens!

We got to our seats and saw the usual familiar faces around us, we don't actually know the names of many of these folk, but they recognise us now, and we exchange the usual pre-match greeting of "How do! Here we go again!" Referring to the likelihood of another rollercoaster ride at Elland Road!

There had clearly been a fair amount of snow on the pitch, as it was still piled up in front of us, against the advertising hoardings, but the surface itself looked OK, if a bit on the heavy side. That might just clip the wings of the usually slick passing Canaries.

After the first quarter of an hour we were well pleased with the display Leeds were putting up. Norwich had very little of the ball, and we were attacking freely on both flanks, with Gradel and Snodgrass both looking in good nick. It had to be said we had missed a couple of good chances though. The best went to Becchio, who headed against the upright, very early doors. Then Jonny Howson ran through a couple of defenders to the left of goal, before hitting a left foot drive that beat the keeper diving to his left. Sadly, it also beat the far post, to run agonisingly wide. In the programme for the Barnsley match the following Tuesday, Ken Bates would refer to Howson's performance today as a "great impression of Wayne Rooney"; referring to the chances he missed! In the 17th minute though, Leeds got the opening goal of the game. Gradel's cross from the left was back headed by Snodgrass at the near post, and it looped over to the back stick where Becchio and defender Adam Drury both jumped together, almost on the goal line. Becchio managed to get the slightest of touches, and the ball dropped into the net. Luciano then proceeded to entertain the West Stand patrons with possibly the worst goal celebration of the season so far, some sort of robot stick man dance. The West Stand patrons probably thought it was marginally better than the display of his hairy arse they got a couple of weeks ago, when he changed his blood stained kit in front of them!

Leeds continued to do the majority of the attacking, and on this display Norwich were not looking a top six side at all. They did have one good shot from distance that Schmeichel launched himself at to tip it round the post. It was one of those saves that Andy Gray would have described as "one for the cameras", were he still broadcasting on Sky TV. He had been sacked a few weeks ago of course, and Richard Keys had resigned, after their indiscretions on an open microphone. They had joked about the talents of female linesman, Sian Massey, and made some unflattering comments about Karren

Brady, the right hand woman of David Gold at West Ham United and assistant to Sir Alan Sugar on The Apprentice TV show.

The Leeds fans were not happy with referee Neil Swarbrick, who seemed to make several poor decisions against us in the first few minutes. The usual chants of "You don't know what you're doing" and "We always get s*** refs" rang round the ground with some anger. Howson then had another great chance to double the lead, as Snoddy put Lichaj through on the right, and Captain Jonny met his low cross. A defender blocked his first shot, but the ball bounced back to him and his next effort crashed off the underside of the bar. We moved into injury time – 2 minutes the board displayed – in the first half, and I turned to Mark and was about to say that we really needed to keep Norwich out, as they always score in injury time. I didn't have chance to finish the sentence though, as the ball was headed down at the back post by Grant Holt, and was thumped past Schmeichel by Henri Lansbury, on loan from Arsenal and presumably a mate of Sanchez Watt. It was heads in hands time again. Every last fan in the Kop was still shaking his or her head, as the referee blew for half time. Leeds had dominated the game for almost the whole of the first half, playing some quite brilliant football at times, and making Norwich look decidedly second best. Yet in they go all square. Un-bloody believable!

It was still bitterly cold, and Suzi made her way down to the concourse for a hot chocolate, while Mark and I chewed over the first half and shook our heads some more. It had been just a one pint lunchtime today, and so we didn't need to seek the relief of the Revie Stand bogs. We guessed though, that there would be just as much shaking of heads down there, as shaking of any other appendage.

The second half got under way, and both sides sensed they could get something out of this game. Leeds were still the more positive, attacking with speed at every opportunity, with Snoddy on the right, and Mad Max weaving his way down the left. Norwich were adopting a far more patient approach, passing the ball back and forth along their back line, and then usually launching a high ball diagonally into our box, (they had obviously done their homework, as that is exactly the ball that has undone us many, many times already this season). Half chances came and went for both sides. Grant Holt hit the post for the visitors, and then disaster struck. Suddenly, out of nowhere, Andrew Crofts was pushing the ball to Wes Hoolahan to the right of goal, and he stabs it towards our net with his left foot. Andy O'Brien swung a leg at it, fell over and missed it completely, while Eric Lichaj could only sky it into the roof of the net, as he slid over the goal line himself. Grayson didn't ponder for long, and on 75 minutes, exactly as he did at Bristol last week, he brought on Davide Somma in place of Neil Kilkenny. Somma has been making a name for himself all season as a 'Super Sub', and once again he lived up to the title. Alex Bruce clipped a hopeful ball up to the edge of the area, where Becchio won the ball in the air. It looped up into the heavy Leeds sky, and came down just outside the box and straight onto Davide Somma's right foot. He hadn't yet touched the ball since coming on seconds earlier, but he met it sweetly, and it just beat the keeper's despairing dive to his left. It suddenly felt exactly like the Middlesbrough game at New Year. The crowd was urging Leeds forward, and trying to suck the ball into the net in front of the Kop for a last gasp winner. The momentum was with us again, everyone suddenly believed again. On 90 minutes, Billy Paynter was sent on to see if he could break his duck, and a very tired looking Luciano Becchio made his way off, to wild applause and his own chant of "Cost less than Berbatov, and he scores more goals". Suddenly, Paynter was in the box playing a one two with Somma, and now only had the Norwich keeper, John Ruddy, between himself and glory. He couldn't fail to score could he? But just like McCormack against 'Boro, with that misguided header in the last minute, so too Billy Paynter just wasn't up to it. He swung his right boot at the ball, but made a poor contact and it bobbled slowly towards the far corner of the net, only for the keeper to tip it round the post. Once again we should've stolen a victory, despite entering the last quarter of an hour behind. Once again, we failed to take the chance. We were left yet one more time, to wonder just how costly that miss would become May.

As we left our seats, several fans asked if we were coming to the Barnsley game and said "See you Tuesday then" when we confirmed we would be here. The other Championship results came up on the big screen at the South Stand end, as we queued to get out. Forest had beaten Cardiff in the big one, to go second, and there was a good win for Swansea over Doncaster. The leaders QPR had been held at bottom club Preston. It was all still very tight at the top, apart from the leaders. The next 5 teams were still separated by just 3 points. Beating Barnsley was now vital, crucial, but it was ANOTHER BLOODY TUESDAY NIGHT!

If it can go wrong...

Ok, I keep going on about Tuesday night games and our inability to win one. When I got home after the Norwich game I sat down at my computer to look at the statistics for mid-week games this season – that was after I discarded the latest e-mail reminder from Bristol City who still want me to sign up for a season ticket! I must remember to de-register from their site! The statistics now tell us, that we have played 9 games on Tuesday nights, and have only won one, the first one, that League Cup game against Lincoln City. The problem though, seems to be bigger than that. Delving into the statistics even further, would reveal that in fact we have only won games played on a Saturday all season, except that Lincoln game. If we were to focus just on League games, we have now played 12 games on days other than a Saturday, and have yet to win one! (In fact, we have played on every day of the week except a Thursday, – so Don Revie was correct about that!). On Saturdays, we have only lost 2 games all season. Clearly there is something going on here, but quite what the problem is, I don't know. I do wonder if anyone at the club has thought about this. Who knows?

I was reasonably relaxed for this latest Yorkshire derby, and travelling up the motorway the only problem I had was a dickhead driver in an old red BMW. There is only one thing that gets my road rage going, and that is when a pillock undertakes me on a motorway. I generally like to leave a comfortable space between my car and the car in front, say 4, or 5 car lengths at 60 or 70 mph. This particular afternoon, the M62 was very busy, and all three lanes were effectively travelling in convoys. I first became aware of Dickhead, when I noticed him getting closer and closer behind me as we were both travelling in the outside lane. You know the score. He was trying to put pressure on me to move over, so he could move up the convoy one position. Then he would do the same to the next guy, and so on. I really do have a problem with this sort of behaviour, so I tried to ignore him. Dickhead's next move, is to dive into the middle lane, and then hope that the middle lane would allow him to get his nose in front of me, to then dive back into the outside lane, filling the gap between me and the car in front. This would cause me to then back off, and try to create the same "safe" gap again. Arsehole behaviour! The only way to stop Dickhead's move, is to get closer to the car in front – too close really. I was getting so pissed off with Dickhead, that I did it anyway. Dickhead's response, was to pull back in behind me, flash his lights, and give me the w***** sign through his windscreen. No problem, I am not rising to that. We travel on a few more miles. Suddenly, Dickhead dives into the middle lane behind me again, and this time, unfortunately, his lane did move on, so that although he couldn't get in front of me, (because I again closed the gap) he did then get in front of the big 4 X 4 in front of me. He pulled over so sharply, and into such a small gap, that the poor sod in front has to brake sharply and swerve to avoid an accident. I could then see that the 4 X 4 driver was flashing his headlights at the red Beamer. We travel on a few more miles. I spot Dickhead again, now two cars in front, dive into the middle lane for his next queue jump. Now anybody who has spent as much time as I have on motorways, would know that each lane tends to have a habit of catching up any yardage it loses, and, as luck would have it, that is exactly what happened this time. I soon found myself sailing past Dickhead in his Beamer, and I resisted the temptation to repay the sign language, tempting though it was. I sensed he would not be a happy bunny though, seeing me go past him, and sure enough he eventually pulls sharply back into the outside lane behind me and once again begins the pressure tactic. At this point I have had enough, so I then put Plan B into action. You don't see many 607's on British roads, and though it doesn't really look like an unmarked cop car, it does have a certain presence, and you might even think the driver has authority in some capacity or another. The sequence is as follows: Look earnestly in the rear view mirror, taking care to adjust it so that it looks like you are trying to see the number plate of the car behind; say the number to yourself out loud, in the mirror, two or three times (it is surprising what you can see, or think you can see, from the car behind); lean across and open your passenger side glove box and take out a pen or pencil (an imaginary one will do if you don't actually carry a real one); make sure the car behind can see the pencil or pen if you have one, and check that number plate again; pretend to write down the registration on a pad on your lap, taking care to stop every other letter or number, to check in that mirror again. I have just finished writing the number, with the imaginary pen, on the imaginary writing pad, when I see that Dickhead has twigged what is going on. He has two passengers who have probably seen more than Dickhead himself, and I can imagine the conversation in the car going something like "Oh, bugger Dick. That bloke in front has just taken down your number mate!" They would probably know that I was not an unmarked police car, let's face it, if I was, I would have pulled him over for dangerous driving long before this point. But more than likely, Dickhead hasn't got insurance, and in any case wouldn't want anyone knocking on his door. Bingo! At last Dickhead pulls back into the middle lane, and slips far enough behind to be out of my line of sight. Mission accomplished. I like to think that Dickhead is now a worried man, I may be kidding myself but, hey, I felt better.

I met Mark in the Pavilion at about 6:15pm, an hour and a half before kick off. I had arrived there about 20 minutes earlier, just in time to see Allan Clarke, John Newsome, and Peter Lorimer, on the stage discussing tonight's prospects and the chances of promotion. Sniffer, (for the younger readers, that was Clarke's nickname, because of his ability to "sniff" out goal chances) felt that we had blown a great opportunity on Saturday, by failing to beat Norwich, and that now, tonight's game was an even more "must win" match. He talked a lot of sense did Sniffer. I queued with about half a dozen folk for Clarke's autograph, on that same team photo I took to last Saturday's game when Mark got Lorimer and Terry Yorath to sign. Three down, quite a few still to go! I had a brief chat with Sniffer, and asked him how he kept so slim, as he didn't look an ounce heavier than that day he dived to head the ball in the Arsenal net to win us the FA Cup, back in 1972. I asked him if he still worked out, and he replied "No way, I'm 65 years old in July you know". I didn't know. It shocked me a bit that one of my boyhood hero's could be nearing retirement age. It is later than I think!

Talking of Leeds legends, the centrefold "Classic Shot" picture in the programme for tonight's game, was a brilliant photo of Duncan McKenzie performing his party piece of jumping over a Mini. I had mentioned this to Mark when we met Duncan at Leeds a few weeks ago, and I don't think Mark really believed me. But there it was, in black and white. Super Mac was caught mid jump, hovering over the roof of the car in front of 12,000 Leeds fans, at Paul Reaney's testimonial match in the 1975/76 season. Can you imagine any manager allowing a player to do that before a game these days? Well actually, the caption for the photo explained that Brian Clough had banned McKenzie from doing it while he was manager, and Jimmy Armfield banned it straight after this particular episode!

I put a quid on a 5 – 2 Leeds win at 100/1, reasoning that it would be ironic if we could reverse the score from the game at their place last September, when we had that late, late collapse, having taken the lead in the 3rd minute with that Howson goal that won Mark sixteen quid. Mark did another one of his accumulators, flushed with the success of winning £20 last night on two Turkish matches, West Ham beating Burnley in the FA Cup, and an Irish league game! Tonight he was on Spurs to beat Blackpool at their place, and Norwich to beat Doncaster, amongst a few others. I suggested that Blackpool might do Spurs and it wouldn't surprise me if Doncaster bounced back after their last two defeats, a 6 – 0 and a 3 – 0. I was to be proved right on both counts, but sadly got our game wrong. Not by much though.

When we got to our usual turnstile, I decided to try to break our poor run of Tuesday night luck, by going in ahead of Mark, thus breaking a previously, strictly adhered to, superstition. Look, anything is worth a try!

Just over 26,000 of us were in tonight, and Grayson had sent out the same team that battled so well against the Canaries on Saturday and at Bristol before that. 4 – 5 – 1 again. It looked a conservative choice against a side we really ought to be beating soundly.

At Oakwell, remember, we were a goal up inside 3 minutes, so I was looking for some sort of symmetry here…and boy, I got it in Spades. 3 minutes gone and … "f*** me, we are a goal down already!"

It has to go in that category of "defence like a sieve" goals. A free kick on the right is curled low into the six-yard area and it goes through a sea of white shirts to the back post where a Barnsley player touches it inside. Jason Shackell is on hand to prod it into the net, and Kasper is on his arse again in the net, thrashing around in his all green kit, looking for all-the-world like a giant, demented frog. It was a messy, messy, goal.

Listening to Simon Grayson being interviewed on BBC Radio after the game, he was clearly angry with some of his players. He spoke particularly about "conceding a bad goal" at the start, and about the way we "keep making silly mistakes", and how we need to be "more professional" in not giving away daft free kicks. But, if we do, we must then defend them properly. He named one or two players, who he considered had made mistakes tonight.

Funnily enough though, I wasn't too worried at this stage, I was still half thinking that this might indeed be a complete reversal, or mirror image, of the scoring sequence up at Oakwell last year. I said so to Mark and a bloke behind overheard me and agreed, "It's too early to be worried," he said, in a very worried sort of tone.

After the initial setback, the Leeds fans shook themselves down and soon got behind the team again, and on the pitch, we were again playing some bloody good stuff. I couldn't help thinking of that Chumbawamba track, "I get knocked down" with its lyric "I get knocked down, but I get up again, you're never going to keep me down". That is what it felt like, we were the better team but they kept knocking us down! Our first good chance came from the right foot of Max Gradel, as he whipped an excellent free kick towards the top left corner of the net, in front of the Kop. Luke Steele, the Reds keeper, somehow got a touch on it before it struck the bar, bounced down, and then cannoned off the back of his head for a corner. Mark is beside himself saying "We never get any f****** luck". It was the first of many contributions from Max, who truly was "here, there, every f****** where" and worked his socks off all night. If any player has embraced what Leeds is all about, he has, and the fans love him for it.

Gradel then played in Luciano Becchio, who made a complete hash of his left foot swinger. On 23 minutes though, we were level. Gradel tormented a couple of defenders out on the left wing, and pushed the ball to Kilkenny. He lofted a cross to the back post, where the keeper missed it, and Becchio was on hand to nod it in. Relief all round. The referee is having a nightmare by this time, and once again the Leeds fans let him know, with a series of relevant chants that are normally aimed at the crop of Championship refs we usually get at Elland Road. Tonight though, we had a so-called "Elite" ref. On 37 minutes, Mad Max was at it again. Howson slotted the ball through to him, and he went down under a challenge from Matt Hill. In normal circumstances, this was a nothing incident, but tonight we had Premiership referee Mark Clattenburg in charge and for some reason known only to him, he awarded us a penalty. I turned to Mark and suggested that this was the bit of luck he thought we never got! In what was fast becoming a one-man show, Max got up, dusted himself down, and clipped the spot kick high into the right corner of the net. 2 – 1, and thoughts turned again to 5 – 2 Leeds at 100/1.

The second half should have seen Leeds building patiently, but it was Barnsley who, within 3 minutes of the restart, made it 2 – 2, as we suffered another Chumbawamba moment. Leeds were again all over the place at the back as the ball was passed across the box to Matt Hill, all on his own, to fire home comfortably. My only consolation at this time was that 5 – 2 was still on, and the game had the feel of that Barnsley away game, or even (God forbid) the Preston home game. Minutes later though it got a whole lot worse for Leeds, as referee Battenberg showed Bradley Johnson a second yellow card for the most innocuous of challenges, and as he walked off even the Barnsley players looked bemused at the decision. Was that an attempt to even up the penalty decision? We will never know, but a visitor from Mars would have assumed so. I couldn't help thinking of that well-worn phrase "If it can go wrong, it will…"

Grayson was 10 minutes earlier with his substitutions today, throwing on Somma and Watt, for Becchio and Snodgrass. But it was our pint sized hero Mad Max, who served up what should have been the winner just 4 minutes later. He was onto a lose ball in the box in a flash, and he curled a perfect right footer just inside the far post. It was a goal fit to win the match. For the umpteenth time this season though, we couldn't see the job through to the end. Leeds were again messing about on the edge of their own box with the ball, instead of lumping it into row Z. It was as if we were daring Beelzebub to knock us back down again. He did! Eventually, inevitably, we give away a free kick. Quite what the wall was then doing, I have no idea, but it looked like a shambles. When the kick is taken by Kieran Trippier, it is struck with neither pace nor accuracy, but somehow it clips Kilkenny on the end of the wall, and then passes Schmeichel to strike the back of the net. Kasper immediately does his Kermit impression again, arms and legs akimbo, clearly upset with his defensive wall. The best one can say, was that Schmeichel was unsighted, but I felt at the time, and still do after watching the replay on TV, that he should have been able to stop it. A bloke stood near us was adamant that it wasn't Schmeichel's fault, and Mark berated me for even suggesting such a thing. In that post match interview, Grayson was clearly upset at the lack of nouse shown at the free kick, and talked of players "turning their backs on the ball". He commented "If the lad had put it in the top corner, you could say well done, good goal" implying that he felt someone was at fault, though he didn't specify whether he thought that was the wall, or the keeper. Whatever, it looked like another example of schoolboy defending. Either that or it was the work of the Devil.

Battenberg blew the final whistle and that was that, another Tuesday night, another 2 points tossed away, another great chance to close the gap at the top of the table wasted. As I sat in the car waiting to get off the car park there were other games still going on. At one point Forest went 2 - 1 up against Preston in the 2nd minute of injury time, and I just thought "Sod it, this isn't gonna be our year". But then 4 minutes later the shout comes from the radio, "another goal at the City Ground", and this time bottom of the table Preston have just equalised. If I was a religious bloke, I might have thought that the Almighty was just reminding me not to give up just yet, and that there is still a long way to go and he can still fix it for anything, absolutely anything, to still happen! It finished 2 – 2 at Forest, and I was right about that game at Carrow Road, as Donny got a draw there. The top three, QPR, Cardiff and Swansea, all won, but there are still 13 games to go for most teams – 39 points worth. It is far too early to assume anything in this league. It all felt uncannily similar to this time last year, when we thought Leeds were tossing it all away match after match, but somehow we were still in that second spot for automatic promotion when the dust finally settled in May.

As we left the Stadium, Mark was really disappointed, and he said "It feels like a bloody defeat tonight". I initially had felt the same, but on the journey back home I was reminded that, at the end of the day, football is just a game. On the radio, there were regular bulletins on the aftermath of the Christchurch, New Zealand earthquake, with eye-witnesses giving stunned reports of churches raised to the ground, huge office blocks reduced to piles of dusty rubble, and roads buckled with the force of the 'quake. The spire of Christchurch Cathedral had collapsed into the road, and it was suspected that many people were buried under the debris. The other news tonight was of the latest peoples uprising, this time in Libya against their long time leader, Colonel Gaddafi. There were reports that his forces were shooting protesters in Tripoli, and many were dead. It put tonight's mere football match into some perspective.

Next up was the long trip to Swansea on Saturday, and a selection headache for the boss, with Johnson now bound to be suspended and Watt not looking quite on it tonight. Maybe this is the time to switch to 4 - 4 -2? Mark and I would be there, and it was another "Must Win" game. Mark's usual comment before every game was "This is a real must win game". But then again, aren't they all?

Swansea

Armed with the AA route finder print out, and the back up of the sat nav in the car, we set out on Saturday morning at 7:45am. Mark had travelled down from Leeds on the train yesterday afternoon, so that he could make the trip to South Wales in the car with me.

The initial chat in the car was about the inexplicable decision of the Football League to move all of the final day Championship matches, from Sunday 8th May at 3pm, to Saturday 7th May at 12:45pm. What is all that about we mused? We had spent weeks planning that weekend, and had just about got it sorted. Mark is appearing in a play at a theatre in Leeds on the weekend in question, on the Friday and Saturday nights. We had arranged for various family members to stay in a hotel in Leeds for the Saturday night, after the final performance, and then Mark and I were driving down to Shepherds Bush for the QPR game on the Sunday morning. We were convinced that we would get tickets under the loyalty scheme, as we had applied for almost every away game this season. We were just surfing the web last night, when Mark spotted the announcement on the Leeds website, that all the games had been switched. The announcement was a copy of the Football League statement on their website, and just said that, in conjunction with the TV authorities and the clubs, the Football League had rearranged all the games for the final day. No explanation as to why or why they couldn't have made the change earlier. Unbelievable! We had worked out that we could still just about manage it, either by driving back up to Leeds straight after the game, or by getting a train, but any delay anywhere was going to potentially mean Mark missed his performance! I e-mailed the Football League to ask them why it had taken them all season to decide to make this change, and I just got a standard e-mail back repeating the website announcement, and a sentence to the effect that they had given 11 weeks notice of the change, so what was I complaining about? Madness!

We put all thoughts about the last day of the season to the back of our minds for the time being, and started to concentrate on today's game. After all, if we couldn't get a result today, it would start to look as if the final day might hold no relevance for us anyway.

The first part of the journey was made in pouring rain, but as we rounded the corner taking us past the Celtic Manor Golf Resort, scene of last years European Ryder Cup victory, onto the M4, the weather suddenly brightened up, and the rest of the trip to Swansea was made in brilliant sunshine. In fact, the South Wales coast looked rather beautiful for the most part, that is until we approached the Port Talbot Steelworks. Then the sky was filled with clouds once again, not of the rain type, but of belching smoke from the various chimneys! At that point we could see Swansea across the other side of the bay.

As always before an away game, I had researched the various stadium guides on the Internet, and for this one it was generally recommended that away fans use the Swansea Vale Park and Ride facility, just off the A4067, which we did. Considering the Stadium is so new, its park and ride facility was obviously an afterthought. It was a fenced off area with a rough hardcore surface, and it was full of huge pot holes filled with rainwater, that were big enough to swallow a small family car. There were also several travellers caravans scattered around the perimeter that looked as if they were fairly permanently sited. We parked up, not really expecting the car to be in one piece when we got back to it later, and then queued with the rest of the fans, mainly Leeds, to get aboard a rusty old double-decker bus. It looked as if it would do well to reach the main road, never mind the stadium that was several miles away. For the privilege of riding on this public transport relic, we were charged £5.

The Liberty Stadium at least, did look impressive when we arrived. It is shared by the footballing Swans, and the rugby union Ospreys, and as it was only opened in 2005, it still looks very clean and tidy. They have a strange policy of not opening up the ground until an hour before kick-off, so we wandered around outside for a while. We popped into the Harvester pub on the adjoining retail park for a quick pee, and then we crossed over the road to Rossi's Fish and Chip shop for a couple of burgers. It was now approaching lunchtime, with this being a 12:45pm kick off, in front of the Sky TV cameras. Before going into the ground, we went looking for the bronze statue of Ivor Allchurch that we located at the South West corner of the ground, back near where we found the Harvester pub.

Ivor Allchurch was a Swans legend who played for Swansea Town (as they used to be known) in two spells, from 1947 to 1958, and then again between 1965 and 1968. All in all, he played 445 times for the Swans, and scored 164 goals. He also made 68 appearances for the Welsh national side. Known as the "Golden Boy of Swansea" (which is the inscription on the plaque beneath the statue), his interest to me, is that in the 1968/69 season he turned out for my "other" team, Worcester City. I was born in Worcester, and lived in the area until I was 18. For many years, I was a junior season ticket holder with the Blue Dragons of Worcester, including that season 1968/69. That was some side, and it was one of the most successful periods in the history of Worcester City. They had won the Southern League 1st Division title the previous season. The late 60's and early 70's often saw former international stars finishing their careers in non-league football, as they tried to earn a few extra bob to supplement their then meagre football pensions, something you hardly ever see these days, because the top players now, all end their careers as multi millionaires, who wouldn't be seen dead on a non-league pitch. When Allchurch left Worcester at the end of the '68/'69 season, he was replaced for the next couple of seasons by Gerry Hitchens, the ex Aston Villa and England centre forward, who was just back in England following a very successful spell in Italy, with Inter Milan, Turin, Atalanta, and Cagliari. Another player I was honoured to watch several times, while he was playing for Hereford United, then also a non league outfit in the old Southern League, was big John Charles, who is also of course, a Leeds United legend. Charles was at Hereford as a player, and then player manager, from 1966 to 1971, and I saw him play several times at St Georges Lane, the home of Worcester City. He was usually played as a centre back in those days, and not a centre forward. I remember him as a huge man with thighs like tree trunks, and a forehead like a house brick. He walked and ran always slightly leaning forward, with his huge backside sticking out! He was still a magnificent header of a football, even at the tail end of his playing career. I saw him plant many unstoppable headers into the back of the Worcester net during those local derby games that were usually played back to back over the Easter Weekend. Incidentally, I have always thought that the Hereford United club motto would be very well suited to our own Leeds United: "Our greatest glory lies not in never having fallen, but in rising when we fall". It would certainly have been appropriate over the last few seasons.

We had a couple of pints of Carlsberg each, in the concourse under the stand, while we watched the pre-amble for the game on the TV down there. Ex Leeds favourite, and now Welsh national team manager, Gary Speed, was Sky's pre-match expert, looking as dapper as always in a dark suit and tie.
We knew that today's game would be very competitive, it is something that's bred into the South Wales folk. Think Cardiff born Craig Bellamy for example! I remember reading, years ago, about 2 lady bingo players at the Castle Bingo Hall in Bridgend, just down the M4 from Swansea, having a punch up, that ended with one of the women going to hospital to have a broken nose fixed! That was over a so-called lucky chair in the Bingo Hall that both women coveted. With that sort of spirit, we just knew we were in for a tough game down here. What we didn't know or expect though, was quite how

easily Leeds would capitulate today. Mark and I failed to factor in another disappointing refereeing performance, as well.

As we half guessed, with Bradley Johnson out suspended, this was an opportunity for Simon Grayson to try 4 – 4 – 2 again, and he did just that, putting in Somma for a start, alongside Luciano Becchio. We would surely need that extra firepower against a side that had only conceded 6 league goals at home all season. As I have reflected before, we conceded six in just one game at home! Other than that, it was the side Simon had stuck with in recent games.

Swansea came out all guns firing, looking every bit the best team we had seen this season, and even the fantastic support being given by the travelling hoards, didn't seem to get our lads started today. The attendance of 19,309 was a new record for the Liberty Stadium, and included 3,000 of us noisy Leeds fans. I made a mental note that helicopter girl (from the Portsmouth away game), and her Dad, were sat right in front of us again, so I made sure I was out of scarf swinging distance during the "Champions of Europe" chant.

We managed to hold out for all of 13 minutes, before the Swans took a deserved lead, having already gone close on a couple of occasions, including a Stephen Dobbie shot that crashed against a post, with Schmeichel well beaten. Neil Taylor burst forward from his left back position, well into the Leeds half, before passing the ball to the left corner of the box to Scott Sinclair. Sinclair continued on into the area, twisting and turning, but seemed to have lost the ball in among three Leeds defenders. The ball though, found its way to Luke Moore, who, spotting Sinclair dodging round the blue shirted Leeds men, back heeled the ball neatly onto Sinclair's right foot, and he made no mistake with a lovely, curling, side foot finish. The commentator on the BBC highlights programme, later that night, would say it was "a goal worthy of the Premiership", and at the moment that ball went in the Leeds net, it really did seem much more likely that Swansea would be going up rather than Leeds, come the end of the season. For the rest of the first half, Swansea continued to pass the ball around crisply, with pace and precision, but even so, Leeds were not without their own chances, and in the last ten minutes of the half, Leeds were on top. Our cause was not being helped much by referee Phil Dowd (why do Premiership refs get all the televised Championship games?), who gave a number of 50-50 decisions the way of the home team. He had already booked Eric Lichaj and Alex Bruce, the latter for a foul when the Leeds man had definitely got something on the ball. Simon Grayson was incensed with the Bruce booking, and Dowd had to go over to speak with him to try to quiet him down. Bad as this all was, it was just about to get a whole lot worse. Rob Snodgrass cut back onto his left foot from the inside right channel, and just as he has done many times already this season, he fired a curling shot that had goal written on every panel of the ball. This time though, it was deflected round the near post, by the left arm and hand of the diving Swansea skipper, Alan Tate. On the recording of the Sky TV commentary, that I watched later, the commentator, Bill Leslie, said, "Ninety nine times out of a hundred you'd have to feel that was a penalty". It was as clear a penalty as you will ever see, but Phil Dowd shook his head defiantly, and pointed for a corner. The Leeds players had given Dowd a hard time over the several decisions already given against them, and it was difficult to escape the thought that this was pay back time. Whatever, it was a shocking decision, and one that could have changed the game. Next to me, Mark was going on about our poor luck again, while Kilkenny continued to debate the point with the linesman, as he prepared to take the ensuing corner. That only served to get Kilkenny a yellow card, from the clearly agitated Phil Dowd, who now had the names of three Leeds players in his pocket. Leeds still pressed whenever they got any ball, and it was then Davide Somma's turn for a frustration attack, as he saw his header loop over the Swans keeper, but strike the crossbar, and not the back of the net. The half time whistle went just as Leeds were putting together this little spell of pressure, but I think the fans, the players, and the officials, alike, all needed the break from a rip roaring first half full of incident.

Mark and I joined the throngs making for the concourse, and discovered that the live Sky coverage had been going out throughout the game on the screen down there, and some Leeds fans had nipped down to check out the penalty claim. They were now passing the word round that there was no doubt...only Dowd.

In the bogs, one Leeds fan was urging the rest of us not to be so miserable. "We are not going to get relegated this season, so what is the problem?" he kept saying, to anyone prepared to listen. It was the same cheerful chap who had been humming a little ditty as he walked down the steps behind one very surly copper. The copper thought the fan was poking fun at him, which I think he probably was! We all stopped, waiting to see what the copper was going to do as he turned to face the jolly jester of a Leeds fan. Fortunately for all concerned, the bobby just shook his head, turned, and went on his way.

We all settled down again for the second half, with at least some optimism that we had to play better than we did in the first half, and after all, we were only one goal down...

Sadly, what little optimism we still held onto was torn away from us, as one became two goals down, after just 10 minutes of the second half. Whereas Phil Dowd steadfastly refused to consider the penalty claim by Leeds earlier in the game, he now had absolutely no hesitation at all in awarding one to the Swans, as Nathan Dyer was brought down right on the edge of the penalty area by the hard working Max Gradel. It was probably a foul, but it was 50-50 whether it should have been called in the box or outside it. Dowd was adamant it was in. Sinclair put the spot kick away, and it looked a long way back for Leeds from here. Somma had a glorious opportunity to reduce the arrears, when Howson chipped a ball through the middle to beat the offside trap, but Somma's usually deadly finishing ability wasn't there today, and with the whole goal to aim at, he managed to pick out the keepers left hand, and it tipped the ball over the bar. Sanchez Watt came on for Becchio on 61 minutes, but Leeds looked well beaten by that stage, and then the rout was complete on 72 minutes, when another very slick passing move by the home team, ended with Luke Moore running through, and steering the ball past Kasper. Immediately Grayson sent on Billy Paynter for Rob Snodgrass, and Ben Parker for George McCartney, who had been tormented by the impressive Nathan Dyer all afternoon. The Leeds fans remained magnificent until the end, with a constant rendition of "We all love Leeds" sung with pride and passion for the last 10 minutes of the game. It was clearly appreciated by the players, who all applauded the fans at the end, as did Simon Grayson, who made a special point of coming over to thank us, as if to acknowledge that he knew the team had let us down this afternoon. As Grayson applauded us, with his hands held aloft above his head, I have to confess a little lump came into my throat. It was a nice gesture by the boss. The fans broke into "There's only one Simon Grayson", and he looked suitably humbled.

We were herded onto buses in the fenced off area behind the North Stand, ironic really, considering this was the "Liberty Stadium", and then we sat there for ages, while the police organised the convoy of coaches behind a "Follow Me" police car. Mark and I were back on the same red double-decker that we had travelled on before the game. We eventually set off away from the ground, second in line in the convoy of what seemed like a couple of dozen coaches, and eventually our double-decker peeled off to the Park and Ride, while the official Leeds coaches continued on their way back to the M4. We caught the convoy up again, once we got going in the car, and as we overtook them, Mark reported that the Leeds fans seemed to be asleep. Hardly surprising really, since they had all been on the go since the early hours and still had several hours more to go, before seeing their Yorkshire homes again.

Mark and I were down, no doubt about that, and as the other games got underway, and we listened to the radio reports of goals going in all around the country, it soon became clear that this was not going to be a good day for us at all. By 5 O'clock we were the only top 6 team to lose today, and only Forest had dropped points, in a 0 – 0 draw at Millwall. Strangely though, we both enjoyed the day out, and those few minutes at the end, with Simon Grayson acknowledging our support, had been quite special. I had really felt in that moment, that I was part of a special group of people, the fans and the club together as one unit. In his programme notes for the Doncaster Rovers game next Saturday, Grayson would write, "Your support was fantastic and you deserved better. Anyone listening to the noise you made during the final minutes, when the game was all-but over, would have thought we were the team who were 3 – 0 up and in second place...to travel all that way and sing like that, even when the team are losing, was nothing short of phenomenal." It was a magic moment for us all Simon.

We sped up the M5 and M6, trying to get to a pub at home in time to see the closing stages of the England versus France, Six Nations match, and we weren't planning on stopping. As we approached Frankley services though, I decided my bladder wouldn't hold on for another half hour. It was the Lucozades we had when we got back to the car I guess, so we pulled in for a quick pit stop. As we were coming out of the Gents, who should be hurrying in but Gary Speed! He was gone before I had chance to acknowledge him, but I nudged Mark, and he concurred it was the very same Gary Speed, in the very same dapper suit and tie, we had seen on the TV earlier in the day. He was presumably on his way home, after performing his duties for Sky earlier in the day down at Swansea. Once back in the car, in conversation with Mark, I shared the thought that it was now going to be a long week ahead, as we waited for the Doncaster game at Elland Road next Saturday, and then after that we were both off to Deepdale, for the Preston away game the following Tuesday.

As the word "Tuesday" came out of my mouth, I looked at Mark and he looked back at me, and simultaneously we both shook our heads muttering "Bollocks, not another f****** Tuesday". Before that though, Donny Rovers would be visiting Elland Road.

Doing it the hard way...again

There are just twelve games to go, and everything is still to play for then. How many times have I said something similar in recent weeks? Leeds are sitting in 6th place on 54 points, and 8 points cover the teams from 2nd to 6th. Top of the pile are still QPR on 67 points, and it is difficult to see anyone catching them now, barring a major collapse in their form or an infringement resulting in a points deduction. All of the top 6 sides have winnable games today, including Leeds, with Doncaster Rovers being the visitors to Elland Road. On paper (yeah, yeah, OK I know that one), we should have too much firepower for them, and perhaps today will be a straightforward 3 points sans rollercoaster ride...did I really just say that?

I journeyed up the motorways again, reasonably relaxed, and I pondered what score I was going to be putting my one-pound bet on today. I was thinking lots of goals, but I would have a look at the odds first and choose a 100/1 shot. The trip was uneventful, with no dickhead BMW drivers this week. I was surprised to pass a bright yellow, 52-seat coach, with a "Shropshire Whites" banner in the window, they obviously had a big turnout for this one, and I assumed the little white minibus was too small. I also passed the "Barrow Whites" coach on the M62. That perplexed me too, as it seemed a strange route to take from Barrow in Furness, to Leeds. Other than that, it was the usual fun and frolics from Fighting Talk, with Colin Murray and the gang, on Radio Five Live, and I noted that my high speed wheel wobble had disappeared, now that I had finally got round to putting 4 brand new Michelins on the Peugeot. The tyre fitter had guessed that the wheel wobble was down to a balance weight having come off one of the wheels, and that with new tyres, correctly balanced, the wobble should disappear. It was somehow comforting that the tyre fitter knew what he was talking about, as I glanced at the speedo and noticed the needle was nudging 95mph.

I pulled onto the car park and parked up, right next to a big black people carrier, out of which were climbing some of the Surrey Whites lads I had spoken to at a couple of games last year. The driver was the Cockney bloke we spoke to at Burnley, and I had spotted one of his passengers last Saturday at Swansea, he had been talking to the police standing next to the Leeds team coach. We were sat on the double-decker at the time, waiting to leave the ground after the game. As I was exchanging greetings with them, Mark and Suzi appeared at the other side of the car.

The Pavilion is starting to become a sort of match day home from home, with lots of people we now recognise on nodding terms. Martin and his lads from Mansfield were there again, they had mentioned at the Norwich game, that they were doing all of the remaining home games, just as we were. We sat at a table with a bloke in a wheelchair, who I had seen many times before.

Suzi, Mark, and I, dined on the usual meat and potato pie, mushy peas, and gravy, and Mark and I washed ours down with a couple of pints of Beck's. We are both creatures of habit! The first Pavilion guest today was Brian Deane, who got a rousing welcome of "Deano, Deano" from the Pavilion fans, as he climbed onto the stage with Peter Lorimer. Brian Deane is a bit of a cult hero with the fans, he joined Leeds for his first spell with the club in June 1993, as a then record Leeds signing, for £2.9 million from Sheffield United. When at Bramall Lane, his main claim to fame was that he was the scorer of the first ever Premiership goal, in 1992, when the Blades beat the Old Trafford lot 2 – 1, on the first day of the first Premiership season. He played 138 games and scored 32 goals in his first spell with Leeds, and then left to go back to Bramall Lane in 1997. In his second short spell with Leeds, in 2004, he played in 31 games and scored just 6 goals, albeit 4 of them came in one match, when Leeds thrashed QPR 6 –1. I also remember him being part of the Sheffield United side we beat, in that famous topsy-turvy game at Bramall Lane in April 1992, the day we won the First Division title when the Old Trafford Yanks lost at Liverpool later in the day. Mark went up and got Brian Deane's autograph on today's match-day programme, and Deano, himself well over six feet tall, asked Mark how tall he was, as my lad towered over the ex Leeds man. Wheelchair Man then told us that Paul Reaney was at the front by the stage as well, and that was my cue to get another signature on that team photo I had been carrying around with me. Paul Reaney was in great form as usual, and he had a good look at the photo before signing across his picture. He then showed it to a nearby table, and he pointed at Don Howe on the picture; "He was a hard bugger" says Reaney "but he was a good bloke, and we had a good manager at the time" he added, pointing to the smiling figure of Jimmy Armfield, a bit further along the back row in the photograph. I now had four signatures on this picture, Reaney, Allan Clarke, Terry Yorath and Peter Lorimer.

The second guest player was Adam Clayton, the young ex Manchester City midfielder, who had made just 4 substitute appearances this season for Leeds, having been out on loan with Peterborough United for a spell. Suzi volunteered to get his autograph as she reckoned he was "well fit". Mark and I responded that he was a bit short! Clayton's signature is another one of those totally indecipherable scribbles that any 3 year old could replicate with a wax crayon. He did include his squad number, 15, for future reference.

We were watching West Bromwich Albion beat Birmingham City 3 – 1, on the big screens, in a Premiership relegation battle, while we munched our way through our pies and peas. Birmingham looked to be suffering a hangover from their shock Carling Cup Final victory over Arsenal, last Sunday. That was just one of a few major football stories this week. The others included a brawl between the coaching staff of Celtic and Rangers, during the latest Old Firm game; Wayne Rooney escaping punishment for whacking a Wigan player with his elbow, because our mate Mr. Clattenburg saw nothing malicious in it; and most bizarrely of all, an incident at the Chelsea training ground, where Ashley Cole allegedly shot a YTS trainee with an air rifle "accidentally". The joke there was "Once a Gunner, always a Gunner!" The funny old game had never been so strange. The one very sad piece of football news from last weekend was the death of another famous "Deano", Dean Richards; the popular centre half, who finally lost his long battle with illness. He had been a player with both Wolves and Spurs among other clubs, and by chance, they would meet tomorrow, in a televised Premier League game. I watched the match on Sunday, and the tribute to Deano before the game was very moving, with a minute's applause, in the presence of his wife and his two young boys. Dean Richards was just 36 years old. The fans of both clubs joined together in one final, poignant chant of "Deano, Deano" during the tribute.

I eventually opted for 6 – 0 Leeds, on my betting slip today. Mark pointed out that 5 – 2 was also 100/1, but I decided to stick with 6 – 0. Mark already had an accumulator placed for today's games; he had Arsenal to beat Sunderland, and Everton to win at Newcastle, as well as several Scottish League games.

The PA announcer then tried to broadcast today's team. It was a different voice to normal, and when the announcer made a complete cods of it, we assumed it was just someone filling in! He had obviously been given a complete squad list with the details, and against each name were the words "Playing" or "On the Bench".... So, PA man works his way down the list from the top, literally broadcasting what was written on his sheet. "Number One, Kasper Schmeichel playing; number 4, Alex Bruce, on the bench; number 6 Richard Naylor, on the bench" and so on. Depending where you put the pauses you got a completely different list of who was "playing" and who was "on the bench"! It sounded like some new peculiar form of football bingo! Of course there was uproar all around the Pavilion, as fans were trying to note

down who was actually playing, so that they could plan their bets! The jeers got louder and louder, as the monotone monologue continued until a chant of "You don't know what you're doing" broke out around the room. The poor bloke on the PA seemed oblivious to the uproar he was causing, as he ploughed on regardless, right through to "Number 44, Ross McCormack, on the bench". Everyone was then checking with the people who had tried to write down the teams, but there were so many crossings out on most fans lists that it was chaos. We had a debate on our table as to whether it was Alex Bruce or Leigh Bromby in the middle with Andy O'Brien. Eventually the plonker on the PA returns, to say it had been requested that he repeat the team news, and this time he managed to do it in the time honoured manner, first listing the team that was actually playing, and then separately the substitutes. It was indeed big Leigh Bromby, of the Rory Delap long throw, who was in, and Bruce who was on the bench. We could only think it was due to the hand injury Bruce had picked up at the Liberty Stadium last week. Bradley Johnson was back in the side, after his one match suspension, and therefore Davide Somma also dropped back to the bench.
We were still chuckling to ourselves over the PA announcement, as we made our way over to the stadium. It was one of the funniest things I have heard in a long time.

Doncaster Rovers had been shipping goals for fun a few weeks ago; six at home to Ipswich, and three away at Swansea, in consecutive matches, but their recent results had seen a huge improvement. Their last three games included draws with Watford and Norwich, and a decent 3 – 1 win at Derby in mid-week. Most of the fans near us in the Kop were optimistic we could see them off today. There was a slight concern that we had been allocated another so-called "elite" referee, for a second consecutive game. Lee Probert was in charge today, and we all hoped he would do a better job than Mr Dowd did last week.

As so often in recent home games, Leeds rampaged forward in the early stages, and we started to pepper the Donny goal with shots. Predictably, it was the dynamic duo of Snodgrass and Gradel, who ripped into the visitors from the off. Gradel had a low shot blocked, and Howson blasted the rebound over the top, and then Snodgrass fired his first effort of the day over the bar as well. In the 12th minute though, Leeds scored their 63rd League goal of this prolific season, more than any other team in the Division. Jonny Howson prodded the ball forward to Mad Max in midfield, and he ran through four Donny players, before driving a right foot shot low into the far corner, from all of 30 yards out. Cue celebrations all around. Max is now the most popular player on the team, due largely to his work ethic, and of course his now frequent goals. His own chant of "He's here, he's there, he's every f****** where" is the most appropriate of all the Leeds salutes, as he really does get all over the pitch. There is one bloke that stands just behind us on the Kop most games, who sings the alternative version of, "He's here, he's there, he's no good in the air, Max Gradel!", but obviously that bloke wasn't at the Walkers Stadium over Christmas, to see Max head our opening goal that day.

Leeds continued to press forward, threatening to overwhelm the shell-shocked visitors, and Kilkenny, Becchio, and Snodgrass, all went close with shots raining in from all angles. The fans were constantly up on their toes thinking we had scored again, and then they were back down on their heels, with their heads in their hands, as chance after chance went begging. It started to get to the point, where a few fans were making "We might rue these missed chances" noises, all around us, and when the board went up signifying that there would be 2 minutes of injury time, I got that Norwich feeling again. Suddenly, having dominated the first half from the first whistle, the Leeds defence started to look jittery. Schmeichel inexplicably starts dawdling with the ball; presumably time wasting, and then looking for a defender to throw the ball to, instead of lumping it up the pitch away from danger. He spots

McCartney on the left touch line, and throws the ball to him, but McCartney too is suddenly struck down with "don't know what the f*** to do with it" syndrome, and he feebly lets the ball slip under his boot, and go out for a throw. From the next passage of play, Doncaster's John Oster, eventually clips a diagonal ball deep into the Leeds area, and little Billy Sharp lives up to his surname and darts between Lichaj and O'Brien to get a foot to the ball, steering it towards goal. Schmeichel does well to parry the first effort, but the ball just bounces up in front of the post and Sharp is able to squeeze it in, from the tightest of angles. 45 minutes of complete domination, 2 minutes of complete stupidity. The half time whistle blows, and as the players troop off, many in the crowd boo them, it was harsh, and one particularly vocal fan, (I think it was the alternative Max Gradel chant man) behind us, made it clear that booing the team off after they had just played one of the best halves of the season, was not acceptable, and those that did it were "twats", as he so succinctly put it. Mark and I agreed, but we were both beside ourselves with disappointment, once again we were being forced to experience that bloody rollercoaster ride, when just a couple of minutes ago we were celebrating a fine performance. Just as with that Norwich game two weeks ago, there was a horrible little nagging voice in our heads saying, "Going to balls it up again, going to balls it up again!" Leeds were once again doing it the hard way, as only they know how.

The players were given a great reception as they returned after the break, suggesting that those who booed them off had seen the error of their ways. Leeds were out first, looking fired up, and presumably with Simon's half time talk, still ringing in their ears. Straight from the restart, Snodgrass thought he had got Leeds in front again, as he stroked the ball towards goal, but it just failed to find the far corner of the net. Then, all our nightmares came at once, a dark shadow enveloped the ground, and football's Grim Reaper suddenly appeared out of nowhere, ready to slice the head from our play off chances, as Doncaster took the lead. Dean Shiels nodded the ball over the statue like Leeds defence, and Franck Moussa was there to hit a left foot bobbler into the corner to give Doncaster an unlikely, and undeserved, lead. For a split second or two, the Leeds players had that haunted Barnsley/Preston look about them, but the Leeds fans were now so vocal and so angry, that they soon snapped out of it, and began once again to battle for the ball, as if winning it back was their only possible salvation, which many of us believed it was. Jonny Howson had had a good game so far, after having been unusually quiet in several of his recent outings. Now the captain looked totally focussed, even possessed, as he fought tooth and nail for the ball with Brian Stock, just inside the Doncaster half. He eventually wrestled the ball away from Stock, and then only had one thing in mind, as he ran on towards goal with 6 Donny players trailing in his wake. He got to about 25 yards out before belting the ball low into the left corner. The lead up to the goal was reminiscent of his effort at Burnley earlier in the season in similar circumstances. It was barely a minute since we had gone behind, and now we were back level, and some sort of sanity had returned to Elland Road. The rest of the game was a blur of scoring chances, (we would have 31 shots during this game) of which thankfully Leeds took three. First, on 75 minutes, Leigh Bromby chested down a Snodgrass cross in the box, and Becchio met it perfectly to half volley it into the roof of the net from 10 yards. Billy Paynter came on for Becchio after 80 minutes, and I for one felt this was Simon Grayson trying desperately to get Paynter to break his duck. The Kop felt the same as immediately chants of "Come on Billy" and "There's only one Billy Paynter" rang out around the ground. Within minutes he had his chance. Snodgrass prodded the ball across the face of goal and Paynter was there, just a couple of yards out. His tentative side foot shot though was easily smothered away by the keeper, but it fell to the feet of Max Gradel, who put it away with ease with his left foot. Billy Paynter had a rueful grin on his face, as he jogged across to join Gradel's celebration in the corner, in front of the Kop. 4 –

2 and at last we could relax, assuming Doncaster didn't get another one back, which they didn't. Leeds continued to look for a fifth and the Leeds fans were begging, no pleading, for Billy Paynter to get one. He knew it too as he was really putting himself about. In the 90th minute, he chased back almost to the half way line, out on the Leeds right wing, to win the ball back with a determined, barely legal tackle, which brought huge applause from the now crazed Elland Road crowd. The ball was picked up by Snoddy, who played it through to Howson, who was now in the clear again on his own. He bided his time, getting the bouncing ball under control, before thrashing it high into the left corner of the net for 5 – 2. I did fleetingly hear Marks voice echoing in my head saying "5 – 2 is also 100/1 today you know" but I soon dismissed it, and continued to join in the chanting of "Come on Billy" as we all tried to will Billy Paynter a first goal. We all know that if he can just get that first one, there will be an avalanche of goals to follow. One bloke near us, with a broad Yorkshire accent, was heard to joke "Ee, ah can just see it nah, 5th minute of injury tahm in t'play off fahnal, Billy Paynter scores first goal for Leeds tah take us in tah Premiership". Stranger things have happened, and many of them to Leeds already this season! It was an emotional end to the game, as Max Gradel made his way over towards us on the Kop, applauding us, as we applauded him, and we once again broke into a chant of "He's here, he's there" and he looked to be genuinely appreciative. Simon Grayson again came over to us as well, and, after giving Max a big fatherly hug, he too applauded us, just as he had done at Swansea, in different circumstances, last weekend. Billy Paynter acknowledged our efforts as well; I look forward to his first goal, and think it isn't far away. In the end, this was a comfortable win, but yet again the team put us through the wringer, and squeezed us dry, in a match we could and should have won nine or ten zip. On the Leeds website on Monday, Simon Grayson commented "Do we make it difficult? I'll need

a health check at the end of the season". Queue forms behind me at BUPA Simon!

We hung around waiting for the scores from the other games to go up on the screen, and in complete contrast to last week it was all good news. Forest had somehow managed to lose at home to Hull City; Swansea had lost 1 – 0 at lowly Scunthorpe; Norwich had contrived to draw at home to Preston; and QPR had beaten Leicester City, who were the closest challengers below us in the table. Later in the evening, Cardiff City increased our joy by losing at home to Ipswich, 2 – 0. Much of the damage done at Swansea last week, had been miraculously repaired. Football's Grim Reaper was trudging off empty handed, and heading off to the likes of Preston and Scunthorpe, and we would sleep soundly tonight knowing that now, just 5 points covered the teams from 2nd to 6th. It really was going to be a nail-biting finale; surely it couldn't be as incredible as last season...could it?

The Premiership results came up on the big screen down at the South Stand end, and Mark shook his head as he spotted that the Arsenal had screwed his accumulator yet again, by drawing 0 – 0 at home to Sunderland.

I was in a little world of my own on the drive home. I was so engrossed in listening to 606 on Five Live, during which Robbie Savage took a call from Ryan Giggs, that I completely missed my junction off the M62. I decided to try to rectify my mistake by coming off at the next exit, but somehow that took me past the massive "Chill Factore" indoor ski slope, and then I found myself in a one-way lane taking me right into the Trafford Centre car park! I was flying my Leeds scarves from the car windows, and I got some very strange looks here on the outskirts of Manchester, as I drove straight through the car park and back out the other side! I eventually worked my way back onto the M6, and continued on my way home. I still had one more daydream though. I dared to wonder what it would be like on Tuesday night, if Leeds could rid themselves of that monkey on their back, of failing to win a mid week league game this season. A victory at Deepdale, courtesy of a Billy Paynter goal, in front of 5,000 delirious Leeds fans would be something special. I snapped out of my daydream as a dickhead in a black BMW pulled out in front of me, causing me to brake sharply.

Come on Billy, Come on Billy

It was another full Championship programme on Tuesday, March 8th, and for Leeds it was a trip across the Pennines to Preston North End. We had some unfinished business with the Lillywhites of Deepdale, following that disastrous night at Elland Road last September, when we contrived to surrender a 4 – 1 lead, to lose 4 – 6, in probably the most incredible game I have ever witnessed. It had been the first time since 1955 that Preston had scored 6 goals away from home, and it was the first time ever that Leeds had conceded 6 on their own patch.

No game is easy in this Division, as recent results had emphasised, and Preston, despite still being bottom of the pile, had ground out some decent results in recent weeks, including draws with Forest, leaders QPR, Watford and Norwich. In fact they had only suffered one defeat in the last five games, and that was to their local rivals, the much-improved Burnley. True, Preston were still looking for their first victory under manager Phil Brown, who had now been in charge for 12 games. This was therefore, yet another game against a team that had changed managers since the first meeting, Darren Ferguson's services having been dispensed with at the end of December.

The Leeds news since Saturday's nerve jangler against Doncaster was of the loan signing of Barry Bannan from Aston Villa, for a minimum period of one month. Villa had included a 28 day reclaim clause, in case they needed him back for their own relegation fight. When Mark texted me to give me this news, I have to confess, that I responded to the effect that I had never heard of the bloke. The Leeds website filled in some of the details for me. He had played 19 times for Villa this season, and was a full Scottish international with a couple of caps, having played alongside Snoddy in the recent international against Northern Ireland. Had he been described as a strong tackling defender, I would have thought "good move", but quite why Simon Grayson needed more cover in midfield, I wasn't sure. The description of his playing style on the Internet, suggested he was left footed, skilful and creative, so maybe this was just cover for Snodds. Anyway, the word was, he would go straight into the squad for the Deepdale clash.

I decided to take another afternoon off work to give myself plenty of time to travel north, and I thought the omens looked really good when a black cat strolled across in front of the car as I drove home to get changed. The omens for the cat were not too bad either, as I managed to miss it. I am not really a superstitious person, but I will always salute a magpie, and will not rest until I have spotted a second one, on the "one for sorrow, two for joy" basis. Any luck coming our way was going to be gratefully received today, as it was another Tuesday, and we would be trying for the 14th time this season to win a game on a day of the week that wasn't spelled S-A-T-U-R-D-A-Y. Thirteen consecutive non-Saturday games had come, and gone, without Leeds tasting victory. Thirteen ...that might just be another omen.

Mark was getting the train from Leeds, and was going to meet me in Preston around 6pm, so I set off up the M6 once more, leaving plenty of time to find a parking spot at the other end, and to be ready when Mark made contact.

As I left the M6 at junction 31, I turned left heading for the centre of Preston along the A59, and I then passed the Tickled Trout Hotel. Back in 1979, the wife, (then girlfriend) and I, spent a wonderful "dirty weekend" at the Tickled Trout, as it was handily placed about halfway between Edinburgh, where the girlfriend was living with her parents, and Derby, where I was based at the time. We even booked in under the false names of Mr and Mrs Smith, (honestly, we did!) and I remember we both felt very guilty, as we signed the register in our assumed names, with rather shaky and unconvincing signatures. We had a lovely room looking out over the river Ribble, and I remember there were dozens of swallows' nests under the eaves, all along the riverside, with a constant stream of birds coming and going the whole time we were there.

This evening I was on a different mission, but still hoping it was a high scoring night! I kept heading on into Preston looking for the Deepdale ground, and somewhere safe to park. I did a few circuits around the stadium, and eventually parked up on Ribbleton Lane, from where I could see the impressive looking white steel structure of the PNE Stadium.

It was only about 5:30pm, but it wasn't long before my mobile buzzed into life, and it was Mark letting me know he had arrived at the station. Unfortunately though, the local Constabulary were taking no chances tonight, and Mark reported that he had been rounded up with his fellow fans as they departed the train. He said they were ordered to climb aboard a double-decker bus, which had been thoughtfully laid on, to take them to a local pub! Mark was able to tell me that the pub was called the Lava, and it was in Church Street, somewhere in Preston, but he was of course unable to direct me to exactly where it was. I could only suggest we meet at the ground, where according to the stadium guides on the Web, we would be able to get a pint. It took me twenty minutes to walk to the ground, and I eventually spotted Mark walking down Tom Finney Way, towards the main entrance opposite Moor Park. He then filled me in with the rest of the story about his little bus ride to the Lava.

He and about twenty other lads were met at Preston station by dozens of Lancashire Police, who were lined up along the platform. All the fans were frisked, and then told to board the bus. Mark was very complementary about the friendly attitude of the police, but did consider it a bit over the top to have so many escorting them, and he reported that the pub only had about 10 people in it, when they arrived to boost beer sales. He managed to persuade a sceptical copper that he needed to meet his Dad at the ground, and eventually he was allowed to leave, being directed up Church Street, and then along Tom Finney Way. By this time it was about 6:15pm, but as we walked round to the Bill Shankly Stand, it was obvious from the crowds of Leeds fans milling around, that the ground was not yet open. Even the burger van on that corner was still not open, although there were some signs of life, suggesting it would be soon. A convoy of about eight Fourways coaches bringing the lads from Leeds arrived, as we stood pondering our next move, and soon the forecourt was bustling with thousands of fans. Eventually, the turnstile doors were opened. We sampled the burgers at the van outside, but we weren't impressed. They were the first poor burgers we have had this season, and the chips could have done with another couple of minutes in the fryer, too. Further disappointment then awaited us inside the ground, when we discovered that, contrary to expectation, the food and drink counters in the ground were not selling alcohol tonight. We asked one of the serving staff why, and she rather sheepishly suggested that it was because the last time Leeds were here, there was "trouble". That meant we had to make do with a couple of bottles of Coke, and I pushed the boat out and bought a Yorkie bar as well. We bumped into Lucas, one of the lads who sits near us on the Kop back at Elland Road, and had a chat with him, and then we made our way up to our seats. We had quite a climb, as we were on row 37, which was three rows from the top. We had the goal to our left, as we looked down onto the pitch. You wouldn't want to be a vertigo sufferer up here. We were so high up, that the pitch looked square, but it was a cracking view. The stadium is impressive, both inside and out, although you have to wonder about the ambition of a club that rebuilds a stadium with a capacity of just 23,000. Having said that, as the game kicked off there were plenty of spare seats on the other three sides, so maybe they do know the extent of their support. The attendance was eventually reported as just 15,269, which I thought was poor. If they had allowed us more tickets, I am sure we would have filled their ground for them. Our end was packed, other than the top 2 rows behind us, and if they ever put people in those, they are probably obliged to supply oxygen to combat the inevitable altitude sickness.

The Deepdale ground is one of the oldest in English football, rivalling Burnley's Turf Moor, and Bramall Lane in Sheffield, but it has been completely modernised on all four sides, and does look smart, if small.

Moor Park, which is just over the road from Deepdale, is described on the Preston City Council website as "the worlds oldest and Preston's largest park" and it has a history going back many hundreds of years. Preston Moor was the site of annual horse racing up until 1833, when it was enclosed and named Moor Park. A cricket team called Preston Nelson, or sometimes, Preston North End, rented a wicket in the park in 1867, and when they moved across the road to Deepdale Farm, after a brief flirtation with rugby, they formed the PNE football club. In 1888, PNE were one of the founder members of the English Football League, and Deepdale is said to be the longest continually used football stadium in the world, having been built in 1860.

The only change to the starting eleven tonight, was the inclusion from the start of Billy Paynter, in place of the rested Becchio, who was on the bench. I thought at the time that this was another clever move by Simon Grayson, coming on the back of the Doncaster game, when the Leeds fans really got behind Billy, and were positively willing him to get that first goal. Grayson knew, just as we all did, how important it was to get Billy off the mark, and if he could do it in front of 5,000 fans here tonight, it would do Billy's confidence no end of good. New boy Barry Bannan was on the bench. A scan of the back page of tonight's programme revealed, that Sian Massey, the lady at the centre of the recent Andy Gray sexism comments, was running the line tonight...

The Leeds fans were, as usual, making all the noise in the early stages, but our lads in yellow were doing their best to shut us up, as they forced us to gasp with incredulity, as chance after chance fell to the bottom of the table side that hadn't won a game since the 11th December. The usual calm and efficient Leigh Bromby, was having a nightmare in the middle, seemingly incapable of heading the ball in the direction he was facing. He then got a bang on the head and was bandaged up with a "Kisnorbo", and that seemed to make him even worse. After just three minutes, O'Brien's careless header away, fell to Keith Treacy just outside the box, and he hammered the ball back against the underside of our crossbar, just down in front of the massed ranks of Leeds fans. The air was blue with every conceivable profanity, aimed squarely at the Leeds defence. A bloke behind us was getting on our nerves, as he hurled abuse at each Leeds player in turn, but mainly Billy Paynter, likening him to a carthorse at one point, and suggesting that he wouldn't ever score "as long as his arse points to the ground". I thought Mark was about to turn round and lamp him one, but the bloke must have realised from the look Mark gave him that he ought to "shut the f*** up".

Leeds started to get going eventually, and Max Gradel was the architect of most that we did that was any good, and most of it was going on down the left wing. Rob Snodgrass was having another one of his quiet games, on the other flank. To be fair to Preston, in those early stages there was not a lot to choose between the two sides. Both were capable at any moment of giving away possession cheaply, or letting the ball escape their control, and letting it slide into touch. These were things that were happening on a regular basis all over the pitch, to the disgruntlement of the fans of both teams. Then on 29 minutes, and completely out of the blue, came a strike of rare quality from …err, Neil Kilkenny! A weak Snodgrass shot was blocked in the box by a defender and the ball rebounded back to Killa, about 30 yards out. He took aim, and then just whacked it towards the right hand post. He hit it so hard, that his little frame visibly shook as the ball left his boot. We were stood right behind the line of the ball, and I could see it was starting well outside that right hand stick. If I had of had the time, I think I would have said something like, "sh**, can you believe our luck" thinking the ball was going to clip the outside of the post, but then in a split second, I could see it was still turning in, and it hadn't yet reached the point of contact. It was like time had slowed to a crawl. If I could have thought that quickly, I would now have thought it would hit the post square on and come back ... but it was still turning. It crashed against the inside half of the post, and then it looked as if it would shoot across the face of goal, and maybe even hit the other post. It was still, in my mind, travelling across goal so slowly that it could have been floating, but then there was that tell tale ripple of the netting at the other side of the goal. It was in! It was bloody well in! The Leeds end went mental, more with relief than anything else, because we all knew we had just got a bit of a break, and it was arguably against the run of play. I tried to shout to Mark, that maybe that was another piece of the luck we had been missing, but he was far too busy loping up and down with his arms aloft, and hugging similarly crazed folk all around. Great shot, great goal, 1 – 0.

It was now a lively encounter, and there were plenty of half chances before the break. Billy Paynter was still coming in for stick from Big Mouth just behind us, but Billy was getting ever closer to that first goal, as he put in a rasping shot that just went past the post. As far as we could see, his arse was still pointing to the ground.

Half time came as a bit of a relief, as there was plenty of tension in the Bill Shankly Stand. As we settled down to enjoy a half time display, from a group of extremely fit cheerleaders, we noticed that it was actually pouring with rain, and the girls were doing well to keep going, with a very long routine. It wasn't only the rain that was hampering them either, the Preston mascot, Deepdale Duck, was also making a complete arse of himself, getting in the way and pretending to do the routine with the girls. I was willing him to slip over.

The players returned, and Sian Massey came out with her fellow officials, to take up her position on the right hand touchline at the far end of the ground from us, exactly as she had done in the first half. Mark and I did wonder, if that was to ensure that she was kept well away from the Leeds fans, and any possible ribbing. They needn't have worried on that score, as Sian Massey was about to become a candidate for "Linesman of the year" in the annual Leeds fan survey.

Preston had already tested Schmeichel once since the interval, but then in the 53rd minute, the ball was nodded to Sean St. Ledger just outside the 6-yard area. He swivelled, and hooked a left foot shot into the net at the far end of the ground, in front of the now delirious Preston fans. Mark was first to spot it. On that right hand touchline, far away in the distance, barely visible through the mist of rain drifting across the night sky, and in the shimmering haze of the floodlights, was a vision of loveliness. Sian Massey, blonde ponytail blowing almost horizontally in the breeze, was stood stock still with her yellow, Leeds yellow, flag held aloft. Offside! The word quickly spreads round the Leeds fans, and after an initial "Ha Ha Ha" shout, and 10,000 hands making various lewd gestures to the Preston fans at the other end, a new chant begins. "There's only one Sian Massey, one Sian Maaaaassey, there's only one Sian Maaaaassey!" It goes on for several minutes, and it rivalled any Simon Grayson chant we had managed all season, in its intensity. It was a magical moment, 5,000 fans, one voice, one experience, and one more unforgettable memory from this already memorable season.

Just three minutes later, and we were raised from joy to ecstasy, as we scored a second. Big Mouth, behind us, was finally silenced. Billy Paynter, arse still pointing to the ground, challenged for a ball in the air outside the box. The ball fell goal side, and he ran on into the area on the right, and then he absolutely blasted a shot across the keeper into the far corner of the net. He stood facing the Leeds hoards, just yards away from us, with both arms outstretched, and a look of total relief on his face, before the rest of the team arrived to join him. Sian Massey was now superseded, as we all joined in a chant of "There's only one Billy Paynter!" just as we had done at Elland Road last Saturday, when we had been urging him on in the final minutes of the Donny game. Another wonderful moment, and for some reason it reminded me of James Milner scoring his first goal at Elland Road, when he came on against Chelsea many years ago. It was just sort of "inevitable" that Billy was going to score tonight, just part of a preordained script.

It didn't yet mean though that this game was over, lest anyone forget, this was a Tuesday night, and this was Leeds United. There was still half an hour to go here, and we hadn't yet had our rollercoaster ride for the night. Just six minutes later though we were strapping ourselves in very tightly!

Out of nowhere, Preston's Iain Hume, suddenly had the ball about 35 yards out, and he just thundered a shot that went like a guided missile, catching Schmeichel completely flat footed. It wasn't exactly in the corner of the net, so some of the lads around us were suggesting Kasper should have got to it, but there was plenty of pace in the shot, and it was totally unexpected. 1 – 2 and loads of time left.

From that moment it was a rearguard action, and real backs against the wall stuff, as the home side piled forward, and bombarded the Leeds defence with high balls. As usual, we were not particularly clever with some of our defending, and we seemed to be running out of steam. The Leeds fans were positively beseeching the players to work harder, to put the ball in row Z at every opportunity, and to concentrate, and I am sure they were trying to do all those things, but they were not convincing the 5,000 on the mountain that was the Bill Shankly Stand. Confirmed atheists were suddenly praying to the Almighty, to forgive a lifetime of sin, and just help the lads get through the next few minutes, and promising to forsake all things bad and evil forever, if he would just do this small thing for them. Billy did almost put the game to bed, when he stuck out a leg to divert the ball onto a post, during a mix up in the home defence, but that was a rare excursion up field. Grayson rang the changes, throwing on Becchio for Paynter, partly, one suspects, to provide fresh legs up front to hold the ball up, partly to waste some time away, and partly to get Billy his moment of recognition. That move worked well, as

Becchio was immediately able to provide a different type of outlet for the Leeds defence. Becchio did infuriate us all though, as he brought a high ball down by cushioning it with both arms in front of his chest, giving away a free kick for handball. We had all seen him do this at least once in every match this season. Bannan got a run out in place of Kilkenny, that was a like for like change, literally, as Bannan is only about 5 foot 7 inches tall, similar to Killa. At the death, Grayson sacrificed Snodgrass, and brought on Richard Naylor, to add some further steel to the overworked back line. The bloke in front of us was tapping away at his Blackberry, and was informing us that Cardiff were a goal down at Palace, Leicester were losing at home to Norwich, QPR were losing at Millwall, Swansea were being held at home by Watford, and most surprising of all Sheffield United were beating Forest. He showed us the scores on the little screen, but we both agreed that we were not yet finished here, and we shouldn't get ahead of ourselves! Preston won a couple of corners, and we gave away a stupid free kick on the edge of the box, but then we hoofed the ball down field, and Becchio won a throw in the corner just below us. By the time Preston got the ball back up field, the ref had decided he had seen enough, and he blew the final whistle. The praying atheists gave thanks, and promised to be good for ever more, and unconfined joy spread all around us. We had at last cracked the Tuesday night hoodoo; Billy had smashed in his first goal; the defence had wobbled a few times, but had ultimately held fast under pressure; and many of tonight's results had gone in our favour.

Billy came back onto the pitch to join the celebrations, as the players all wandered down towards us, and we saluted them all heartily. We gave a rousing rendition of "There's only one Simon Grayson" when the manager strolled over to give his thanks to us. As Billy turned to head for the tunnel, at the other end of the ground, he proudly beat his chest three times with his right fist, giving our own special salute.

Tonight, there was absolutely no doubt, just like the Almighty, Billy is Leeds too.

In his "Simon says..." spot, in the programme for the Ipswich game next Saturday, Simon Grayson would write: "The 5,000 at Preston on Tuesday were magnificent and I wish you could have seen yourselves after Billy scored his goal. It really was a sight which summed up this club and the togetherness we have."

As we struggled down the steep steps, leaving the stand, I said to Mark "Bloody fantastic night, how could it be any better?" After a pause Mark replied, "A decent burger, some properly cooked chips, and a couple of pints come to mind!" He had a point.

By the end of tonight, the gap from 2nd to Leeds now in 5th was down to just 3 points. Simon Grayson had said after the Swansea defeat that people could write us off if they wished, but there was still a long way to go. He was right! Next up, Ipswich Town at Elland Road on Saturday. Bring it on!

...when all around are losing theirs

The world news this week was dominated by yet another natural disaster. Coming hard on the heals of the flooding in Brisbane, cyclone Yasi, and the recent earthquake that devastated Christchurch in New Zealand, the latest disaster involved another earthquake, this time in Japan. This 'quake was one of the strongest ever recorded at 9.0 on the Richter scale, but the major death toll came as a result of the ensuing tsunami, that battered the north east coast of Japan, with waves 10 metres high in some places. A nuclear power plant had been damaged, and there was now a real danger of a major radiation leak. Whole towns had been obliterated, and thousands were believed dead, although the authorities were only giving details of confirmed dead of around 1,300 at this stage. Listening to radio reports in the car driving up to Leeds for the Ipswich game, it was hard to get too excited about a mere football match. Once I had parked the car and met Mark though, it was the football that became the centre of our thoughts again, at least for the next few hours.

A new little ritual has been formed between Mark and I; Mark got into the habit of saying "Today's game is massive" before every Leeds game, and so I would now remind him of this before each match, by mimicking him saying "Massive game today Mark", and he would respond with a grin, and say something like, "Yeah, huge, absolutely huge!" There was some truth in the statement of course, as from now until the end of the season every game is indeed "massive". After taking 6 points from the recent encounters with Doncaster and Preston, this was a great opportunity to at least cement our current place in the play off positions. Our fellow teams in the top 6, all had winnable games again this weekend, so we felt that a failure to win today would undo the good work put in this week, and would mean we failed to capitalise on a whole raft of games, where our rivals had failed to beat lesser opposition. It was uncanny how all the top teams were stumbling, very reminiscent of what happened in the League One promotion race last season, when the leading teams seemed intent on self destructing, and letting us through to take one of the automatic promotion spots, despite our own stuttering run.

Ipswich is yet another team who have swapped managers since our previous meeting, having dumped Roy Keane in favour of Paul Jewell, around the turn of the year. The Tractor Boys had been in the middle of a decent run when we went there in October last year, and we suffered a rare 2 – 1 defeat. After that though, the East Anglian outfit struggled, and were sinking rapidly when Jewell came in. Since his arrival, results in general had improved, although they were still inconsistent. They recently went to Doncaster for example, and came away with a 6 – 0 victory, and also famously beat Cardiff 2 – 0 at their place, though they did ride their luck a bit in that one. In mid-week though, they lost 3 - 1 at home to Reading. They do have a few, more than useful players, Jimmy Bullard, recent loan signing Kieran Dyer, and Jason Scotland, to mention but three. It was anybody's guess, which Ipswich Town team would turn up today.

The usual crowd were in the Pavilion. Martin from Mansfield was there, with his three lads, and he came over and had a word. He was particularly disappointed that he had been unable to get tickets for the away game at Bramall Lane, next weekend. We were in the same position, but were hopeful that Leeds would secure more tickets next week, as they indicated they might do, in today's programme. We sat at a table with the couple we had spoken with last Saturday, the guy in the wheelchair and his partner. He was telling us how he was one of the fans having a running debate with Ken Bates, over the use of the disabled parking spaces outside the Pavilion. Bates mentioned in his programme notes earlier in the season, that they were seldom all used, yet this guy told us, that he always had to arrive 4 hours before kick off, or he couldn't be sure of getting a space! He had apparently written to Ken to mention this. He was also very helpful to us last week looking up Deepdale on the web on his mobile, when we were discussing where the ground was in relation to the station, in preparation for Mark's train journey to Preston.

The guest ex player today was John Hendrie, who played for Leeds for just one season, in 1989-90. I didn't have anything with me suitable for Hendrie to sign, but decided instead to ask Peter Lorimer to sign my Chelsea versus Leeds FA Cup final replay programme, which he kindly did. That programme now had Lorimer's and Jack Charlton's autographs, signed across a centre spread photograph of the goals from the original final at Wembley.

Lorimer came back to the Pavilion stage later, this time with Paul Connolly and Lloyd Sam, who both reckoned they were fully fit, and ready to play, but neither was even on the bench today. Both Connolly and Sam had Leeds down to win, with Billy Paynter as first scorer, so when the team was announced, it was no surprise that it was exactly the same side that took the field at Deepdale, with "Come on Billy" being given another chance to improve his goal tally, now that he was off the mark. Becchio was on the bench again just in case, as was Davide Somma. Davide must have wondered, just what he had to do to get a regular place in this side. New boy Barry Bannan was again on the bench. We were all pleased to note, that our usual trusted announcer was back behind the microphone today, and not the nutter we had last Saturday!

Elsewhere in the country this weekend it was FA Cup quarter final time. On the screens in the Pavilion we watched Lee Chung Yong of Bolton Wanderers, (you wouldn't have seen a statement like that 30 years ago would you?) get a late winner at St. Andrews, to beat Birmingham City 3 – 2, and later today Arsenal would have to battle at Old Trafford. The remaining two games were Stoke v West Ham, and Manchester City v Reading, and they were all playing tomorrow.

The game today was a tense affair, with few clear-cut chances. Once again the referee was dreadful, even by comparison with the many other useless pillocks we have seen at Elland Road this season. Mr Deadman (Why would a bloke with a name like that, become a referee?) took poor to a new 4th dimension this afternoon. He got numerous decisions wrong, both for and against us, he wasn't biased, he was just crap. At one point, an Ipswich defender, out near the touchline on the Ipswich left, had no choice under pressure but to hook the ball back to his keeper, who inexplicably picked it up. Deadman just waved play on, while the Leeds fans bayed for a back pass decision. He booked Billy Paynter in the 4th minute, for the first challenge of the game, and he booked Andy O'Brien for a foul, when O'Brien was fully 3 yards from the Ipswich man, who had actually tripped over his own feet! At one point Simon Grayson was so incensed with Deadman's performance, that he got another ticking off from the official, just as he had done at Swansea, when that other plonker, Phil Dowd, had to do the same. For the umpteenth time this season, we broke into a chant of "We always get sh** refs" and "You don't know what you're doing" but Deadman went merrily on his way, making awful decisions throughout the game.

Truth be told though, we were not very good today, but thankfully neither were the Tractor Boys. We were nearly given a shock as early as the first minute, when we allowed Tamas Priskin to get through for a shot on goal that luckily skimmed the far post, with Schmeichel struggling to get there. Max Gradel had several good efforts from distance, but Billy Paynter was guilty of missing a number of good chances, as he continued to look very tentative in front of goal, despite him having got off the mark in mid-week with that stunner. The second half saw Leeds well on top, but we just couldn't find the net. We had a total of 17 shots, and a massive 61% of the possession, but we just didn't have the creativity to break down a resolute Ipswich side, that was well organised, if lacking in ambition themselves. Grayson waited until his favoured 75th minute before making any changes, and then he brought off Paynter and Howson, replacing them with Becchio and Bannan. New boy Bannan immediately injected some urgency in midfield, and he put in some good ball winning tackles, but still we couldn't find a goal. The final whistle went, and we just had to accept that we weren't quite good enough today. It was therefore with some trepidation that we stood on the Kop waiting for the other Championship results to come up on the big screen. At half time it had not looked too bad. As the results came up the noise level increased, as the fans took in the fact that yet again, most of our rivals had stumbled. QPR had won, but Swansea had lost to lowly Derby County, Forest had only managed a goal less draw at home to Doncaster, and Burnley, who were coming up fast behind us, had been thrashed at home by Millwall. It would get even better on Sunday, when Cardiff would fail to beat Barnsley and have to settle for a 2 – 2 draw. So, despite our failure to beat Ipswich, we were actually now in a better position, than we were before this round of matches, and we were now just 2 points behind the 2nd automatic promotion spot. How things had changed in the two weeks since that abysmal performance at the Liberty Stadium! True, Norwich City were now in a position to move into that second spot, if they could beat Bristol City, on Monday night, but even so, we would still only be 5 points adrift of them. The fact that Norwich City were in the mix with us, was another similarity with last season. There was also much talk in the press about various investigations being held into goings on at QPR, in particular, the possibility of them being docked points for fielding an ineligible player. If that happened in the next few days, then the whole climax to the promotion race would be thrown wide open.

Thinking about today's results in the Championship, I could not help but keep remembering those famous opening lines from Rudyard Kipling's poem "If". It begins:

>If you can keep your head when all about you
>Are losing theirs and blaming it on you,...

We just need to keep our heads, and who knows where we might get to this season. So it was in positive mood that I drove home on Saturday night, and not even the fact that I had to listen to Arsenal losing their FA Cup quarter final tie at Old Trafford, would dampen my mood. I was heading home to meet three ex school mates, and their wives, and we were going out for a meal in our village to celebrate one of the couples 25th wedding anniversary. I was very much looking forward to sharing a couple of bottles of wine, and a few beers with them all, and celebrating not only the anniversary, but a pretty good day out as well.

This was shaping up to be some end to the season. I would make a point to check my diary for possible play off dates.

No fun in the sun

We had a problem. The next game, on Saturday 19th March 2011, was Sheffield United away. Leeds had announced in the match day magazine for the Ipswich game, that they were expecting a second allocation of tickets from the Blades, on the Monday before the game. We assumed that we had been unsuccessful in the first allocation, as no tickets had yet arrived in the post. Leeds announced on their website, on the Monday morning, that they were processing the new tickets, but due to the scale of the task, they would not be able to let the fans know by e-mail if they had been successful. This was the problem. We did have a plan B, but that would involve Mark, Suzi, and I, all sitting in with the Sheffield United fans, but obviously that was a last resort. Suzi, a psychology student at Sheffield's Hallam University, had a friend who had purchased Sheffield United tickets before, and he was therefore able to buy tickets for this game. The Blades, in an effort to stop Leeds fans buying tickets this way for the home sections, had come up with this "prior purchasing history" requirement, and that meant it wasn't just a matter of me registering on the home team's ticketing system, as I did for the Bristol game. However, how would we find out if we had tickets from Leeds or not, and when? Obviously there was a deadline, after which Suzi's contact wouldn't be able to get tickets in time. We left it until Thursday morning, and I still hadn't received any tickets in the post, and I knew nothing had gone through on my credit card, as I had checked that online as well.

Ignoring yet another e-mail from Bristol City, reminding me once again, that I was running out of time to get my season ticket for Ashton Gate, I e-mailed the Leeds ticket office. I asked if there was any way they could tell me, if I had been successful in getting tickets in the second allocation for the Bramall Lane game, which had now boosted the Leeds total

to 3,600 altogether. I didn't expect to get an answer back, but I did! It wasn't the news I wanted, as it just said:
"Dear David, unfortunately, your application this time has been unsuccessful."
But at least we now knew, that we needed Suzi to put plan B into action. I sent a text to Mark, explaining the situation.
Friday morning, and the eagerly awaited message arrives from Suzi, saying, "...picked up the tickets...in one of the side stands near the front..." Sheffield here we come. I had read on the Blades website, that the club were going to be very hard on any Leeds fans they found in the home sections, threatening to hand them over to the police, and have them ejected from the ground. So, I texted Suzi, to tell her to make absolutely sure that neither she nor Mark wore any Leeds colours to the game, and how important it was going to be to keep quiet. For me, it was Bristol City all over again, I just hoped the result would be similar.
The difficulty we were experiencing, in just getting tickets for an ordinary league game like this, highlighted to me yet again just how important it was for Leeds to get back in the Premiership as quickly as possible, so that, with the generally bigger grounds, Leeds could satisfy more fans.
Leeds had announced this week the arrangements for the play offs, should we end up in the top six. The biggest problem the Club had to face was that in the event that they got to the Wembley Play Off final, the Football League was only going to give each club 32,000 tickets. Wembley has a capacity in excess of 90,000, so where the hell do the other 30,000 tickets go? Anyway, Leeds had now calculated, that Members and Season Ticket Holders, together totalled just over 40,000! Clearly, 8,000 Leeds fans were going to be disappointed, should we have our day in the sun. Leeds had decided to use the loyalty scheme for the final, and probably the away semi final, meaning that any member or season ticket holder who had been to at least 4 away matches was guaranteed a ticket, but the rest would have to go into a ballot. At least Mark and I were OK on that score, although it

might mean that He That Can't Be Arsed, and his mum, might miss out.

The encounter with the Blades was another lunchtime kick off, with a one o clock start, at the request of the police. So, it was another early start for me. I set off on a chilly, but sunny morning, at 9am, with the aim of meeting Mark and Suzi, at Suzi's student home, on Ecclesall Road, Sheffield, at around 11am. It's just a fifteen-minute walk across town to Bramall Lane from there.

I followed the shortest route on the map, up to Sheffield, and that took me through Leek and Buxton up the A53. It brought back memories of that trip along the A628 to Barnsley, back in September. That also had been a journey made in lovely sunshine through some fantastic scenery. Today, I found myself wondering why we hadn't holidayed in the Peak District recently, as some of the views were stunning. Particularly the stretch of road from Leek to Buxton was amazing. It is another dangerous old road, as it, like the A628, also has to follow the contours of the landscape, and it undulates up hill and down dale in equal measure. There is though no escaping the beauty of that landscape, with great clusters of rocks hanging precariously over the roads, and the fields all marked out by mile upon mile of dry-stone walls, as far as the eye can see. My route took me over Blackshaw Moor, and then through Hope Valley, and I made a mental note that we must visit the area this summer to explore it further. The local pubs looked well worth a trip.

As I drove through the town of Leek, in Staffordshire, I was reminded again about those lines in Kipling's poem. The reminder came in the form of the map book that was lying open on the passenger seat next to me. Kipling was named 'Rudyard' after Rudyard Lake, and I could see that if I branched left and took the A523, Macclesfield Road, that would lead me straight to Rudyard Lake, or Reservoir, as it is now known. Mr and Mrs Kipling were so taken by the beauty of the Lake, that back in 1865 they named their first born after it. I couldn't help thinking how lucky the little fellow was, that his folks hadn't met at, and fallen in love with, Tittesworth Reservoir instead. That is only a few miles further to the East, on the A53, Buxton Road, that I was taking out of Leek today.

The journey should only have taken about an hour and a half, but I stopped a couple of times, just to note down some place names for future reference, and so it actually took me a couple of hours, before I arrived at Suzi's. I rang Mark when I thought I was vaguely in the right neck of the woods, and he directed me the last few hundred yards to a space he had saved in a neighbours driveway, where I could park the car. We popped into the house, and I noted that it was a typical student abode. I think I upset Suzi, when I pointed out the odd chip lurking on the floor, on the rather grubby green carpet, and the baked bean stains splashed up the cupboard doors and on the lid of the pedal bin! As I say, it was a fairly typical student house! I tried not to touch anything, as I wasn't sure my inoculations were up to date. Suzi's excuse was that they had all had a take away late last night.

We set off on our walk to the ground, with the sun now very warm on our backs, and our first stop was the Scholar Bar, on London Road. Mark and Suzi had been in there a few times before, as during the week it is a student haunt. Today, there was a sign taped on the door stating "Home fans only", but as we were going to be honorary Blades for the next few hours, we marched straight in. It was bursting at the seams with Sheffield United fans, but there were shirts of other clubs hung around the walls. Apparently, they will let you have a free beer if you donate them a club shirt, though I can't think of many shirts that are only worth the price of a pint, other than the obvious red rags worn by the Yanks from Old Trafford. Hanging right over the centre of the bar, was a huge red and white Southampton flag, which we couldn't quite understand. The beer was decent, I had a pint of Bombardier, and Mark had a pint of Beck's to keep his Leeds pre-match ritual going! Suzi had a J2O, and the whole lot only cost £6.35, which was excellent value, and more proof that it was a student watering hole.

We only had the one drink in the Scholar though, and then we made our way to the ground, as I wanted to find the Railway Hotel, which a contact at work had told me was run by his brother or brother in law (couldn't quite remember which!). As we passed a bookies window, I suddenly understood the significance of that Southampton flag in the Scholar. A huge advert in the window proclaimed that Southampton were playing the Blades' arch-rivals Sheffield Wednesday, later today, in a 5:20pm kick off. There is no love lost between the Blades fans and the Owls of Sheffield Wednesday, and a defeat for the Owls is celebrated as much as a win for their own team.

When we got to the Railway Hotel, a little pub right on one corner of the ground, we were told that admittance today required a "Railway match day pass" which obviously we didn't have. I enquired with the "enforcer" on the door if he knew the landlord, but I think he thought we were just trying to con our way in, so I still don't know if this was the right place or not. We adjourned instead to test the local burgers, at one of the many burger vans located along Bramall Lane, behind the away end of the ground. We were at least mixing with the Leeds fans at this point. The burgers were first class, and on a par with those we sampled at Pompey a few weeks ago. Strangely though, there were no chips available, so we couldn't have a chip buttie, the famous staple foodstuff that's mentioned in the Blades anthem, "The chip buttie song", of which more later. We stood munching the excellent burgers, and watching as the Leeds coaches arrived in their dozens. The fans disembarked, and were all frisked, as they lined up to go through the turnstiles into the ground. There was a fairly relaxed atmosphere outside the ground despite of, or maybe due to, the dozens of South Yorkshire Police who were on duty. The mounted police were very much in evidence here, as the piles of horse dung scattered all over the pavements, frequently reminded us.

With half an hour to go before kick off, we decided to make our way into the stadium, as it was rumoured that alcohol would be on sale, albeit we had heard that many times before this season, only to be disappointed once we got inside the grounds. We walked three sides of the ground, to find the South Stand, or GAC Stand, as it is currently known, and then we squeezed ourselves through the narrowest of turnstiles I have ever seen, I couldn't see how fat fans would fit through them, but Mark pointed out they did have signs directing our larger brethren to some wider ones further along.

Once inside we had a pint of something purporting to be lager, but tasting of pond water, and we then contemplated putting a bet on with 188Bet, the sponsors of the away fans stand. However, the odds were not particularly attractive, 4 – 0 Leeds, was only 33/1 for example, which we thought was a bit stingy, so we passed on that, and eventually just made our way to our seats. We were on row c, the third row from the front, just about level with the edge of the penalty area, and on the South Stand side of the pitch. To our right was the home Kop, that was pretty full, and away to our left, at the Bramall Lane End, were the massed ranks of the Leeds fans, taking the upper and lower tiers of the 188Bet Stand. What really pissed us off though, was that one whole block of the stand at that end, and the whole of the South West corner, was completely empty, both upper and lower tiers! I reckoned there must have been upwards of 3,000 seats not being used and here we were, stuck in with the home fans, compelled to remain silent throughout the match, simply because we couldn't get away tickets! Crazy, absolutely crazy, and I was sure the Blades could have done with the extra revenue. At £25 a seat, those extra 3,000 seats would have brought in another £75,000. We took 6,700 fans to Barnsley on a Tuesday night, so I am damn sure we could have sold 6,600 for this one.

It was hard to know what to expect from the game today. Sheffield were in trouble, second from bottom, and with a poor run of recent results, except for an eye catching win over Nottingham Forest here, eleven days ago. Manager Micky Adams, had been saying how he refused to give up the fight, but in a manner that suggested he thought the task was beyond his players and beyond his powers. They were struggling with injuries and suspensions, but were sure to be up for this game against their famous Yorkshire rivals. The Blades (or Blunts, as they are often referred to by Leeds fans) had several players in their squad with Leeds connections, including Welsh international striker Sam Vokes, who had a spell on loan with us last season, when he was next to useless; Micky Doyle, who keeps cropping up all over the place, having also been on loan with us last season and then playing against us for Coventry earlier this year; Shane Lowry, another loan player from last season; and Richard Cresswell. They would all have points to prove. As for Leeds, we stuck with the tried and trusted 4 – 5 – 1 formation, with Becchio preferred to Paynter this time out, and Barry Bannan getting his first start, in place of Neil Kilkenny.

There was a decent atmosphere inside the ground, which apart from those sections right next to the Leeds fans, looked pretty full. The attendance was later announced as only just over 23,000, which, in a ground with a capacity of over 32,000, is poor for a major derby game like this, and just showed again how daft it was to limit Leeds to just 3,600 tickets. The record crowd inside Bramall Lane, albeit before it became an all seater stadium, was in 1936, in an FA Cup, 5th round tie against Leeds, when over 68,000 were crammed in. In the current, all seater format, the record is 32,604, against Wigan Athletic in a league game in 2007.

Just before kick off, we got the first rendition of the "Chip Buttie" anthem of the Blades, sung with great gusto by the fans to our right. It is set to the tune of John Denver's famous hit ballad from 1974, Annie's Song, and it goes like this (in a broad Sheffield accent):

> You fill up my senses
> Like a gallon of Magnet
> Like a packet of Woodbines
> Like a good pinch of snuff
>
> Like a night out in Sheffield
> Like a greasy chip buttie
> Like Sheffield United
> Come thrill me again

I had thought that the Cider, or *Zider,* song down at Bristol, was the worst anthem I had come across, but this one runs it close! The Leeds fans did their best to compete, with a rousing rendition of MOT, but sadly we couldn't risk joining in.

In terms of lack of quality on display, today's game was very much like the reverse fixture at Elland Road. By half time today Leeds had not troubled the Blades keeper at all, though Schmeichel had been called on several times, to get us out of the brown stuff. One particular chance came when Bogdanovic was left all on his own, in the middle of our box, but he took too long to get a shot away, and Schmeichel smothered the effort. On the BBC's Football League programme later on that night, the commentator described the opening by saying, "If you ever wondered what the meaning of 'unmarked' is, watch this". Max Gradel had Leeds' best effort, when he should have scored with a free header, but he put his effort wide of the post. At half time, we glumly made our way to the bogs and back, with very little to say for ourselves. The sun was still shining, but only into the stand opposite, and in the shade where we were, it was damn chilly, as was our mood.

The second half confirmed our worst fears, as we still failed to carve out more than a couple of half chances, while the Blades were looking much sharper (oops, sorry). The inevitable happened just 9 minutes into the second half. Nick Montgomery hit a speculative ball low across the front of goal, past Schmeichel at the near post. Eric Lichaj was sliding in at the back post, and just couldn't avoid pushing the ball into his own net, right in front of the jubilant home Kop support. Everyone around us was jumping for joy, and thankfully, they were all far too preoccupied with their own celebrations, to notice three forlorn figures in their midst just sat slowly shaking their heads. The Blades fans really got behind their team from that point, and it was difficult to hear our lads at the far end, not that we had much to cheer about anyway. Leeds toiled away, and our mate Billy was sent on to replace a very much below par Becchio. Despite a chorus of "Come on Billy", from the travelling Leeds contingent, he made little difference to our cutting edge, and in the 74th minute, we went two down. As so often this season, it came again from our left back position. Bjorn Helge Riise, somehow got himself time to strike a shot that went through Kasper's legs, low into the far corner of the net. Davide Somma was immediately sent on in place of left back McCartney, as we tried 4 – 3 – 3, and later on Sanchez Watt got a run out in place of Snoddy. But Leeds never looked likely to snatch anything from this game, and to cap it all, Billy Paynter got himself sent off in the last minute of normal time, for allegedly head butting a defender. The way Billy stomped off, and the way his teammates just accepted the decision, summed up a very lack lustre performance, that is best confined to the history books, and not dwelt on for too long.

The PA announcer was clearly overjoyed, as he congratulated his Blades for their performance, but he then went beyond the call of duty, by wishing the Leeds team and fans a safe journey home, and then stating "we look forward to welcoming them all back here next season". That would depend on two things. Leeds failing in their bid to get promoted, and the Blades succeeding in their bid to avoid relegation. We will see.

In a radio interview after the game, Simon Grayson was clearly very annoyed by the lack of passion and commitment shown by his boys, talking of his side playing too much as individuals, and not together as a team. As always though, he was already thinking of the next game, at home to Forest, in two weeks time after the international break, when he would be looking for a response from the team similar to the reaction he got following the Swansea defeat.

The three of us trudged back to Suzi's house, and I said my farewells before climbing into the car for the journey home. It was still only 3pm of course, so I had the dubious pleasure of listening to the goal alerts throughout the afternoon on the car radio. As it happens, the results in the Championship were yet again not too unkind to Leeds today. QPR won again, to go further ahead at the top, but Swansea beat Forest, Norwich drew at Hull, Millwall got a draw at home to Cardiff, and Leicester, Watford and Burnley, all lost. Once again it was so, so, reminiscent of last season, with most of the top teams unable to string together a series of good results that would propel them clear of the pack.

Hence I was able to enjoy my journey back through the Dales and the Peaks, despite the latest setback to our promotion hopes. Later in the evening, I heard that Southampton had beaten Sheffield Wednesday 2 – 0, so I guessed that Blunts fans would be well pleased with their weekend's work, and would probably be celebrating with a greasy chip buttie and another gallon of Magnet beer. Sadly for Blunts fans, I spotted the other day that Heineken UK, the Dutch owner of Scottish & Newcastle Breweries, announced in 2010 that it would be stopping production of Magnet beer, so maybe the Chip Buttie Song will need a rewrite.

A fortnight off from Championship football then, during which we'd see if the England football team could avoid embarrassment against the Welsh, next weekend in the European Championship clash.

8 games to go now, and it was looking more like the play offs than automatic promotion, but even to make the play offs we would need to find some better form than we showed today. There was no rollercoaster ride today, just a very flat performance. Our momentum had been halted for a couple of weeks at least, but somehow, you just knew there were more twists and turns to come in this oh so unpredictable journey. Next stop, Elland Road on April 2nd for the visit of Nottingham Forest. They, like Leeds, had been doing their level best to cock up their season in recent weeks.

Chopping down the Forest

It had been a long couple of weeks. Seven Leeds players had been involved on international duty, although only Bannan and Snodgrass for Scotland, in the 2 – 0 defeat to Brazil at Arsenal's Emirates Stadium, had spent any time on the pitch. The others, Nunez, Somma, Lichaj, Gradel, and Kilkenny, had all remained on the bench for their respective nations. England had managed to beat Wales comfortably at the Millennium Stadium, to go top of their group in the European Championship, in a game that was, to all intents and purposes, over by the 14th minute, when the second goal went in. England then drew 1 – 1, in an unusually competitive friendly at Wembley against Ghana, the following Tuesday.

At Leeds there wasn't much going on, apart from the arrival of another loan signing, and hopefully plenty of training for our still overly porous defence. Jake Livermore, the young Spurs midfielder, had been signed on loan until the end of the season. He had played against Leeds when on loan with Ipswich Town, earlier in the season, and did in fact set up the opening goal in their 2 – 1 win, with a defence splitting pass. I still couldn't understand why Simon Grayson couldn't manage to persuade a decent Premiership defender to join us; surely that was the real need. We already had more midfielders at the club than you could shake a small stick at.

On the ticket front, it was all looking good. Mark and I had got our tickets for the remaining four home games, and we had got them for the trips to Derby and Palace as well. We were still very hopeful that we would be successful in the ballot for the QPR game at Loftus Road, on the last day of the season, although those had still not yet been allocated. We had only missed out on the allocation for the Millwall game next week, so we should be at seven of the last eight games...or of course there could even be another three after that...

The fortnight break had given me a chance to catch up with some football reading, and in particular I re read the Sheffield

United programme, "The Blade". It is a darn good read, and its' "Stat Pack" statistics page, is fascinating. On the "Where to see goals" section, Elland Road was 10 goals ahead of the next most plentiful venue, which was Vicarage Road at Watford. 71 goals had been scored at Elland Road, in 19 games, at an average of 3.74 in each game. There was no doubt that Leeds was the place for excitement this season, as Mark and I well knew. Another stand out statistic, was that Leeds were also well ahead of the pack for most shots on target, (269, prior to the Blades game) and for most times hitting the woodwork, (15). We also had most yellow cards, with 72 prior to the Sheffield game. Thankfully, there was no record of "most defensive cock-ups", although there is no doubt we would be at the top of the table for that one too.

Despite our excellent goals for tally, (Leeds had scored 69 in their 38 games so far, which was also the best in the Championship) I was concerned that we were going into the Forest game having failed to score in the last two matches. That was a first for the season so far, and my concern was that we had now lost our own ability in front of goal, but still hadn't solved our problems at the back. At least so far it hadn't really mattered that we kept conceding, because we usually managed to score more than we let in.

The Forest game was to be shown live on TV, this time it would be on the BBC, and it was another lunchtime kickoff at 12:45pm. Hence it was an early start for me once again, and I left home this time at 8:45am. I had a great run up the motorways, and pulled onto the car park at about 10:15am. I sat in the car, waiting for some contact from Mark, and whilst waiting I saw the first of the coaches bringing in the Forest fans arrive and park up. The Forest fans looked cheerful and optimistic at this stage; I looked forward to seeing them a good deal more miserable, at about 3 O'clock this afternoon!

Mark eventually called, and he explained that he and Suzi were getting a lift in with a couple of mates, who had been stopping with him last night. Joe, the lad driving his bright red pick-up truck, had now got them lost in Leeds, and they would be a while! I made my way down to the Pavilion.

The Cricket World Cup final was being shown on the big screens in the Pavilion, so I sat and watched as India began their reply to Sri Lanka's 274 for six. India would go on to lift the trophy, winning by six wickets, with a couple of overs to spare.

Eventually Mark, Suzi, and their two guests, Will and Joe, arrived, after their tour of the city centre, and the three lads were clearly still suffering following a boozy night at the Leeds University Union. Joe is a Leeds fan, but Will, who lives near to us, is a Stoke City fan. This week he had decided to watch a real team though.

The guests on stage in the Pavilion today were Allan Clarke and Frank Worthington, who both provided us with plenty of banter, and clearly didn't need any prompting from Peter Lorimer. Once PL had introduced the two former strikers, he couldn't then get a word in edgeways! I had spoken with "Sniffer" before the Ipswich game of course, but I still went up to get another autograph, and Mark took my photo with him as he signed. Frank Worthington hasn't changed much since his playing days, with his long black hair and Teddy-Boy styling still in evidence today. Frank played 35 games for Leeds in 1982, scoring 15 goals, but in total he played 757 league games and scored 234 goals, for a whole host of different clubs. He was one of the great characters of British football, and led a high profile life both on and off the pitch. The double entendre title of his autobiography was "One Hump or Two", referring to his alleged fondness for the ladies, rather than the way he liked his tea! There are very few characters like Frank in football today.

Billy Paynter was the other guest today. He was serving the first game of his three match suspension today, following his dismissal at Bramall Lane, a couple of weeks ago. Billy is another Scouser like Paul Connolly, and he is also a bit of a "mumbler", so we have no idea what he said up there on the stage.

The team was announced as unchanged from the starting line up at Sheffield, perhaps Grayson was giving them a chance to atone for that poor display against the Blunts. Looking at a sportingbet betting slip in the Pavilion, the odds were not particularly attractive for a big Leeds win, but I eventually plumped for 4 – 2 to Leeds at 50/1, and I also had a quid on 3 – 1 with Snodgrass to score first, that was offered at 70/1.

When I watched the recording of the game on Sunday afternoon, it was being given a big build up by Gaby Logan, who was filmed outside the ground in Lowfields Road, and in front of Billy's statue before the game. That had obviously been recorded, because the coverage then switched to Logan interviewing BBC pundit Steve Claridge, and ex Leeds hero Danny Mills, in front of the West Stand, alongside the Championship trophy, which stood proudly on a plinth. At one point Logan turned to Mills and asked "Do you get down here often" as if using a well worn chat up line! All this was happening while we were still in the Pavilion of course, so the recording was the first time I had seen it.

When we got to our seats, I spotted one of the great characters of the Kop, seated just behind us. Joanne can always be found on the Kop on match days, usually sporting her distinctive yellow and blue striped Leeds jacket, which is absolutely covered with autographs of Leeds players. I asked her if she would mind being mentioned in my book, and she said it was fine...as long as I didn't say anything derogatory about her! My main memory of Joanne, who told me she was at one time a partner of one of the top English referees, is from the Preston debacle earlier this season. We were 4 – 6 down near the end of the game, when Joanne spotted that a couple of lads near us were texting on their mobiles. She was looking over their shoulders, and could see them typing in "we are sat with the white shite", giving away that they were Preston fans. When she broadcast this to the Kop, the lads soon made a hasty exit.

Joanne kept us amused throughout today's game with her comments, particularly her very informed insight into the performance of today's ref, Mark Halsey. As today's game was live on TV, Halsey had been allocated to us as another one of the so-called 'elite' group of ref's. Joanne reckoned he was one of the better ones.

The game kicked off in bright sunshine, and it soon became quite uncomfortably hot in the Kop, with the sun beating down on our faces. Forest annoyed the Leeds fans by winning the toss and turning the teams around, so that Leeds would attack the Kop in the first half, never a popular move by the opposition skipper!

On the pitch the football wasn't anywhere near as hot as the weather, as Leeds struggled with a very physical, and cynical, Forest side. It quickly became apparent that the Forest players were going to stop any Leeds man getting past them, by all means possible, whether fair or foul. Mark Halsey was too lenient by far in the opening minutes, and a few chants of "We only get sh** refs" broke out from the Kop. Joanne shrugged and said "well, he's usually alright!" Gradel blasted a free kick over the top in the first couple of minutes, after Halsey did consider one challenge too harsh, but then Gradel got clattered a couple more times without any further reward.

Then a five minute spell probably determined the outcome of the game. Firstly, after 30 minutes, Forest playmaker, Paul Anderson, was injured, and he was replaced by Garath McCleary. 5 minutes later, Tudgay hit the ball at Bromby in front of goal, when he should have scored. Then out on the Leeds left, Chris Cohen jumped into a tackle on McCartney with both sets of studs showing, and, after consulting a linesman, Halsey sent Cohen off. Forest didn't hold back though, even when down to ten men, and Tudgay then went into the book for yet another cynical ankle tap on Howson. Kris Boyd then joined in, and he got a yellow for barging Schmeichel over, when the Leeds keeper was trying to get the ball away quickly. As the teams went off for the break, I certainly felt this game was there for the taking. Forest were undoubtedly the most cynical side we had seen so far this season, and they had paid the price with Cohen's sending off. To get any payback for my two bets though, we needed the goals to fly in to the Forest net in the second half.

The half time score at Upton Park went up on the big screen, for one of the other lunchtime kick offs. West Ham were leading the Red Yanks 2 – 0, and a big cheer went up from the Kop. I couldn't help thinking though, that one wasn't over yet, as it was only a few weeks ago we watched Aston Villa lose to the Yanks, after themselves going 2 – 0 up.

The sun was now positively burning our faces, as the second half got underway, and Leeds were about to warm our hearts as well. McCartney and Lichaj had clearly been given instructions to bomb on down the flanks to support Snoddy and Max, and Lichaj in particular, was lightening quick. 6 minutes into the new half, and Snodgrass chipped the ball forward to Eric Lichaj on the right wing. From the bye-line, Eric clipped the ball to the near post, and Jonny Howson was there to control the ball with his first touch, and smash it into the net with his second.

On 57 minutes, Leigh Bromby rose at the back post to head a corner against the woodwork, and when the ball came back Becchio was on hand, to nod it in for 2 – 0. Luciano then wandered over to his favourite West Stand audience, and entertained them with another very strange goal celebration. He stuck out his ample belly, and made 'I am pregnant' gestures by rubbing his stomach with the palms of his hands, presumably to let us know his missus is with child? Either that, or he was still suffering from an over indulgence of pasta last night!

2 – 0, and Leeds are in command. As usual though, we then contrived to let the opposition back into the game, just to keep it interesting for the millions of viewers on TV, or so it seemed.

McCartney challenged for a high ball outside the area, and it broke to McCleary on the right. McCleary then did a magnificent impersonation of Snodgrass, by curling a delicious left foot shot into the far top corner of Kasper's goal. It was almost identical to Snoddy's goal at Coventry, earlier in the season, and indeed Snoddy had a similar effort hit the Forest bar in the first half today. Nervous tension then engulfs the Kop, and we start to think the unthinkable might happen against 10 men. A corner for Forest on their left then gives us all heart failure, and Kasper a chance to shine for the cameras. Big Wes Morgan, the Forest number 5, gets his left foot to the ball six yards out, but hits it into the ground and it bounces up heading for the roof of the net. Kasper is going to his left as the ball is heading past him on his right, but he swings his right arm at the ball, and just touches it over the bar. Andy Gray would have said "one for the camera, son". Many of us in the Kop said "F****** Hell that was close!"

The Kop collectively breathes a huge sigh of relief. Morgan then joins the growing band of Forest hit-men in the book, by blocking Howson in mid-field, in yet another cynical, professional foul. Seconds later though, and we are bouncing again, as Max Gradel hooks the ball inside the keeper's right hand post, at the far end of the ground. Comfortable again, and this time the Forest players seem to accept the inevitable, as they cease to harry and chase quite as readily for the last twenty minutes. Jake Livermore came on for Bannan, as Simon made his usual 75th minute change, and the Spurs youngster was quickly on the pace. In the 87th minute, he cut in from the right and fired in a left foot shot that Camp, in the Forest goal, could only parry out. Becchio followed up, but again Camp blocked the shot. It was third time lucky though as Mad Max was next to latch onto the loose ball and he made no mistake. I suddenly remember that I have a quid riding on 4 -2, and I turn to the folk behind me to explain that I now need Forest to score just one more. Joanne, of the yellow and blue jacket, tells me to be satisfied with the win, and give up the stake money! With seconds left on the clock, a Forest player is taken down in the area by Mad Max, and it looks for all-the world a penalty. But Halsey gives the decision the other way, and someone behind taps me on the shoulder and laughs, "unlucky there mate!" I didn't mind. The final whistle blew and we roundly applauded the victory. On the pitch Jonny Howson was being interviewed for the TV show, to a background of "There's only one Jonny Howson" from the Kop, and then Max Gradel, always last to leave the pitch, is pulled over to join Howson, and we try to get another chant to be heard on the TV. "He's here, he's there, and he's every f****** where, Max gradel!" echoes around Elland Road, but I guess they muted the microphones at the Kop end at that point! It was a nearly perfect day so far, but then the full time score from West Ham goes up on the big screen. Somehow, the Old Trafford mob have won 4 – 2. Incredible, absolutely, bloody incredible.

We drove over to Mark's place in Leeds to pick up his washing, and then headed home. By this time the 3 O'clock kick offs were in full swing, and there was more good news, as Preston pulled off an unlikely victory over Swansea, while 'Boro got a last minute equaliser against Leicester at the Riverside. Cardiff and Norwich both had big wins, but overall it was another good day for the promotion challenge from the Mighty Whites.

QPR comfortably beat Sheffield United 3 – 0 on Monday night, while Reading just shaded it against Preston 2 -1 on Tuesday. So the standings were now: QPR, 79 points; Norwich, 70 points; Cardiff and Swansea, 66 points, Leeds, 64 points; and Reading 63 points. Seven games left and *still* anything could happen. Next up for Leeds though is a difficult looking trip down to the Den, to play in-form Millwall.

Lions and Tiger

Mark and I had known for a few weeks that we had not been successful in getting tickets for the Millwall game. It was also one game where I was not prepared to sit in with the home fans, for the reason that I am quite enjoying life at the moment, and saw no reason to put that at risk with any bother in Bermondsey. There is absolutely no love lost between Leeds and the Lions of Millwall, and as mentioned in an earlier chapter, trouble is never far away from this encounter. As it turned out, this game was a sell out, with a best of season 16,724 turning up at the New Den, including just over 2,000 Leeds fans.

With the weekend now free, Mark had decided to go on a last minute jaunt to Gothenburg with six of his mates. It was a birthday bash for one of the lads. They had cheap Easy Jet flights out of Manchester, and were going to sort some accommodation when they got there. Mark was still getting his fix of football on Saturday afternoon, watching GAIS beat Trelleborgs 4 – 0, in the second round of matches in the new Swedish Allsvenskan season that kicked off last week.

My gut feeling was that we would get beat at the New Den, Millwall had been on a decent run of late, and I just couldn't see Leeds keeping them from scoring. In fact I couldn't see Leeds keeping any team from scoring.

Where to be on Saturday afternoon then? It turned out to be a scorching hot day, with the sun out and a clear blue sky all day long. So that decided it for me and I spent the day doing jobs in the garden, cleaning down and jet washing the conservatory, and mowing the lawns. I didn't dare switch the TV on until well into the second half, and when I did the news was pretty much as I expected. As the Championship scores rolled around the bottom of the screen on the Gillette Soccer Saturday programme, I could see that Leeds were 3 -1 down. Leeds had gone 2 – 0 down in the first half an hour, and then Becchio had pulled a goal back, early in the second half. A third Millwall goal looked to have won the game for them. I sat watching the scores come in at around 4:50pm, as we football fans do, hoping that Jeff Stelling would suddenly shout "late drama at the New Den". Imagine my surprise therefore when he did say exactly that. Andy O'Brien had headed a goal in the 5th minute of added time, to reduce the arrears to just one goal, but within seconds the game was over, and that was that.

Simon Grayson had made a couple of changes to his side for this game, George McCartney was out injured, and so Paul Connolly made a return at right back, with Eric Lichaj switching to the left, and Jake Livermore got his first start in place of Barry Bannan. Grayson had then switched from 4 - 5 – 1, to 4 - 4 – 2, by introducing Davide Somma for Snodgrass at half time, and that had given Leeds a much greater threat, according to match reports.

Watching the BBC's Football League Show later that night gave no real indication of the nature of the game, other than the fact that Millwall's first goal was a well taken free kick, and their second was a soft effort from a corner. Becchio's effort was just a toe poke at the back post, and Millwall's third was scored by the prolific Steve Morison, just nipping in to beat Schmeichel to the ball. There was little comment from BBC pundit Steve Claridge either, just a note that Millwall had got themselves to within 4 points of Leeds and the 4th play-off spot, as a result of the win.

On the Leeds website on Monday, I read that there had been some distasteful antics by some Millwall fans during the game. They were apparently flying Turkish flags, and waving Turkish soccer shirts, to taunt the Leeds fans over the deaths of Christopher Loftus and Kevin Speight, in Istanbul's Cumhuriyet Street, in 2000, almost exactly eleven years ago. Chris and Kevin had been in Istanbul to watch the Uefa Cup semi-final between Galatasaray and Leeds, when trouble broke out between the two sets of fans that resulted in Chris and Kevin both being fatally stabbed. Millwall had quickly denounced the actions of those fans responsible for the flag waving, and reported that they had ejected 4 Millwall "fans", and had banned them indefinitely from the ground. Six Leeds fans had also been arrested, during and after the game. It was disappointing to have missed my first Leeds game since the Arsenal FA Cup match at the Emirates, way back in the first week of January, but if I had to miss one, then in hindsight this was the right one.

This was a big weekend of Sport around the world, with the Grand National taking place at Aintree, the second Grand Prix of the season in Malaysia, and the Masters golf at Augusta. When Mark arrived back from Gothenburg on Sunday evening, we both sat down to watch the Masters as it played out to a climax, just after midnight. We are both great fans of Tiger Woods, (for his golf, not his recent off course misdemeanours with the ladies) so it was another disappointment to us that he was beaten by 4 shots by Charl Schwartzel, despite having two storming rounds on the Saturday and Sunday. In fact, Mark pondered that it had not been a great weekend for him from a sporting perspective. Leeds had lost, Tiger Woods had missed out, and Mark and I are both keen followers of Ferrari in Formula One, and they were outpaced yet again by the Red Bulls.
Oh, and the horse Mark tipped to win the National was Dooneys Gate. He fell at the 6th fence, and was fatally injured!

In terms of the race for promotion, the defeat at the New Den had not had a major impact. Second place Norwich had been thumped 3 – 0 at Swansea, just as we had been a few weeks ago, and so we were still just 6 points shy of second spot, and Forest had been beaten at home by Reading, who had now swapped places with Leeds. We remained 4 points clear of the chasing pack that was now led by Millwall.
Not the best weekend then, and I quickly wanted to forget it and move on to Pride Park on Tuesday Night.

Despair

I had been looking forward to the trip to Pride Park for many weeks. I took my accountancy exams in Derby, at the then Derby Lonsdale College, (now the University of Derby) over three years from 1979 to 1981, and I got to know the area quite well. I lived in a house on the Ashbourne Road, just north of Derby in the first year, and then rented a place in Mickleover. I went to Derby's old Baseball Ground many times, including the First Division games against Leeds in March of 1979, (won 1 – 0 courtesy of a John Hawley goal) and in April of 1980 (lost 2 – 0). Despite the Rams beating us that year, Derby were relegated at the end of the 1979/1980 season, and finally that ridiculous pitch they had, was removed from top flight football. I have tried to explain to my sons just how bad the pitch at the Baseball Ground used to get, but they don't believe me. Any football fans that lived through the 1960's and 70's, will remember the mud patch that it always was.

My most vivid memories of Derby from my time there are of the days and nights spent at the Beer Festivals that took place each spring, at the Kings Hall. It was a time when various friends would descend upon my rented house, and we would sample some of the best ales in the land, over a boozy weekend. I still possess the half pint commemorative glasses from each of the three festivals I attended. The Beer Festival is still an annual event to this day, as is another great attraction that takes place in Ashbourne, the Royal Shrovetide Football match.

I made the trip up into Ashbourne one year while I was in Derby, to see this age old tradition in action, and I would recommend that everyone should see it at least once in their lifetime.

The game is played in the streets of Ashbourne, on Shrove Tuesday and Ash Wednesday; it lasts 8 hours each day, and is played out between the two halves of the town, the

"Up'Ards", and the "Down'Ards". There is no limit to the number of players on each team, and basically there is very little, if any, football that takes place. It more closely resembles a giant rolling maul, in rugby union parlance! The aim of the game is to score a goal, by bashing a large hand painted ball three times against one of the two mill stones that act as "goals", and which are set 3 miles apart, at either end of the town. The shops are typically boarded up for the duration, to prevent any damage from the marauding players, barrelling along the narrow streets, but the pubs are open throughout, and it is a lovely day out if the weather is fine. I particularly like the main rule of the game that states:

"Committing murder or manslaughter is prohibited. Unnecessary violence is frowned upon."

Not a game for Roy Keane then, allegedly!
The game has its own anthem as well and part of it has echoes of our own MOT:

>Through the up's and down's of its chequered life
>May the ball still ever roll,
>Until by fair and gallant strife
>We've reached the treasured goal.

Would tonight's game at Pride Park be full of yet more "ups and downs"? I wondered, as we set off along the A50, going past the Britannia Stadium, home of Stoke City, heading for the East Midlands.

Mark and I arrived in Derby at 5:30pm on Tuesday night, the 12th April. We parked up in a modern little trading estate, just a few minutes walk away from the ground. The locals had cunningly sealed the area off, and were charging a fiver to access the car parks that are normally used by employees of the firms on the estate during the day. We then walked back up Pride Parkway, past the many car dealerships that are situated either side of the road. We lingered at the Derby Audi salesroom that had a magnificent Audi R8 in the window and a stunning new A5, in brilliant white, on the forecourt. We noted the prices, and walked swiftly on to the Harvester pub, just a few yards further along the road.

The Harvester had been recommended in one of the stadium guides on the internet, as a place that usually allows away fans in on match days, and sure enough when we got there, we could see dozens of Leeds fans already supping pints in the bit of a beer garden to the one side of the pub. It was a gloriously sunny evening, but it was still mighty cool outside, and the stiff breeze was threatening to blow down the sun umbrellas. Fans of both teams were happily mingling, both inside and out. I tried the Marston's Pedigree, while Mark had a Stella, and we joined the fans sat outside in the sun, to soak up the atmosphere. I must pay tribute to the bar staff in this place, there was so much beer being pulled, that barrels were going off, left, right, and centre, and all the beer was so lively, that it took an age to pull some of them. All the staff were in good humour though, despite the stress of trying to keep dozens of thirsty fans happy, and thanks to the efforts of Lorna and Kerry in keeping an eye on who was arriving at the bar, and in what order, there was no queue jumping.

The discussion amongst the Leeds fans, was mainly about tickets for the QPR game, and the Play Offs, in the event that we have to suffer that eventuality. I was convinced that defeat tonight would end any hope of getting that second automatic promotion spot, and that the Play Offs would then be our only hope.

After a second round of pints, we made our way back towards the ground, stopping just long enough to take a couple of photographs of the statue of Brian Clough and Peter Taylor, which stands proudly at one corner of the ground. One of the stewards kindly stepped to one side to let us get a better shot, saying something like, "make sure you get a good picture of our famous duo". Quick as a flash, Mark turns to him and says, "Why, who are they?" and grins! Next stop was a burger van, and this time we gave the chips 9 out of 10, as they were almost perfect, the burgers were good, but still not in the Pompey league. While we were stood eating, we got chatting to a group of local coppers. The Leeds coaches had arrived in a long convoy, while we were waiting at the burger van, and we overheard one of the coach drivers talking with a police officer who had a blue panel on the back of his jacket. He was asking the officer, why he had not been able to get away from Millwall at the weekend until 6:30pm, after the game. We deduced therefore that the coach driver a) recognised the policeman and b) the copper must have been at Millwall. That meant that there were obviously police from Leeds, who regularly travelled with the fans to away games. We asked the Derby police if that was the case, and they told us that it was usual practise for the big teams to take police "spotters" with them, to help the local police identify the away fans. They told us it was a much sought after role, particularly for the police covering the teams playing in Europe, as they got to travel all over the continent. The chap we spoke to added, "Not that we will ever get the chance here at Derby!"

We made our way through the turnstiles and into the South Stand, to join our 3,800 fellow Leeds fans. Only for the Swansea game, had Leeds failed to sell out the ticket allocation for an away game this season.

We made straight for the bookies counter, and I had a couple of £1 bets for 2 – 1 Leeds, (13/2), and 4 – 2 Leeds (50/1). It seemed a long time since I last won anything, at the Bristol City home game, back in November, when I correctly called it 3 - 1 to Leeds.

We climbed up the concrete steps to our seats in Row N, and we were well pleased when we turned round to look at the view we had. We were quite high up, but we were almost directly behind the goal, and the view of the pitch was perfect. The main core of Derby fans appeared to be in the corner to our right, similar to quite a few grounds we had been to this year. We seemed to outnumber them.

Simon Grayson had made a couple of changes to the side that lost at Millwall at the weekend. Barry Bannan was in for Bradley Johnson, who dropped to the bench, and Neil Kilkenny came in for the injured Robert Snodgrass. It was the trusted 4 – 5 – 1 again, but the 5 across the middle was a new combination of Howson, Gradel, Kilkenny, Bannan, and Jake Livermore. Jonny Howson had still maintained his 100 per cent appearance record for the season, this being the 45th competitive game. George McCartney was still injured, so Eric Lichaj continued at left back, with Connolly on the right.

Leeds looked sharp from the start, and Derby looked like a side low in confidence, that had won just 2 of their last 17 games. Connolly and Lichaj were overlapping down the wings, and several good crosses were put into the box. Max Gradel, as always, was in the thick of the action, and he got several decent efforts in on goal. In the 39th minute, it looked as though that long run of consecutive appearances by Jonny Howson might come to an end after this game, as he was nearly chopped in half with a poor challenge by Daniel Ayala, who was booked. Howson was down for a long time, but eventually, to the relief of everyone around us, he struggled to his feet, and began to try to run the injury off. The half time whistle brought to an end a mostly satisfactory 45 minutes, with few clear chances having fallen to the home side, and their fans having been kept fairly quiet. I sat down in my seat for the first time; as usual all of the Leeds fans had remained standing throughout the first half, despite the match tickets proclaiming "Persistent Standing Is Strictly Forbidden".

During the interval, I was reminded very much of the game up at Deepdale, Preston. The colour scheme was the same of course, black and white, and on the pitch a troupe of cheerleaders was going through a dance routine. I thought that might be an omen, and that we *might* get the same result and I *might* be picking up at the bookies for a 2 – 1 Leeds victory.

There was then an audible stirring amongst the Leeds fans, as Seth Johnson was introduced on the pitch, to make the half time club lottery draw. Seth Johnson was transferred from Derby to Leeds in 2001, for a huge fee of £7 million. At the time, Leeds were spending money like it was going out of fashion, in the Ridsdale and O'Leary era, and the fee for Johnson was just a part of almost £100 million that O'Leary spent, in a little under four years as Leeds' manager. It was this spending, and the subsequent failure to turn it into results on the pitch, that began the decline that culminated with our relegation to League One, in 2007. Johnson spent four years at Leeds, but largely due to injury, he only played 54 games, scoring just 4 goals. In 2005 he was released by Leeds, and he went back to Derby. Johnson was not a popular fellow with the Leeds following, and I felt a bit sorry for him today as he suffered all sorts of abuse from the fans, despite having two young kiddies with him, that I assumed were his children. "What a waste of money!" Was the first chant sung with feeling by the majority of the South Stand, and then even worse came "You're too sh** to play for Leeds". Johnson pulled the winning ticket out of the drum, and then made the long walk down the touchline, holding the hands of his kids, one on each side, as the verbal battering continued. He bravely stuck out his chest and gave a little wave to us, but it was an embarrassing moment.

Flicking through the mammoth 83 page Derby match day magazine, the Ram, I spotted an article by one time Derby hero Roger Davies that brought back memories for me. Roger Davies was discovered while he was playing with my home side Worcester City, way back in 1971. The story of how he was discovered, and how he went from amateur with Bridgnorth Town, to superstar with Derby County, in a few short weeks, is the kind of stuff that would get rejected for a Roy of the Rovers script as being too far fetched. Worcester City were in severe financial difficulties in the summer of '71, and hence looked to bring in Davies, a young striker from Bridgnorth Town, as an amateur. However, it was quickly apparent that Davies was an exceptional talent, and Worcester gave him a professional contract just before the start of the season, and as it turned out, just in the nick of time. He played just 7 games but scored 7 goals, before Brian Clough pounced, and Derby paid Worcester a then non-league record fee of £14,500, to take Davies to the Baseball Ground. I can still remember the four home league games that Davies played that August, and the coverage he got in the Worcester Evening News. The interest in Davies was so great, that I managed to persuade my Mother to go with my Dad and I to the home game against Wimbledon, a game City won 4 – 1, thanks to a hat trick from Davies. I will never forget one of the goals he scored that day. His reputation was such, that 3 Wimbledon players were marking him when a ball came over from the right wing, at the Canal End of the ground. Somehow, Davies rose in the middle of them all, and smashed a header into the net. Amazing! It is the only time my Mother has ever been to a football match with me, and it is likely to remain so, as she is now 95 years old and walks with a Zimmer frame!

I stuffed the monster programme back into my jacket pocket, as the two teams emerged back onto the Pride Park pitch. The feeling was, that it was just a matter of time before we got a goal, and that we could then go on to win this comfortably. Shouldn't be any rollercoaster ride today...
It took us an hour, but eventually that all important opening goal arrived, and once again it was that Duracell bunny, Max Gradel who got it. He played a lazy one-two back to Kilkenny, outside the box on the left hand side, and then he turned, took aim, and fired a rasping shot inside the keeper's right hand post. We were right behind the line of flight, and it was a corker. The South Stand went absolutely bonkers, and you could feel the concrete stand actually rocking beneath our feet. For a couple of minutes we were all dreaming of promotion again. "He's here, he's there..." rang out loud and clear, as Max skipped back to the half way line in tune with

his own anthem. Now was the time to work doubly hard, to put pressure on a Derby side whose confidence was now shot. Don't give the ball away; don't play too open, keep it tight. I had heard coaches saying this for years, even on a Sunday morning, when either of my lads' teams had just scored. Always remember, a team is at its most vulnerable immediately after it scores. It was just basic stuff. . .

Jake Livermore, a player with Premiership experience at Spurs, had the ball safe in the centre of midfield. He played a loose, aimless pass forward, that was easily intercepted by a Derby player. The ball was fed forward to Stephen Pearson, who immediately sprinted down the Left wing. He managed to outpace Connolly, and then clip the ball across the face of goal behind the Leeds defence. Jamie Ward, running in at the far post, just had to make contact to score. He made contact. He scored. We were stunned. Two minutes ago we were jumping for joy, now we were in deep despair. Two minutes ago automatic promotion was a distinct possibility again, now it was as likely as my 95 year old Mum appearing in the 100 metres final, at the 2012 London Olympics. That old rollercoaster had indeed visited us again; it was as if those football gods were teasing us, punishing us even. Maybe we had been too hard on poor old Seth at half time, embarrassing him like that in front of his kids, and this was the retribution. In my mind, I promised to be good in the future in the hope of pleasing the gods, so that they might help us get back in front. This was a desperate time, and it called for desperate measures. The Derby players visibly grew a couple of inches taller, became two yards faster, their fans doubled their decibel level. The Leeds players had shrunk; it looked like we had eleven Barry Bannan's on the pitch, not just the one, and they all looked forlorn, empty, and as if they didn't now know what to do next. The dream had once again turned into a nightmare, and my head was swimming. Suddenly, Derby had won a corner on the left wing at the far end of the pitch from us. Stephen Pearson swung it across with his left foot, and we watched in total disbelief, as Ben Davies met the ball on the full, and volleyed it into the top right corner of the net. The Derby crowd was now going mental all around the stadium, the noise was deafening, while we all stood open mouthed, gasping at what we had just witnessed in the last 5 minutes. We had moved from ecstasy to agony in the blink of an eye. I am sure that there was only one thought in the minds of the 3,800 Leeds fans at that moment. There was no way we were going to get that second automatic promotion spot now, and the only way we would be going up, was if we could get into the play offs, and then somehow navigate our way through to, and win, a Wembley final. That seemed as likely as my Granny coming second to my Mum in that 100 metres final...and she has been dead for over 40 years!

A couple more chances came and went at both ends, and then the Derby keeper went down in a heap, I am sure just to break up the game. While he was being bandaged up, Robbie Savage walked over towards the Derby fans to our right, and he urged them to sing up even louder. Their fans responded with a rendition of "There's only one Robbie Savage", so we fought back with "Robbie Savage, is a w*****, is a w*****" no longer caring if the gods were watching us or not. Savage then bent over with his ample arse facing towards us, pretending to stretch, but we knew what he was up to, and anyone who hadn't joined in the "Robbie Savage is a w*****" the first time, certainly did now. The final whistle went to signal defeat again, 2 - 1, just as it had been in the opening game of this unbelievable season, up at Elland Road last August. We had left Elland Road eight months ago full of optimism, that despite the defeat that day, we had more than held our own, and would perhaps have a decent season. Of course few Leeds fans would have thought at that time, that we would have been 6th in the league with 5 games to go, and in with a chance of making the Play Offs. But having got this close, it would be a gut wrenching disappointment if we now threw it all away. In his interview with BBC Radio, after the game, Simon Grayson was clearly annoyed by his team's naivety. He said that after half time "We were just naïve in what we did straight from the kick off, and must have given the ball away 3 or 4 times" He bemoaned the fact that his players were not able to "take a different stance at different stages of the game" noting that once we scored "we should not have been playing 'Tippy-Tappy football' in the wrong areas of the pitch" and that "Someone switched off at a set piece, and that just drives me mad". He sounded as depressed as I have ever heard him, but he did then start talking about the upcoming game with Watford, and how we just needed to re-focus and go on again.

Roger Davies isn't much of a football pundit either. Included in his piece in today's programme was the comment "We can't afford to start slowly because I don't think Leeds are the sort of side that will let you get back in". Wrong!

It took an age to work our way out of the traffic jams around Pride Park, and we had plenty of time to absorb the night's other results. QPR had won again, this time 1 – 0 at Barnsley. Forest had got back to winning ways by beating Burnley 2 - 0. Swansea and Norwich had drawn their games with Hull and Watford respectively, while the form team, Reading had won again at Scunthorpe. We were clinging on to that 6th spot, but were now only 1 point ahead of Forest in 7th, and now a full 5 points behind Reading in 5th. 15 points still to play for, and that Watford game at Elland Road on Saturday was now "massive". That was going to be another very nervy old afternoon.

That might just be the end of that!

If I needed any reminder as to how important the Watford game was, it came by e-mail from the Leeds United ticket office on Friday morning. They had sent out the unique pin numbers, that members would need in the event of Leeds reaching the Play Off final. I optimistically moved the e-mail into my "Leeds United" folder, in the hope that I would have to retrieve it next month. I then angrily hit the delete button, to get rid of another one of those bloody season ticket reminders from Bristol City. I must cancel my registration with them.

It was another big sporting weekend in the UK, with the London Marathon, and two FA Cup semi finals taking place in the capital. The two Manchester clubs were doing battle on Saturday evening, and our local side, Stoke City, were playing Bolton Wanderers on Sunday, both games taking place at Wembley. As Mark and I drove north up the M6 on Saturday morning, the southbound carriageways were full of coaches and cars travelling down for the first semi final. Most were flying Manchester City colours, as no doubt the majority of the other lots supporters would be jumping on the tube to Wembley, from their posh London homes.

We had to chuckle when we heard on the radio that the M1 was shut in both directions between junctions 1 and 4, due to a scrap yard fire, and the danger of some gas cylinders exploding. Something else had clearly happened on the M6 southbound as well, as just as we were listening to the M1 problems, we noticed that the traffic was stopped on the opposite side of the barrier. It was going to be a long day for those Manchester fans.

Northbound we had no problems, and it was another lovely spring day. We went past the Crawley Town Supporters coach heading for Southport; they had wrapped up their promotion to the football league a couple of weeks ago, and would enjoy another thumping win this afternoon, 4 – 0. Not surprisingly the fans on the coach looked to be enjoying their day out.

We arrived at the ground, and we were able to park in our usual spot, despite being a bit later than normal. It was about 12:30pm as we arrived, and we got a cheery "Hello mate" from the bloke taking our £6 at the gate. Walking down to the Pavilion, I calculated that I had spent £111 on car parking at Leeds so far this season, no wonder he recognises me!

Martin and his lads were arriving at the door of the Pavilion just as we were going in, and he asked me where Worcester City were playing this afternoon, as he had just seen their team coach. Embarrassingly, I couldn't recall who they were playing, but later in the weekend when I checked, I saw it was Harrogate Town. City lost 1 – 0. Worcester had lost a few games recently, but were safe from relegation, and so should take their place in the Conference North again next season. When we got inside, I asked Martin if he was going to the FA Trophy final between Mansfield and Darlington. Mansfield was Martin's local team, and he confirmed he would be there on May 7th, and not at the QPR game. Our good friend Brian, from Darlington, was bound to be at Wembley, and I wondered if their paths might cross.

The first guests on stage with Peter Lorimer today, were Paul Reaney and Carl Shutt. Paul Reaney was a fairly regular visitor to the Pavilion, but Mark got yet another autograph from him, this time on the back of that 1969 Arsenal versus Leeds programme. Carl Shutt joined Leeds in 1989, and played a part in our First Division title winning team of 1991/92. Peter Lorimer reminded us of one of his greatest goals, in the Nou Camp in 1992, in a replayed European Cup match against VfB Stuttgart. Carl was looking quite portly today up on the stage, in stark contrast to Reaney, who looked as if his first Leeds strip would still fit him, despite it now being forty odd years old.

Carl Shutt forecast 3 – 1 Leeds, while Reaney went for 2 – 1 Leeds. I decided to have a quid on 1 – 0 Leeds (the same score by which Leeds had won down at Vicarage Road, that day last summer when we had been at Wembley, watching Leeds Rhinos get hammered by Warrington Wolves). That was only offering a 13/2 payout, so I also went with another quid on Leeds to win 6 – 1 at 80/1... I admit that was a tad optimistic, although this Watford team had shipped plenty of goals so far this season, 60 in the league, not so far behind our awful tally of 66.

The other guest player to appear later in the afternoon was Billy Paynter, so that gave us the first clue as to the likely front line today. Billy was available again, following his three match ban for the head butting incident at Bramall Lane, but was clearly not in the squad at all. Sure enough, when the team was announced, Billy was not involved, but there were a couple of surprises. Snodgrass and McCartney were both back from injury, and Eric Lichaj moved over to his preferred spot at right full back, so Connolly, Livermore, and Bannan, dropped to the bench. Bradley Johnson was back in the starting eleven, but the main surprise was that Davide Somma was starting up front, instead of Luciano Becchio, who was also on the bench.

As we took our places on the Kop, the usual faces were there, including Joanne, who, in deference to the warm weather, didn't have her famous blue and yellow striped Leeds jacket on.

The first half saw Leeds attacking the South Stand, and the best chances of the half fell to Max Gradel, including a snap shot while at full stretch from close range, that clattered the bar, and a header that he put wide, when he probably should have done better. Danny Graham always looked lively for the visitors, as he tried to add to the 24 goals he had already bagged this season, as the Championship's top scorer.

At half time, in the bogs, the feeling was that this had not been a vintage Leeds performance, and most voices were proclaiming that the sooner Becchio was brought on, the better our chances would be. Somma had only had one glimpse of goal in the first 45 minutes, and he made nothing of that chance.

After just 11 minutes of the second half, Simon Grayson came to the same conclusion as the urinal philosophers, and on came Luciano to replace Neil Kilkenny. I was pleased with myself, as I had called that exact change, whilst Mark was convinced Becchio would be a straight swap for Somma. There is no doubt that we are a better side with Becchio marauding up front, and he immediately began causing problems. Even the huge figure of Martin Taylor, in the centre of the Watford defence, was now looking concerned. Just 16 minutes after arriving on the pitch, Becchio rose unchallenged on the 6 yard line. He buried a powerful header in the net from a Barry Bannan free kick on the Leeds right. Bannan had replaced Somma a few minutes earlier.

One Leeds fan, wearing a blue away shirt that must have been at least a size XXXXL (if they do one that big), managed to get on to the pitch, and he waddled across the goal right in front of us. He had initially tried to grab Becchio, presumably to congratulate him on the goal. I counted eight stewards in purple "emergency response" jackets all hanging on to him, and eventually wrestling him to the ground. As they got him back on his feet, he still managed to give the Leeds salute with a free arm, before all 9 of them fell to the ground again. In his programme notes for the Reading game on Good Friday, Ken Bates wrote:

"The season is over already for the former fan who ran on the pitch to embrace Luciano Becchio; he is banned and may in fact face charges if his actions show to have been a contributing factor to Becchio's injury. In a further blow, after looking at him we may have lost our best customer for the famous Elland Road pies!"

The Kop was jubilant, but at the same time everyone was now demanding that the Leeds players didn't repeat the mistakes of Tuesday night, when a similar late one goal lead was squandered. A reasonable man would have assumed that

Grayson would have been working on just this potential situation all week, so surely we had learned the lesson.

Apparently not! This time we held the lead for just 6 minutes. A long hopeful ball (yeah, another one of those) was crossed into the Leeds box, where Lee Hodson, a five foot six midget of a full back, ran on to the ball to head it down and into the Leeds net. From the replay on the big screen, it looked another appallingly soft goal to give away. Quite what Kasper Schmeichel was doing at the time, I have no idea, and many far more knowledgeable fans than me were very angry with young Kasper, who just looked too slow to react.

Lady luck was clearly not supporting the team in white today, as the next calamity was an injury to Luciano, who took a blow on the knee which left him in no fit state to carry on. Ross McCormack was then pressed into service, as Becchio left the field. We were still bemoaning this latest set back when the unthinkable happened, and Watford took the lead. It came yet again from weakness in our left back area. First Danny Graham evaded McCartney, and then he did well to avoid a lunging challenge from O'Brien, that would have resulted in a certain penalty had the two collided. He rolled the ball across the 6 yard line to Andreas Weimann, who just had to sweep it into the net. 2 – 1 down and just 4 minutes of normal time to go. I start to feel personally responsible for this disaster, and try to remember what I have done today that has so enraged the football gods. Was it those comments I made about all those Manchester fans only getting through the traffic jams in time for the Stoke Semi on Sunday, and not their own, later on today? Had I failed to salute any magpies today, or accidentally killed a spider? Whatever it was, it didn't deserve this degree of retribution. Mark was obviously feeling the same and he turned to me and said "That might just be the end of that!" meaning promotion I assumed. We had patiently ridden the rollercoaster up to the top of the run, and when Becchio scored we had once again dared to look across to the horizon, and we saw Wembley beckoning. Within minutes we had plunged down again, and were now thinking the worst. Then the gods had second thoughts. Bannan took a corner out on the Leeds right wing, and Watford's number 9, Troy Deeney, hammers the ball into the corner of his own net from no yards at all! 2 – 2 and perhaps all isn't yet lost. The Kop no longer knows whether to laugh or cry, whether this is the end, or the beginning of a promotion journey. Even the referee is unsure what is going on. The ball is down in the North West corner, and the ref is pointing to the centre circle, but surely it's a throw to Leeds? No, he is trying to say the game has finished. It finally registers with the players and the fans. Many of us slump down into our seats, trying to make sense of what we have just seen. The other Championship results go up on the big screen, and most games have ended in draws today. Cardiff have won, but Swansea and Millwall have lost. Somehow we will end the day still in that 6th spot. We live to fight another day, next Friday, Good Friday indeed, against Reading, back here at Elland Road. Can the heart stand it?

We listened to the Cup Semi final, on the radio in the car, and we took a small crumb of comfort from hearing City take a one goal lead. We headed straight for a barbeque that Suzi's Mum was hosting, and shortly after we arrived there to see the closing few minutes on TV, Paul Scholes was sent off, and then Mike Dean blew the final whistle to signal a City win. That made me feel a bit better.

There were several Stoke City fans at the barbeque who were going down to Wembley for the second semi tomorrow. We wished them luck, as they left ready for an early start on Sunday, as the M1 was still closed, and it would be a long tortuous trip. They would be happy with the result though, as Stoke demolished Bolton 5 – 0 on Sunday evening, to set up a Stoke City versus Manchester City final. As for us, well we were really not sure of anything anymore. Four games to go and we knew that we would grab a Play Off spot if we won them all. Anything less and we were relying on others to drop points. I was mentally ready to accept that this was not to be our year, but while there is a chance, let's keep hoping.

Final thought on the Watford game. As I walked with Mark across the car park, he spotted that Watford appeared to have brought just two supporters coaches. Mark shakes his head and says "Two bloody coaches, is that all they brought? They should forfeit their point for that!" I looked at him and waited for him to realise the implausibility of that suggestion ever being implemented as a Championship rule. He started to grin.

Alarm bells ring

Good Friday, April 22nd 2011, is a day I will remember for a very long time, and not only for the game against Reading played at Elland Road that evening, another "must win" game if promotion was to remain a possibility. It was a 7:45pm kick off, and was being shown live on Sky.

The day started normally enough, with me going for a short jog. We were in the middle of an early spring heat wave and so it was a struggle, but in our house we were on a bit of a fitness drive, so I didn't want to miss a day. As I arrived home I was met by the local Avon lady, delivering the wife's latest order, and I was surprised to see that a little clip-on pedometer was among her purchases. I didn't even know that Avon sold such things. Karen doesn't run, but she loves to walk, and had decided to set herself some fitness targets of her own, and hence the pedometer to measure how far she was walking. It also had a personal alarm function, so it was a useful addition to any woman's hand bag or belt.

Mark had stopped at Suzi's the previous night, and he was next to arrive through the door, announcing that we needed to leave early for today's game, as he needed to pay a visit to his student house in Leeds. He had received a call from another of the students, telling him that the house had been burgled, and Mark now wanted to check if anything of his had been stolen. The house had been ransacked, but it was believed that all that had been taken was the TV, a big flat screen unit that they had all clubbed together to buy when they first moved in. Mark's iPod was also missing, but he wasn't sure whether it had been in the house or not.
So Mark and I set off in the car at 2pm, and by 4pm we were pulling up outside his Leeds home, having battled with the M6 bank holiday traffic. Mark's house mate, Sam, met us at the door and he showed us around pointing out the damage

and disruption caused by the intruders. First, he took us down to the basement to show us Ralph's room, and I gasped when I saw it. There were piles of clothes all over the floor and cupboard draws hanging open, papers were strewn everywhere, and empty beer cans were randomly scattered about. It was a real mess. I started to mutter something about why burglars would do this to a student's room. Sam looked at me quizzically. "No, the burglars didn't do it." he said, "His room is always like this. I only brought you down here to show you the window where they got in!"

All of the rooms had been thoroughly searched by the thieves, presumably looking for cash, and so they were all in a mess. If it was cash that they were looking for, then a student house was a strange target, I thought. Mark was relatively lucky in that his room didn't take too much time to tidy again, since most of his stuff went home with us after the Forest game. It didn't appear he had lost anything, apart from maybe the iPod, but he still thought that might be at home somewhere.

Sam explained that he had called the police, and they had been round to inspect the damage and take details of what had been stolen, but were otherwise not too interested. They had established that the basement window in Ralph's room was the point of entry, and they had barricaded it shut as best they could. Sam would later inform the landlord, who would have to do a more permanent repair.

We bade farewell to Sam, who was to be at the house on his own for a few days, until the others returned after the Easter break. He wished us well, telling us it was "a must win game" as we already knew.

It was still only 5pm when we pulled onto the car park, and we were just about to get out of the car when my mobile rang. It was the wife in a very distressed state, telling me that the house alarm had suddenly started to sound for no apparent reason, and neither she nor He That Can't Be Arsed could stop it. They had tried to enter the usual code into the alarm panel, but it still hadn't stopped. I could hear the alarm in the background and it sounded peculiar to me, I asked if they had set off the smoke detectors, which were also linked into the alarm system but gave a different sound. It had been a very hot day, though I still thought the problem unlikely to have been caused by the weather, but Karen sent Adam off to check if the sound was coming from the smoke detectors, or from the alarm boxes on the outside of the house. It sounded as if panic had set in as Adam was trying to describe to me where the sound was coming from. "It seems to be moving around the house from one detector to another" he told me, and then "It seems to be outside now". He held his phone out of an upstairs window, and sure enough the alarm noise got noticeably louder. "Where's Mum now?" I asked. "She's gone outside to check the alarm boxes" Adam tells me. I told Adam to get his Mum to find the paperwork relating to the alarm company, and to ring the emergency number to ask what they should do. Adam rang off. I felt completely helpless as there was little I could do from 100 miles up the motorway, but I hoped that the emergency number would have some advice. Mark and I made our way down to the Pavilion, and I tried to rack my brain as to what could have set the alarm off. Half an hour had passed since we got into the car park, and I was having trouble turning my thoughts to tonight's game. In the Pavilion we sat at a table near Martin and his boys, who we exchanged greetings with, but I was still focussed on the problem at home, and waiting for the next call. When it came it was even more confusing. I wandered over to one corner of the Pavilion where it was a bit quieter. Karen was beside herself now, and I could understand why as the alarm was still deafening, even to me through my mobile 'phone. She explained that the emergency contact had suggested that she take the covers off the smoke detectors, and that she should remove the batteries, but even before she told me that it hadn't made any difference, I had realised how barmy that suggestion was, and that whoever she had spoken to didn't understand our system. The smoke detectors ran off the electric, and so didn't have batteries! He That Can't Be Arsed was for once doing his bit, and he had removed the covers anyway, and he reported that now the display panel just said "check", but the alarm was still going. I began to wonder if the wiring itself was on fire, and I told Karen to get up in the loft and make sure there was no smoke up there, which she did with HTCBA, while I waited on the phone. Then suddenly the ringing in my left ear went much quieter, and Karen told me the alarm had almost stopped, and was now just making a slow squeaking noise, that I could also just about hear. Then that too stopped, and all was finally quiet. I said I would look at the system when I got home, but instructed that in the meantime, they should continue to regularly look round the house to make sure there was no fire smouldering anywhere, if indeed it was the smoke alarm that had been set off. Karen told me she would, and she then told me to "enjoy the game". Some chance! I was going to be watching a football match, while my house could be burning down! In the back of my mind something was telling me that it wasn't the house alarm, or if it was then somehow it had been triggered by something either K or HTCBA had done. I went back to our table still pondering the possibilities, and informed Mark that the alarm seemed to have stopped for the time being. Mark was obviously deeply concerned. "Two pints of Beck's then?" He asked nonchalantly!

We had a couple of pints, and the usual pie and peas, while browsing through today's match day programme. In the "Away Days" section I noticed two pictures. The one showed a girl standing on London Bridge, with Tower Bridge in the background, while the other one showed a bloke inside Millwall's New Den ground, before the recent Leeds game. It was Helicopter Girl and her father! You will remember that I first came across them at the Leicester away game, and then we were again stood near them at both Pompey and Swansea. As luck would have it, I then spotted Lily and her Dad, Andy, as I now knew them to be, sat at a table just a few feet away. I went across to speak with them to explain that I was writing a book and how Lily had nearly taken my eye out with her scarf at the Leicester game and that I had nicknamed her "Helicopter Girl" because of the way she impressively twirled her scarf during the "Champions" chant. I asked if they would mind me including this detail in the book, and they seemed to be keen that I did. Andy asked me what the book would be called and I told him the provisional title was "Leeds United in pursuit of the Premiership" but that depending on how the season unfolded I might have to change it. We wished each other "enjoy the game", and I went back to our table.

On the big screens, the Forest versus Leicester Championship game was being shown. It had kicked off at 5:15pm and was now well into the second half. It had been locked in a 1 – 1 stalemate since Matt Oakley equalised in the 20th minute, and a draw would not be a bad result for Leeds, as both Forest and Leicester were snapping at our heals in the table. The one result we didn't want was a Forest win, as that would push us out of the Play Off positions, at least until we could beat Reading. *If* we could beat Reading. In the 73rd minute of the Forest game, there was a huge collective groan from the Pavilion fans, as Rob Earnshaw gave Forest the lead. We were all just starting to mutter about a wasted season and being pushed out by Forest, when up popped Darius Vassell to equalise yet again. As the ball hit the net, the Pavilion roof nearly came off with a mighty roar of approval. Maybe our luck was changing, and this was an omen for our own game later. Sadly not! With just six minutes to go, Forest captain Paul McKenna hit a soft, speculative shot, low to Chris Weale's left hand post, and somehow the Leicester keeper contrived to let it squirm under his body and crawl into the net. If that was the moment that decided Leeds would not be in the Play Offs, then it was somehow appropriate. Weale looked devastated as he lay on his back pondering how he'd missed the ball, but only the thousands of Leeds fans gathered in the Pavilion at that moment, truly knew the meaning of devastated. Forest held on to win the game 3 – 2 but as we all knew, it didn't matter as long as Leeds could win tonight.

Paul Reaney was again on stage this evening, joined as usual by Peter Lorimer and this time by big Mel Sterland. I reminded Mark that it had been Sterland who had scored that winning goal at Roker Park 20 years ago, when Mark was an unborn spectator! Of all the ex players we had seen, Mel had worn the least well, having put on a significant number of pounds since his playing days. Both Reaney and Sterland predicted a win for Leeds, Reaney going for 2 – 1, and Sterland 2 – 0, and both went for Jonny Howson to score the opening goal. I opted for 2 – 0 and 5 – 1 on my betting slip, hoping for the latter and an 80/1 payout. The final guest today was Paddy Kisnorbo, and the news was that he was rapidly getting close to a come-back. He suggested that being fit for the last game of the season at QPR was not out of the question. In the context of tonight's team news, that was interesting, as Richard Naylor had been recalled to replace Leigh Bromby. That was obviously an attempt to bring an experienced head in, to navigate us through another difficult game, and Kisnorbo also had great experience if we could just get him fit. To be fair, the announcement that Naylor was back in the side was not met with universal approval in the Pavilion, with lots of head shaking and raised eyebrows. I think the issue is that some fans are concerned about his age and lack of pace. There was similar disgruntlement over the news that Jake Livermore was being given another start in midfield, alongside Snodgrass, Johnson, Howson, and Gradel. Billy Paynter was up front in place of the injured Becchio. At the back, Connolly was in on the right, with Eric Lichaj again filling in on the left. Livermore was not a popular choice with the Pavilion faithful, probably due to his misplaced pass at Derby the other day, which led to the first Derby goal.

The reverse game at Reading earlier in the season had ended 0 – 0 and I had wondered, whether that would have been a better bet. Funnily enough, I reminded Mark that the only other game this season we had played on a Friday night, was also live on TV, and that had ended goalless too, at Doncaster Rovers, way back in September. To some extent a draw with our opponents tonight would have been an excellent result, as they were on a run of eight consecutive victories that had propelled them into a safe Play Off spot, above Leeds. A draw for Leeds was now though not good enough, if we wanted to keep our destiny in our own hands. Anything less than three points, and we would again be relying on others, particularly Forest, to drop points in the last three games.

As we took our places on the Kop, we greeted Joanne, who was in the seat behind me with her usual friends, and Lucas, who was in his normal seat to my right. I was starting to feel a part of this Kop family. I took the opportunity to ask Joanne how long she had been sitting on the Kop, and she reckoned it was about 19 years, but she had been following Leeds longer than that, she said. We all settled down to what was going to be yet another nervy old night.

Leeds looked solid at the back from the start, and there was no doubt Naylor's experience was useful. O'Brien seemed more comfortable just doing his own job, rather than having to be the backline organiser, a task that Naylor quickly slotted back into. Up front Billy Paynter worked hard, but somehow he just doesn't give the impression that he is about to score, which he did all the time at Swindon last season. He looked ponderous and just not sharp enough. Gradel was his usual self, buzzing here and there, and he and Snodgrass had the best efforts in the first half, though both were well saved by England's under 21 keeper, Alex McCarthy, who must be one of the reasons for Reading's recent run of victories. 0 – 0 at half time, and the main discontent in the crowd was over Jake Livermore's lack of creative contribution, although he had put himself about, with a number of crunching tackles, one of which earned him a booking. Simon Grayson obviously felt it was a risk leaving Livermore on the pitch, and Neil Kilkenny replaced him at half time.

Kilkenny seemed to give Leeds more impetus and creativity, and we really took the game to the visitors, but clear cut chances were few and far between. Bradley Johnson should have won it for Leeds, when he broke through and only had the keeper to beat, but he smacked his shot against the cross bar. With 10 minutes to go Grayson tried his luck with Somma and Watt coming on for the hapless Paynter, and the very tired Howson, but other than an effort by Watt that went close in the dying seconds, it was not to be, and the game ended goalless.

Leeds slipped to 7th in the table, behind Forest on goal difference, Leeds being just 1 goal worse off. It would now take a Herculean effort by Leeds to win their remaining three games, and hope that in the process Forest dropped points, or at least scored fewer goals than we did. It all seemed unlikely now, and I resigned myself to writing a sequel book next season – "Leeds United *still* in pursuit of the Premiership".

I didn't have time to look at the alarm system on the Friday night, it was half eleven by the time we arrived home and Karen didn't want to risk setting it off again so late at night, for fear of upsetting the neighbours! So we just did a final check around the house, and then trusted that the house wouldn't burn down as we slept.

I was having a shave on Saturday morning when Karen came into the bathroom. She looked rather sheepish and began "Do you want the good news or the bad news?" I thought for a moment, and then decided it would be good to get the bad news out of the way first. "I think the alarm problem is my fault" she confessed, adding, "You remember that pedometer I got from the Avon lady?" "Yes", I said slowly, wondering what the hell that had to do with anything. "Well, I just set off the personal alarm in the garden, and I suddenly realised it was that and not the house alarm at all that was going off last night". "You cannot be serious" I said with my best John

McEnroe impression. It did suddenly all fall into place though. She had the pedometer clipped to her belt, and she was now aware that the little tag she noticed on the floor, at the exact time the alarm went off, was the personal alarm tag that you pull out if attacked! The noise though was so intense, that both He That Can't Be Arsed and the wife thought it was the house alarm. Now I also understood why Adam had been telling us "The sound seems to be moving around the house". It *was* bloody well moving around the house, everywhere in fact that the wife went, even outside. I remembered Adam holding his 'phone out of the bedroom window, to prove to me that the sound was at that point coming from outside. Well, it would wouldn't it, because Karen was outside at the time checking the alarm boxes on the walls of the house! I could only laugh out loud at all of this. The good news was that when I put all the smoke detectors back together, and reset the house alarm, all was fine and dandy. We will dine out on that story for many years to come, but at least it means no more alarm bells at home. For Leeds promotion push though, the alarm bells were now well and truly ringing. Mark, Suzi, the wife, and I, were all off to Selhurst Park on Easter Monday for the Palace game. A defeat there, and I could write my final chapter with certainty.

Eagles Soar

Our longest trip of the season was to the Borough of Croydon in South London, the home of Crystal Palace. It took nigh on three and a half hours to get to Thornton Heath, and then a further half an hour to find a road side parking spot. There is absolutely no formal parking at Selhurst Park and lots of the roadside parking is either for residents or is time restricted. It was chaos everywhere. Still, on this Easter Monday bank holiday, the weather was glorious. It was 22 degrees, we had a clear blue sky, and there was hardly a breath of wind. My passengers, Mark, Suzi and the wife, were all asleep for most of the 180 mile trip down the M6, M5, M42, M40 and M25, but I enjoyed the solitude and marvelled at the scenery, including the brilliant yellow fields of rape set against the blue sky. Was that an omen for this afternoon? Would Leeds be turning out in their yellow and blue away strip, and would they clip the wings of the Eagles of Crystal Palace? It wouldn't be easy as Palace needed the three points themselves, to just about ensure they would avoid relegation to League One.
We parked in Davidson Road, which was obviously going to be easily remembered, my name being David and my son being with me! We then had a 10 minute walk to the ground, taking us up Tennison Road, and then a further 10 minutes to The Prince George pub that we had driven past earlier, noting that plenty of Leeds fans seemed to be drinking there.
On Tennison Road, we had spotted a blue plaque on the wall of a house, proclaiming it to have once been the home of Sir Arthur Conan Doyle, author of the Sherlock Holmes stories. He lived there from 1891 to 1894 and allegedly wrote several of the Sherlock Holmes novels in that house, number 12, Tennison Road.
When we got to the Prince George, it seemed to be full of Leeds fans, including some of the Surrey Whites folk that we had seen many times before in the Pavilion and on various away trips. This was probably their shortest trip of the

season. We had also bumped into Lucas, who often sits next to us on the Kop in Leeds, just as we walked past Selhurst Park. We had asked the police if alcohol was being served in the ground, and the negative response caused us to retrace our steps back to The Prince George, even though we were all bursting for a pee having not stopped at all on the way down.

It was Karen's first taste of Leeds away, and she got into the spirit wearing He That Can't Be Arsed's white Leeds top. With 6,000 Leeds fans descending on the area, there was a brilliant atmosphere and daft as it sounds, the hour or so we spent at the 'George, standing on the pavement outside in the sun, supping pints of Stella, and eating pizza bought from a shop a few doors down the street, was one of the highlights of this season for me. When we got back to the ground it was an amazing site to see the queue of Leeds coaches stretching up Park Road as far as the eye could see. I had the camera with me and I took plenty of photos and when I got back home, I e-mailed a couple to the Leeds "Away Days" e-mail address. I got a reply saying that they might use them in the summer edition of the programme.

We were later than we would have liked getting back to the ground, and so we went straight to our seats. Mark and I were about 5 rows from the front of the Arthur Wait stand, about level with the half way line, while the girls were right at the very back in line with the edge of the penalty area to our right. When we realised that there were a few spare seats around us, we got the girls to come down and join us for the second half. The only thing we could have done with was some sun protection, as we gradually roasted in the blistering sun. It was just too low in the sky to be blocked out by the roof of our stand.

The pre-match entertainment included the famous Crystal Girls, a group of scantily clad cheerleaders. They had caused some debate at Selhurst Park a few games ago. Some fans wrote in to the club, saying they thought they were distracting the players who were ogling them when they

came out of the players' tunnel! They certainly distracted me for a few minutes, as did the display of a real live Eagle, that flew from one end of the ground to the other in front of our stand a few times, seemingly oblivious to the 6,000 chanting Leeds fans. We don't often get given the bird by the opposition even before a ball is kicked! (Sorry, again!).
The Leeds team was announced and surprisingly it was the same starting eleven that took to the field against Reading last Friday night. It was surprising to me, in that Jake Livermore was starting again. For me, he just hadn't looked the part, but obviously Simon Grayson thought differently.

So everything was perfect and 6,000 lightly oiled (inside and out) Leeds fans cranked up the volume as the game started, with Leeds kicking off in their all yellow strip. For once, the usual opening long diagonal pass to the left wing, found Billy Paynter's head, and Leeds had an early few seconds of possession. Then, 90 seconds into the game, we yet again committed football suicide. A nothing ball into the box, Bradley Johnson swings a boot at the ball but hardly connects, and the ball comes to Neil Danns on the edge of the Leeds area. Danns had scored up at Elland Road earlier in the season, and this time his shot takes a huge deflection off Andy O'Brien, and dolly's past Schmeichel into the Leeds net. For a second or two the Arthur Wait stand, all down one side of this fine old stadium, was silenced, while Palace fans, some 14,000 of them, went berserk all around us. We shook ourselves down and began to get behind the team again, but even as early as this we were all thinking the worst. For the rest of the half, Leeds tried hard enough, but almost everything we did was only "nearly" right. Too often passes went awry; the ball would balloon off a players boot instead of stopping dead; crosses were either too long or too short. Snodgrass in particular just couldn't do anything right, and when he did get past the full back, he was usually upended. Poor old Billy Paynter looked as if Treats would melt in his hands before he ever scored again. It was poor enough for the Leeds faithful to boo the team off at half time, and with their next breath a chant of "Kilkenny, Kilkenny" sprang up which Mark and I did join in with. We didn't go as far as to chant "Livermore off", but it was clear that was the player we wanted replacing. Whether that influenced Simon Grayson or not we will never know, but before the second half got underway, both Kilkenny and Sanchez Watt were ushered onto the pitch, with neither Livermore, nor Paul Connolly re-emerging. At the end of the season there would be a hilarious entry on the Leeds United Facebook group, listing a number of spoof "End of Season Awards". There was one for the "Who's that? And why is he wearing a Leeds shirt?" award. Jake Livermore won it.

Kilkenny made some difference, as he had done up at Elland Road on Friday, but the individual failings were still there, and I for one felt we could have gone on playing until Tuesday week, and still we wouldn't have scored. Another entry on that spoof awards list was the "Couldn't score in a brothel" award, and King Billy Paynter won that one.

One or two fans were very irate at the final whistle and were making an array of hand signals to our own players, none of which you'd want your Granny to see. The rest of us applauded the team as if to say "we know you did your best lads, but it just isn't good enough". Even Simon Grayson didn't wander closer than the centre circle, as if embarrassed to look us in the eye. Still, we managed to sing out "We're Leeds and we're proud of it, we're Leeds and we're proud of it" and it was another pretty emotional moment as 6,000 Leeds fans contemplated that this was nearly the end of the season, and it wasn't going to have a jubilant finale.

As we trudged slowly up the steps to leave, we were grateful to be in the shadow of the roof of the stand and out of the ferocious sun. We turned around to see the other results go up on the big screen to our right, high over the stand at that end of the ground. We all knew they were no longer important and that was confirmed when the screen then displayed the Championship table. Leeds had slipped to 9^{th,} with Forest now three points ahead in 6^{th,} and both Burnley and Millwall now a point ahead in 7th and 8th spots. It was not mathematically over, but the fat lady was all dressed up and had the microphone in one hand.

It is hard to explain to a non football fan just what following a football team is all about, and why we get so attached to our own team. Non football people are surprised by just how important it can become to a fan, how it can get at your emotions and make you so irate, tearful, and deleriously happy by turns. I can only try to explain it in terms of comradeship, sharing with thousands of like minded people the ups and downs of your team. Sure, at the base level, we all wanted to be footballers and failed to make it, so the next best thing is to watch it. But more than that, it is the fellowship you find with your own group of fans. As we were making our way out after the game, there were literally thousands of us slowly edging towards the exits. Suddenly, just ahead of us, two Leeds fans started a bit of a fight with each other. It was handbags at dawn really, but one lad got hold of another by the throat and pushed him up against a security fence. Almost at once a voice comes from out of the crush somewhere shouting "Hey! We're all Leeds aren't we? What are you doing? Leave the lad alone!" Within seconds many more voices pipe up echoing the first, and then every last fan there spontaneously began to chant "We are Leeds, we are Leeds, we are Leeds". Not for the first time this season, a lump came into my throat and a tear welled up in my eye, as somewhere deep in my subconscious, I was reminded again just why we all love this game and everything about it.

Nearly, but not quite.

From the Palace on Monday, to the Royal Wedding on the Friday. As the whole world fell in love with Kate Middleton's sister, Pippa, in her sheer white, sexy, Maid of Honour outfit, thoughts in our house turned to the home game against Burnley on Saturday lunchtime. It was yet another TV game and therefore yet another early start. A win for Leeds in this 12:45pm kick off was the only result likely to take the season to the final round of games next Saturday, and even that depended on results elsewhere. Leeds began the penultimate Saturday of the Championship season in 9th spot, and only a particular set of results around the country would get us into the 6th and final Play Off spot today. The other key game today was Forest at home to Scunthorpe. If Forest won that, then even if Leeds beat Burnley, they would then need to win at likely Champions QPR on the last day, and rely on Forest losing at Crystal Palace in their final match. It really was looking very unlikely. First though, we needed to focus on Burnley.

As this was the final scheduled home game we had 5 tickets. One each for our family of four, and one for Suzi. That meant that He That Can't Be Arsed would be journeying up to Leeds with us, though he was distinctly unimpressed by the 9am start. Mark was already in Leeds, having gone back to University on Wednesday evening, so Karen, Suzi, HTCBA and I, drove up on the Saturday morning. We had an uneventful trip, with the only highlights for me being a sighting of the Hinckley United coach, on its way up to Workington Town, and the Vauxhall Motors FC coach, on its way down the M6 towards Boston United. Both those sides were in the Conference North, the same league that Worcester City are in. Both Hinckley and Vauxhall would lose their games this afternoon, but Worcester City would finish their season with a fine 1 – 0 home victory over Blyth Spartans. By a strange and rather spooky coincidence, the final Conference North table tonight would list Hinckley, Worcester and Vauxhall in 15th, 16th and 17th positions respectively. Weird or what?

We met Mark in the car park at 10:45am. Fortunately, he was there at the agreed meeting time, because we had no way of contacting him, since he dropped his mobile phone in the toilet at his house in Leeds the previous day. In 2007, a piece of research by SimplySwitch, the price comparison and switching service, reported that a staggering 855,000 handsets are flushed away each year in Britain. The problem seems to be that the units are getting smaller and smaller and it is easy to drop them or for them to fall out of pockets. A further 810,000 handsets are left in pubs each year; 315,000 in taxis; and 225,000 on buses. Dogs eat over 58,000 as well! In total, we Brits lose around 4.2 million handsets every year. So, Mark was in good company. He had actually rescued his mobile (we didn't ask at what point he fished it out, but I refused to shake his hand when we met him!) but it no longer worked.

In the Pavilion, it was business as usual. Allan Clarke met us at the entrance, he was having his photo taken with fans as they arrived, and Luciano Becchio and Paddy Kisnorbo were also there later on. The fact that Becchio was there, meant that he was still not fit to play and when the team was announced, it was clear that Simon Grayson was making his last throw of the dice, by including both Billy Paynter and Ross McCormack as a dynamic duo up front. Rob Snodgrass was the midfielder to step down, with Kilkenny joining the usual suspects, Howson, Johnson, and Gradel, across the middle. It was no surprise that Snoddy wasn't playing, as he had looked really tired last Monday at Palace. Richard Naylor continued his run of games, partnering O'Brien at the back, with McCartney and Lichaj as full backs, and Kasper in goal. With just the QPR game to go after today, Jonny Howson looked likely to get through a whole season playing every match. It was Howson who had scored the winner up at Turf Moor just before Christmas, and Allan Clarke reckoned he was a good bet today for first goal scorer. Mark plumped for Ross

McCormack to score first but he paired that with a 3 – 1 Leeds win. Ever the optimist, I went for a 5 – 1 Leeds victory at 100/1.

Allan Clarke was surprisingly forthright in his assessment of the season when he was up on the Pavilion stage. He had joked that all was well when he went away on holiday to Disneyland with his family. That was straight after the Forest game. He then couldn't believe the results he was being sent while he was out there. He told us he thought it must be his fault, and he certainly wouldn't go on holiday at this time of the season next year! He then went on to give his own assessment as to what had gone wrong. He considered that to get promoted to the next level, any team needed half a dozen or so players that could hold their own in the higher division. That meant that for Leeds to go up, he believed we needed 6 or 7 Premiership quality players. He felt that we currently only had three. Someone in the Pavilion shouted out asking him to name the three he thought were good enough and to everyone's surprise he then listed them. Schmeichel, Howson, and Snodgrass. When he mentioned Schmeichel, there were a number of heads shaking on the table next to ours, and Sniffer noticed. He told them "I know, I know what you mean. He is what I call a "liner", staying on his line rather than coming and getting the ball at corners and crosses, but I'd give him a chance". We shouldn't forget that Clarke spent 12 years as a manger himself, including a couple of years in charge at Elland Road, so he knows a thing or two about what is needed. It was an interesting insight and I didn't disagree that we needed to significantly strengthen the squad in the summer, with a few Premiership quality players.

Allan Clarke wished all the fans in the Pavilion a good end to the season, whatever it might hold, and he said he would be back to see us all next season. He mentioned that his great striking partner, Mick Jones, had recently had a triple heart bypass operation, and he looked forward particularly to sharing the Pavilion stage with Mick, when the new season started. I looked forward to that too, as Mick Jones is one of that great Revie team that I haven't seen in the flesh, since his playing days.

The sun was once again beating down on the first few rows of the Kop, and I judged that by the time the game ended, at around 2:45pm, it would still be baking anyone in row GG, where we were sat. I had remembered sun glasses, but none of us had any sun protection, despite having suffered just the same problem at Selhurst Park earlier in the week. Again we had neither hats nor sun block. It was all in stark contrast to that game up in Burnley when there had been snow on the ground.

Burnley won the toss and annoyed the Kop by turning the teams around, so that Ross and Billy would be attacking towards us in the first half, but at least that meant they would have the sun at their backs for the first period. Just over 31,000 were in Elland Road, the game having sold out a few weeks ago. The atmosphere was surprisingly good, considering the long odds we faced to ensure that this game actually meant something. The Leeds players looked up for it from the start, and there was a pleasing pace about the play. Maybe that was the impact of Ross McCormack, who, whatever you might think about his poor finishing, did at least put himself about. Leeds had a few decent efforts on goal early on, with Kasper having just one big save to make at the other end, before we took the lead in the 33rd minute. Bradley Johnson sent an exquisite ball through the defence in the inside left channel, for McCormack to run onto. He steadied himself before picking his spot at the near post, and then rifled the ball past the Burnley keeper, Brian Jenson. It was McCormack's first start since January, and his goal meant that both he and Billy Paynter now had one each in the Leeds record book. They had both come to Leeds with such great reputations as goal scorers, that it is hard to believe they only had two all season between them, albeit neither had had a sustained run in the team. Never mind, today's goal could still be priceless.

It was still 1 – 0 at half time, as we tried to cover our now partly roasted faces, while listening to The Soldiers, beating out their rendition of We are the Champions, out in the middle. Had Leeds still been in contention to win the division, I am sure the Leeds fans would have joined in with the classic Queen anthem, but today we let the three lads do it themselves. There was a bit of comedy when The Soldiers finished their performance. The boards were set out for the usual half time competition and as soon as The Soldiers had finished the Leeds announcer fetched a bloke out of the South Stand. However, just as he was about to take his first shot at goal, the players started to make their way back onto the pitch. They had to quickly abandon the competition, but not before the Kop broke out with a rousing chant of "You don't know what you're doing!"

The second half was a tense affair, but Leeds had most of the possession. We carved out a few more good chances but all went begging, either due to poor finishing, or often with some excellent saves from the impressive Burnley keeper, Jensen. Snodgrass came on for Paynter near the end, and then Sanchez Watt replaced Gradel. Sanchez Watt had two glorious chances to put the game out of reach, but he couldn't hit the target with either. Then Leigh Bromby was brought on to replace McCormack for the final 5 minutes of added time, as Leeds, somewhat nervously, closed the game out.

1 – 0 it ended, and while the Burnley fans wended their way out, the Leeds fans all remained to give a final thank you to the team. The players briefly left the field before returning to do a lap of honour, and apart from one crazy lady; everyone else complied with the pre-match requests to keep off the pitch. The lady in question, who was no spring chicken, was bundled away unceremoniously by two burly stewards, and will presumably face a ban from the ground. The applause

from the fans was heartfelt, but it was also given with the realisation that this was in all probability the last time we would see the team at Elland Road this season, and that there would be no Play Off games for us in the coming weeks. Today's game was live on TV of course, and at the end Simon Grayson was interviewed just in front of the Kop, not a wise choice, as the Kop belted out "There's only one Simon Grayson" at the top of their voices until Grayson gave us a wave. Kasper went round the pitch carrying his little baby, the one that had been born the night before the Coventry away game that meant he missed that game!

We gave Mark a lift back to his house before setting off down the motorway, and then we listened to the scores coming in from the 3pm kick offs. Millwall eventually lost at home to Swansea, so they were out of contention, but Forest steadily built themselves a solid lead at home to Scunthorpe, and eventually beat them 5 – 1. What that meant, was that Leeds would have to win at Loftus Road next Saturday, and hope that Crystal Palace could beat Forest. That alone though was not enough. In doing so, we also needed to close a 6 goal gap that now existed in the goal difference between Forest and ourselves. Hence a 5 – 0 win for Leeds and a 2 – 0 defeat for Forest, would get us into that 6th spot, or anything similar. Such things had happened before, and no doubt will happen in the future, but to all intents and purposes, the season was done. QPR had secured the Championship title today, with a 2 – 0 win at Watford, although there was still the small matter of the FA enquiry into alleged rule infringement by the Loftus Road club that was due to be held next week. That might still be significant if any drastic action was taken such as points being deducted.

I wasn't going to Loftus Road, as we didn't get lucky in the ballot for tickets. Instead, I would be in Leeds with the family, to see Mark perform in a production of Bugsy Malone at the Carriageworks Theatre on the Saturday night. Before that,

Mark and I would be looking for a Pub in Leeds in which to watch the final day's events...just in case.

What if?

On Monday 2nd May, Cardiff City surprisingly lost 3 – 0 at home to Middlesbrough, and at the same time Norwich City won by a goal to nil at Portsmouth. That meant that Norwich had sealed their return to the Premiership, and would go up as runners up, with QPR as Champions, regardless of the final day results. Cardiff, Swansea, and Reading, were all also certain of a Play Off place, with the last place then going to either Forest, or with a footballing miracle, Leeds United.

The world news this week was dominated by death, which was not a good omen I didn't think. Osama Bin Laden was shot dead by a team of US Navy Seals, at his safe house in Pakistan. Nearer to home, British sports fans were saddened to learn of the death of Sir Henry Cooper, possibly our most celebrated boxer. Our 'Enry was famed above all else for flooring Muhammad Ali, (then known as Cassius Clay), with a typical "Enry's Ammer", in a bout in 1963. The golfing world was mourning the death of Seve Ballesteros, in the early hours of Saturday. Seve was born just 16 days after I was in 1957, and that just served as yet another reminder to me that this life of ours is not a rehearsal, and we should all get out and enjoy it while we have it!

On Thursday we all went to the polls to say "No" to the Alternative Voting system, choosing instead to stick with the time honoured "First Past the Post" system. 6 out of every 10 of us couldn't even be bothered to vote! I am fascinated by elections, and this one had some intriguing statistics. For example, did you know that 10 of the 440 areas of the UK actually voted "Yes"! These were mainly London boroughs, but Oxford and Cambridge also voted "Yes", as did Edinburgh Central and Glasgow Kelvin. Very strange us Brits!

For our household though, it was all about Leeds this weekend, the team and the city, and that tiny glimmer of hope that still burned...

I was all ready for the trip to Leeds on Saturday; I had even forked out for a new Leeds replica shirt, the current home shirt that was being sold off at just £10, prior to the new home strip being launched! It was a bargain, even if it would be out of date in less than a week; I could always use it for my daily jog.

My new Leeds shirt was delivered by our regular postman, Steve, on Friday morning, together with some other stuff that I had to sign for. Steve has been our postie since we have been at this house, about three years now, but I had never got to speak to him about football before. He noticed the shirt, and he told me he was a mad keen Shrewsbury Town supporter who goes to all the games he can, both home and away. Like all real fans, Steve was passionate about "his" team, and I think he would have gladly stopped on my doorstep for hours discussing the current situation of the Shrews, and to hell with the other folks' post for the day. He explained that this was a huge weekend for the League Two outfit, as they could still clinch automatic promotion to League One. They just needed to record a better result than Wycombe Wanderers on the last day. If the Shrews won, and Wycombe drew or lost, that would do it, and even a draw for Shrewsbury at home to Oxford would be enough, as long as Wycombe lost at home to Southend. If Wycombe won, then Shrewsbury would have to go into the Play Offs regardless of their own result.

We both wished each other the best of luck for the weekend games, although Steve agreed with my assessment, that Leeds would need a miracle of the order of the Loaves and Fishes, to get above Forest and into a Play Off spot. As I closed the door I felt that I had just made another football obsessed friend for life. I consider myself very fortunate, that I can count among my friends and acquaintances, really dedicated fans of many different teams in the current Football League, and even a few fans of non league outfits! By fans I do mean true fans that actually travel to games to follow their team and "feel" the emotions of win, lose or draw; promotion and relegation; success and failure, and not just people who call themselves supporters but really are just "interested" in the results of one particular team or another. There is nothing wrong with that, don't get me wrong, but those folk will not truly "get" what football can be about and they are probably not bothered about that.

In fact, as I opened the package containing my new Leeds shirt, I suddenly remembered that I have an ex business acquaintance who is a fanatical supporter of Southend United, the team Postie Steve needed to get a positive result at Wycombe this weekend. Andy Leeder looks after the pension administration for my former employer, and when I retired, back in March of this year, he sent me a lovely e-mail wishing me well. He also playfully included a downloaded picture showing the scoreboard from the Southend versus Leeds, League One game, in October '08, when Southend somehow beat Leeds 1 - 0. He suggested I could use it as a screen saver, cheeky bugger! I am rambling a bit here, but the point was, that if I had remembered at the time, I would have passed on to Postie Steve the comments Andy made to me earlier in the season, in respect of the form and capabilities of the current Southend team... and I could have assured Steve that there was no bloody way that Southend would get anything but a hiding at Wycombe!

Andy is another guy who fully understands the meaning of the game of football to its real fans; he signed off his e-mail to me as follows:

"Enjoy every minute, continue to enjoy the wildly unpredictable, frustrating but so captivating, game of football...should you ever feel inclined to get in touch, are ever down this way and want to visit, or just want to get a ticket when Southend play Leeds in the final game of the 2015/16 season for the Premiership title, you know how to get in touch..."

As soon as our teams' paths do cross and they most surely will again one day, rest assured Andy, I will be in touch.

Saturday morning, and Karen and I set off on yet another trip to Leeds. Mark had appeared at the Carriageworks Theatre last night, and the reports from Suzi, who was there to see his first night appearance in the Devonshire Hall production of Bugsy Malone, were excellent. We were therefore very much looking forward to seeing the show for ourselves this evening. The wife's Mum and Dad were travelling down from Edinburgh on the train, and we were meeting them late morning at the Hilton Hotel, where we were all stopping tonight. The first challenge though, was where Mark and I would be watching the QPR game, which was being screened live on BBC at 12:45pm.

We arrived at the Hilton at noon, and had only been there a couple of minutes before Mark and Suzi wandered into reception. The missus was going to wait for her Mum and Dad, and so Mark led Suzi and I, in search of a pub or bar showing the game.

We settled on Shooters Sports Bar, on the Headrow in the centre of Leeds. We got there in time to secure a table in their VIP area, right in front of the giant cinema style screen. It cost £5 just for the table, but it is a great screen. We had the added bonus that two smaller screens either side were showing the Rangers versus Hearts game (on the left), and more importantly, the Palace versus Forest game (on the right). Mark and I settled down on the leather sofa with a pint each and Suzi curled up in the corner with a J2O.

The first bad news was that the BBC was reporting that there was to be no points deduction for QPR after all. They were going to get a large fine, but any hopes we had of turning our 7th spot into 6th, purely as a result of a 17 point deduction for the "R's" was gone. It was all now down to a big win for us, and a big defeat for Forest.

Becchio, McCartney and Snodgrass were all still injured, and so the side was the team that started against Burnley, but with Connolly back in at full back for McCartney.

Leeds kicked off and played the usual long diagonal ball to the left wing. It ended up, as it has done virtually every time this season, in touch. We were still getting used to the surroundings, and I was just savouring the first sip of my pint, when QPR broke away down the left. The ball arrived with Tommy Smith who shot with his right foot. Schmeichel got down to his left and stopped the ball, but merely shovelled it out a bit further to his left. Heidar Helguson was the only player there, and he had the easiest of tasks to tap the ball home. From the replays it looked as if Helguson could've been in an offside position when the first shot came in, but the goal was allowed to stand. It was déjà vu. If anything, this was even quicker than the goal we conceded down at Palace on Easter Monday. That was in the 90th second, this was in the 26th second of this game! Schmeichel was once again red faced; a keeper at this level just has to be able to hold a shot like that. Unbelievable! I couldn't get my head round this situation at all. I couldn't help thinking that someone up there was telling us that we shouldn't even have been considering a positive outcome from today's games. But we had, and so this was The Almighty just making sure we understood the situation!

On the left hand screen, Rangers were steadily scoring against Hearts, and I soon lost interest in looking over there. The Forest game on the small screen to our right though, was now also giving cause for concern as Forest were clearly the more dominant team in the early minutes.

17 minutes into our game and I hear Mark say "It's all over now" and I glanced to the right to see the Forest players celebrating a goal at Selhurst Park.

From then on it was somewhat academic. To complete the story, Palace had Dean Moxey sent off on 25 minutes, and with two further goals in the second half, Forest ran out comfortable winners to secure that all important 6th spot in the final Championship table. Leeds gradually played themselves into the game at Loftus Road, and in the 38th minute Mad Max got on the end of a ball from Richard

Naylor, right down the centre of the QPR defence. The keeper ran out to try to get it, but Max's right boot was there first, and he just poked it up and over him, and it bounced nicely into the net. It was not celebrated at all by any of the Leeds players, save for a brief clenched fist from Max. He had recently carried off all of the club awards for player of the year, both from the fans and his team mates, and there was some element of "rounding the circle" as he closed the book for good on his indiscretion at the final game of last season, that so nearly cost us promotion.

Shooters had gradually filled up since we had arrived, and when Ross McCormack's shot in the 68th minute ballooned off a defender, and ended up in the top corner of the QPR net, there was a big cheer. But it was just a big cheer, not the start of any prolonged celebrations. Leeds played well in the second half and could have scored more, but with Forest comfortably ahead it was of little importance. Mark Clattenburg was the referee, and other than one handball shout for Leeds that he refused to give, we couldn't really complain about his performance for once. And Paddy Kisnorbo got a run out in the 79th minute, complete with "Kisnorbo" head bandage. He was very ring rusty, and made a couple of dreadful attempts at clearances, but it was good to see him back on a football pitch. It remains to be seen now if he is offered a new contract.

So that was it. We watched the QPR fans celebrating on the big screen in front of us; they would be watching Premiership football next season. We could see the 3,500 Forest fans at Selhurst Park, celebrating on the little screen on my right; they would be trying to overcome Swansea, in a two legged Play Off semi final. Cardiff and Reading would battle out the other semi final, and one of those four sides would also be a Premiership club come the end of May. Who it will be, I really couldn't care less, except that I might enjoy it if Forest manager Billy Davies doesn't get to celebrate. All Leeds fans will remember the smug manner in which he confidently said

"Job Done", after his Preston side had drawn 1 – 1 in the Championship Play Off semi final, first leg, in 2006. Spurred on by the little Scotsman's rather arrogant comments, Leeds won the second leg up at Deepdale 2 – 0, to get through to the final, and to ram Mr Davies' words so far down his throat...well, you get the picture. So yes, an all Welsh final would probably suit most Leeds fans. But really, who cares?

We didn't have much time to reflect on today's results, as we were heading straight off to meet up with my missus and her folks. We all went to Jamie's Italian, the restaurant on Park Row, just around the corner from Shooters. The restaurant is unsurprisingly owned by Jamie Oliver, and is housed in an old bank building. It is pricy, but the food was very good, and it is worth knowing about as there is no need to book, you just turn up, get your name on the list, and they will fit you in as soon as they can. We only had to wait 30 minutes on this busy Saturday, mid afternoon, despite Leeds being full of hen parties that seemed to be everywhere you looked! We had a lovely meal, and then Mark had to leave and get to the theatre, ready for the evening's performance. We all popped back to the hotel for forty winks, before setting out again, this time heading for the Carriageworks Theatre, about a 15 minute walk back into the centre of Leeds. Mark did us proud with his performance as "Knuckles" in Bugsy Malone, and as far as I can remember, I didn't think about football once all evening.

It was only when we all retired for the evening, after another pint in the Hilton's bar with the in-laws that I switched on the TV in our room. First I checked out the Darlo versus Mansfield result on teletext, and was slightly surprised to see that it would be our friend Brian who would be celebrating a 1 - 0 Darlo victory, and not Martin, the Leeds fan from Mansfield.
I then flicked the teletext off, and settled down to watch the BBC's Football League Show. Karen was sound asleep, as I relived the day's events. I watched long enough to see that

Steve the Postie wouldn't be happy tonight. As I had guessed, Wycombe easily beat my old colleague Andy Leeder's beloved Southend, 3 – 1, so despite Shrewsbury doing their bit and beating Oxford 3 – 0, it was only the Play Offs for the Shrews. At least they still have a chance of promotion.

When I eventually switched off the TV, and lay back on the bed, I did just for a few moments start to think of what might have been. What if we had been able to close out that game against Preston, when we had gone 4 – 1 up; what if we had hung onto that two goal lead at the Walker's Stadium, the two goal lead at home to Pompey, or that one goal lead at Derby just a few weeks ago; what if, what if, what if... I then remembered one of my favourite sayings though; "If my Auntie had of been a bloke, she would have been my Uncle". Forget it, move on.

This had been a wonderful season. 50 games, 88 Leeds goals scored, and 76 conceded. Some of those goals were world class. I will not forget BJ's goal against the Arsenal at Elland Road, or Killa's thunderbolt at Deepdale, that Bostock rocket, for Hull, or Andy King's screamer at Leicester. We had experienced virtually every emotion, from joy to despair, from hope to expectation; we had seen some fabulous goals and some awful defending. We had laughed often, we had been angry, annoyed and appalled, and I had sometimes welled up with emotion. Other than your partner and your children, what else can do all of that to you?

I switched off the bedside lamp, and idly wondered where we would be journeying next season. Who was coming down? West Ham, maybe? Wigan? Blackpool or Blackburn? Any number of Premiership clubs were still possible candidates for the drop. And who was coming up? Brighton and Southampton were definite already; they would both be good trips. I wondered if first thing tomorrow would be a good time to break the news to the wife, that Mark and I were getting season tickets for next season. On reflection, it's also a bloody good job I didn't cancel that Bristol City website registration isn't it? I may need it again next season after all.

A NOTE ON THE AUTHOR

David Watkins spent 33 years in industry working as a Finance Director for various organisations before he "retired" in 2011. *Leeds United in pursuit of the Premiership* is his first published work. He has followed the fortunes of Leeds United since the 1960's and has held a club membership for many years.

www.ingramcontent.com/pod-product-compliance
Lightning Source LLC
Chambersburg PA
CBHW071223080526
44587CB00013BA/1477